NOW THAT I'M DEAD, HERE'S THE REAL DIRT

THE POSTHUMOUS MEMOIRS
of Johnny Fratto

NOW THAT I'M DEAD, HERE'S THE REAL DIRT

JOHNNY FRATTO
& MATTHEW RANDAZZO V

THE
ISAAC OLIVIA
COMPANY

*This book is dedicated to the memories of
Luigi Fratto, Frank Fratto, Barbara Farrell,
and Johnny Lew Fratto.*

This book is published by The Isaac Olivia Company.
For more information, visit IsaacOlivia.com and MatthewRandazzo.com

ISBN: 0692956581
ISBN-13: 978-0692956588

Cover image courtesy of Tyler Shields
Cover and interior design by Danielle Deschenes

CONTENTS

Coming Dirty

By Johnny Fratto Jr.
with Matthew Randazzo V

If it were possible for the dead to communicate with the living, this foreword would provide the decisive evidence. Forget me—*you* would be able to hear my dad screaming from the other side for me to get out of his spotlight.

I hear ya, Dad; I'll make this quick. I just need to explain how this book full of dangerous secrets and outrageous stories overcame great odds to reach readers worldwide.

For 25 years, I watched as Dad turned down tens of millions of dollars from a variety of TV, film, and radio offers to share "the truth" about his life. Everyone from Oprah Winfrey to Merv Griffin to Howard Stern asked him to come clean—and Dad in his words would "come dirty", giving them just enough to tease and keep them chasing.

That was Dad—Mr. Hard to Get.

Like a burlesque dancer, my dad thought he couldn't afford to ever give his audience the goods. To a stranger, he was the most charismatic guy you'd ever meet. But the closer you got to him, the more you realized how deeply buried, and hidden, and protected his true personality and thoughts and secrets were. Any revelation he made to you was just misdirection to get you to chase the three new mysteries he introduced for you to obsess over. There was a reason for this: like a magician or pro wrestler, exposing Dad's secrets could kill his business, not to mention *him.*

My dad grew up the son, brother, nephew, and cousin many-times-over of men some might call "Mob Bosses" of various degrees. In those days, our family name was dangerous and sexy like a black pirate flag. It came with a sort of inherited tabloid infamy that could ruin your life, but, on the plus side, also got you laid. When he was still basically a kid, there were news reporters calling him "Handsome Johnny" and "Johnny Diamonds"—and my dad always told me that receiving nicknames in the press was the inevitable prelude to prison.

It was Dad's great innovation to figure out how to monetize our family name and bad reputation without going to prison, or betraying his relatives and values. It was an extremely delicate hustle based on blurring the lines between outlaw and civilian so thoroughly that no one else could quite tell where he stood. His footwork had to be precise, or he'd step into a federal prison sentence. Dad's entire life was based on this paradoxical two-step: attract attention, then cultivate mystery and mystique.

He made millions of dollars using this strategy—and walked away from tens of millions of dollars more. Any deal that involved more than a little personal exposure from Dad would, inevitably, die a gratuitously painful, bitter, and nasty death. Even if a deal was originally his idea, Dad would eventually get paranoid about telling his life story—and then he wouldn't just kill the deal, he'd torture it, as if to punish everyone for thinking they could take away his precious secrets.

This book was the classic example of such a deal. He received the best imaginable opportunity in the book world: a tell-all published by mega-powerhouse HarperCollins, managed by bestselling authors and *Rolling Stone* editors Neil Strauss and Anthony Bozza, edited by *Esquire* editor Bill Tonelli, and written by Matthew Randazzo V, the best and most knowledgeable young author specializing in organized crime stories. Hell, Neil even called in favors to get the world's hottest fashion photographer, Tyler Shields, to take the book's photos.

It was a perfect deal, but it required Dad to come clean. So it was also the world's worst deal, with the most predictable ending.

Once I talked to Randazzo, and realized how many secrets he'd extracted from Dad that even I had never heard, I immediately pitied him. I had seen this before; I knew what would happen, and I even warned Randazzo. As soon as the book was completed, Dad had to come to terms with dropping his mystique and showing the world what he really was—and decided instead to put the Evil Eye on the project and everyone involved.

He didn't need much of a reason. Dad manufactured silly disagreements over what photo of him would be used for the cover and what the title would be, and then set his mind to playing his writer against his editor against his publishers. With his special talents, Dad caused this tiny disagreement to detonate into a mushroom cloud of drama, bitterness, and threats.

By the time it was over, the book was aborted, and every relationship involved was a radioactive crater. Everyone besides Johnny Fratto had to invest in lawyers and psychiatrists, but I was just relieved the cops didn't get involved.

A few years later, in 2015, Dad was suddenly and unexpectedly diagnosed with terminal cancer. Only 61 years old, he had only a few months left to live. I'd love to say that he launched a grand farewell tour—righting all of his old wrongs, coming clean with old partners, and reconnecting on a new level with all of his closest friends and family. I wish he would have solved the countless family mysteries he kept to himself, no matter how many times I begged.

I think my Dad had that kindness somewhere deep in him, but it would've required him to confront and deal with the inevitability of his death. He couldn't do that—he loved life too much. Here was a guy who truly adored waking up in the morning and contemplating the hustles, mayhem, and fun the day would bring.

In his last days, this book was one of the few touchy subjects I dared to bring up with him. In a lot of ways, along with his kids, it was his legacy—a tangible and complete testament to the fascinating, unique, and entertaining creation he made of himself. My Dad was an artistic guy, and his masterpiece was Johnny Fratto—the persona, the hustle, the story. This book was the closest anything ever came to capturing it for posterity.

So, gently, I asked him if I could bring the book back, if I could make something happen with it. I could never say, "once you're gone", but I didn't need to. He didn't make it easy, but eventually he gave me The Nod.

Luckily, the book was still great, and Randazzo was an unusually forgiving Italian like I am. All that was left was settling on the title that we never figured out the first time around.

The title had to reflect who my Dad really was: a hilarious storyteller and showman, "a master raconteur" according to the great comedian Artie Lange. Dad was a shameless P.T. Barnum-style promoter who would capture attention by any means necessary. He insisted from the beginning that he wasn't going to lend his name to a serious, uptight, meticulously documented history of the Midwest underworld from our family's vantage point because it would be both dishonest (because he wasn't going to rat on living family, so he'd have to lie) and boring.

Dad didn't do boring.

Dad wanted a hilarious page-turner that would be true to his story, and to his views, but would make no claims of being the objective work of a journalist.

Forget the rest of you: my Dad knew our very opinionated, very egotistical, and very confrontational Italian family would eat itself alive if he claimed that Johnny Fratto's version of events was the only valid interpretation.

This book is Johnny Fratto's experiences, his views, his life story—crack open a can of beer, or light up a joint, and enjoy a master storyteller holding court. If you take it too seriously, that's on you.

After all, how are you going to argue with a dead man?

We were thinking that very thought when the perfect brand came to mind. When I first told it to my family, they laughed and nodded their heads— Signature Johnny Fratto!

Without further ado, please enjoy *Now That I'm Dead, Here's the Real Dirt: The Posthumous Memoirs of Johnny Fratto*.

1

A SMILING MUDDERPUCKER

"They might be Chicago's First Family of the Mob: The Frattos."

CHUCK GOUDIE
March 12, 2010 ABC-7 News Report

"**FRANK FRATTO**
AKA. Frank Frappo, One Ear Frankie, Half-Ear.
RECORD: Record dates back to 1941, more than 10 arrests: fugitive, theft, assault to commit murder...A suspect in the 1957 murder of Willard Bates and the 1963 murder of Alderman Benjamin Lewis...
MODUS OPERANDI: A syndicate terrorist on the North Side who muscled his way into the aluminum siding and storm window business."

OVID DEMARIS
Captive City

"Johnny, come quickly! Your uncle's massacring a Shriners' convention at the Des Moines Hilton!"

This is the sort of phone call that goes a long way to explaining what it means to be a Fratto.

I had enough experience in the family business to immediately know which of my many gangster uncles was laying waste to a peaceable assembly of Shriners. Frank Fratto: you only said the name with disrespect once.

After that, you learned if you lived.

I should have seen Uncle Frank's showdown with the Shriners coming: the charitable offshoot of the Freemasons had been riding on his nerves ever since I could remember. Frank's hatred of the Shriners arose entirely from his macho disgust for their gimmick of riding in Midwestern parades in tiny toy cars. It jiggled Uncle Frank's rage switch; he had probably killed people for less.

"I didn't know midgets threw gay rights parades," he'd yell from the sidewalk, as he lifted a huge jeweled hand and expertly flicked a lit cigarette into the face of the closest passing Shriner. "My *dick* couldn't even fit in those cars, you fuckin' goofs!"

Uncle Frank may have been Dad's little brother, but the emphasis was definitely not on "little." My uncle Frank was 6'2", a full foot taller than Dad and as thick as an oak tree, and every pound and every inch was dedicated to causing others pain. Uncle Frank was an artist—his medium was confrontation, and his style was maximum violence. The man went from zero-to-psychopath *fast*, thunderclap fast. The man couldn't wait to throw a punch. Uncle Frank was the sort of guy who chased fights like most men chased women.

You could call him the toughest man on Earth, and he'd shoot back, "What? Are you saying I'm a pussy on Mars?" Whenever he walked into a room, he intentionally bumped into every guy and openly stared at the tits on every girl. The most poisonous, insulting comments would fall out of his mouth as nonchalantly as shit out of a circus elephant's ass.

I've never met anyone who acted like him, who treated every single interaction with another human being as a fight to the death for domination. In the course of a normal day, Frank Fratto would set rude waiters on fire, sucker punch unsuspecting traffic cops "out of principle," shoot a gun into the ceiling in order to get a lazy bank teller's attention, intentionally piss on the shoe of any celebrity he encountered at the urinals in Chicago's hottest nightclubs, and drink enough vodka to kill the entire military command of the Soviet Union.

No mercy, no shame, no humanity—that was my Unc. There was no internal conflict; the Gangster cannibalized the Human in him many years before. You just ducked for cover. If you stood in Uncle Frank's path, he'd beat you right down the evolutionary chart until you changed species.

That's why I was particularly thoughtful and calculating as the Des Moines Hilton concierge continued to shriek into my enormous late 1980s cellphone. As I considered my strategy, I took to scratching my stubble and contemplated the proposition of a good, long, thoughtful scratch under my nutsack. I could not risk wrinkling my ageless forehead over this bullshit, or adding any laugh lines by sucking harder than usual on the cigarette in my mouth. My prematurely silver Beethoven hair only worked if the rest of me stayed young.

I was in my early thirties, but I was more seasoned than a Chicago-style Italian sausage. Wisdom comes with fielding phone calls like this and getting away with causing phone calls like this. It's this sort of shit that puts silver in a man's hair, sense in his head, and cops up his ass like a blue enema.

A lifetime spent squashing emergencies made me cold, calm, and lucid in absolute chaos. Thanks to my childhood, my natural habitat is where conflict and chaos roam. After the death of Dad and my older brother Frankie, I inherited the responsibility of putting out the fires that my family started.

I looked at my watch and told the Des Moines Hilton concierge I'd be there in five minutes. "Any longer—one long red light at an intersection—and everyone will be dead!"

I was *probably* being melodramatic for effect.

Three minutes later, my older brother Tommy and I screeched up to the front entrance of the Hilton in Tommy's brand new MG Midget (yes, my five-foot-tall brother defiantly drove a car called a "Midget") and sprinted inside the lobby. I immediately tripped over an unconscious old man who smelled of piss.

George Patton would have been nauseated by the carnage. It was like Shriners Gettysburg in that hotel lobby. The carpet was littered with red fezzes, upturned toy cars, and bleeding old men crawling desperately like half-stomped roaches.

Hopping over the carcasses, Tommy and I followed the comic book sounds (*thwack! bash! phlunk!*) to the convention room where the remaining Shriners had retreated like the doomed defenders of the Alamo.

The first sight we saw as we turned the corner into the room was Uncle Frank throwing one of his signature punches. Though tutored by the best boxers in Chicago as a kid, Frank never had much time for the proper form of throwing a punch. Instead, he would launch his fist with a deep, elaborate windup, like baseball legend Sandy Koufax. These haymakers could have shattered the face of the Statue of Liberty. When he made a fist, it was the size of a Christmas ham, and anything on the wrong end of it was demolished.

Even Rocky Marciano, undefeated heavyweight boxing champion of the world and honorary Fratto, would not take up Uncle Frank on his frequent requests for a street fight. "You could hit 'im four or five times for every one of dose haymakers he trows," Rocky would say in a whisper so Uncle Frank could not hear, "but God forbid one of those crazy motherfuckers actually *lands.*"

Uncle Frank was reducing an elderly Shriner's nose to powder when

Tommy and I entered his line of vision, our arms waving frantically. The sight of his fuckwit nephews instantly woke Uncle Frank up from his blind rampage. We were the hypnotists: we snapped our fingers, and Uncle Frank was back.

It wasn't like he had any particular respect for us, or anyone else alive for that matter. Tommy and I were just useful spectators. Uncle Frank was happy that members of the Network had arrived so we could vouch for his master-piece of mayhem to the other gossips in the Midwest underworld.

"Uncle Frank, why did ya go and do that?" I asked, reasonably.

Shrugging, Uncle Frank massaged his profusely bleeding knuckles for a moment and then said, "I overhead them whisperin' about me."

This was classic Uncle Frank logic: if one person in a large social or ethnic group said something against him, then Frank felt justified in bludgeoning *all* of them. Uncle Frank had a problem with discrimination. If some Japanese guy in Chicago had told Uncle Frank he was ugly, he would have hopped on a plane to Tokyo and laid waste to everything in sight like Godzilla.

After all, Frank Fratto was part of a family and culture that was all about guilt by association.

The next question came from my brother Tommy, and it was a good one.

"Um, Uncle Frank, which ear heard them whispering?"

There was a good reason Frank Fratto was called "Frankie One-Ear" in Federal Bureau of Investigation press releases. The motherfucker only had one ear! Back in the day, some quickly deceased prick shot off Uncle Frank's right ear, leaving a shredded lettuce leaf of flesh behind.

"If you nosy pricks have to know, I heard dem fuckers in my right ear."

I should have known: Uncle Frank had assaulted two dozen innocent old men over a whisper he heard in an ear he no longer had. It could be no other way. He was the Van Gogh of Violence, a demolition artist with a missing ear. Uncle Frank wouldn't be Uncle Frank if he committed atrocities for anything but the most ridiculous reason imaginable.

Though he was responding to Tommy's question, he really was responding to me, since he knew my reaction would be amusingly over-the-top. It was our routine—after I flipped out, he'd threaten me like Ralph Kramden and then we'd all move on from whatever crimes against humanity he had committed.

"You're a fuckin' nut!" I shouted. "You are a sick, demented individual! You've got issues I don't even understand! Don't you think you should fucking make sure you *have* an ear before you rely on what it's hearing?"

"Whatever," Uncle Frank said, dismissing me with a suggestive upward scratch under his chin. He had gotten precisely the reaction he wanted, and now he could respond with threats. "Keep talkin', smartass. Keep writing checks your fists can't cash, pretty boy!"

Just like Uncle Frank, I abandoned my previous posture and advanced to the next step in our decades-long sideshow act: defiantly smiling in his face like an annoying little kid. Our relationship always had a juvenile streak since we had both competed like siblings for my father's attention—Frank as Lou Fratto's neediest brother and most attention-starved Mafia enforcer, and me as Lou Fratto's neediest son and most attention-starved Mafia apprentice. Decades after my father's death, we were still going at it like Itchy and Scratchy.

"I don't know what you're smiling about, you smiling motherfucker," he grumbled. Without the option of killing his own nephew, Uncle Frank's only recourse was to impotently mutter insults after being bested in any confrontation with me. "If I were a smiling motherfucker like you, I wouldn't trick myself into thinking I had anything to be smiling over."

We left the Des Moines Hilton—not together, of course. Can you imagine Uncle Frank, all 6'2" of him, accordion-ing himself into a goddamn car called a Midget? As he screeched off in his own luxury sedan, he screamed loud enough for all to hear over the approaching police sirens: "FUCK YOU, SMILING MOTHERFUCKER!"

Tommy and I couldn't help but laugh as we sped off—the Frattos had gotten away with it again.

That was always Uncle Frank's most devastating insult against me: Smiling Motherfucker. In our underworld social circle of misshapen, deformed, scowling Dick Tracy villains, I was a bizarre anomaly because I actually went about my day smiling like an ad for teeth. This inexplicable quirk motivated a Chicago journalist to nickname me "Handsome Johnny", much like *his* dad had branded *my* dad "Cock-Eyed Louis" decades earlier in the same newspaper.

We're all about history in the Midwest.

For example, I'm not the first Chicago underworld figure who made it out West and was nicknamed "Handsome Johnny." The first Handsome Johnny was dismembered, tossed into an oil barrel, and dumped into the Gulf of Mexico. If it were up to Uncle Frank, the same sentence would have been appropriate for the second Handsome Johnny . . . if only his last name weren't Fratto.

Since I was a Fratto, the worst thing that could happen to me was getting called names like "Smiling Motherfucker". . . or to be honest, "Smiling Mudderpucker."

With his stylish suits and gorgeous mistresses, Uncle Frank cut a glamorous figure, but his constant two-fisted drinking undercut his suave image.

Consumption of booze had an inexplicable side effect on my uncle: it caused his F's to come out as P's. You'd never expect this distinguished, senatorial gentleman in a $2000 suit to slur "Hey shithead, don't you puck with Prankie Pratto!" at strangers.

If you heard Uncle Frank mispronounce his own name, it was hard not to laugh—and then it was hard not to die. If you pissed him off, you were a "mudderpucker!" and, if he caught you—a "dead mudderpucker!"

Uncle Frank would corner me at family get-togethers and yell out aggressively, "Look at the smiling mudderpucker, everybody! Look at mudderpucking 'Handsome Johnny'! Look at 'Johnny Diamonds'! Puckin' vain Mudderpucker! Puckin' Prick!"

This screaming assault was this lunatic's version of "Hello!"

"Pirst you were a hippie with long sissy hair, girl clothes, and a crush on those puckin' Beatles," Uncle Frank would slur with a jiggling screwdriver cocktail in either hand, enumerating for the thousandth time my sins against masculinity.

"Then you were some tight leather-pants-wearin' pruitcake," Uncle Frank continued, "and *then* you were a disco-dancing pairy paggot, then you were a pashion magazine editor, then a puckin' art dealer, and here you still going around smiling that mudderpucker smile, all excited that they call you 'Handsome Johnny!'

"You vain prick! I was better looking than you, and you never heard me goin' around calling myself Handsome Prankie, didya?"

That's what it was all about: Uncle Prankie deep down wanted to be known as Handsome Frankie. This was a man who had checked into Zsa Zsa Garbor when that was world-class five-star accommodations, and he didn't want to let me forget it. Uncle Frank would always look incredulous behind his psychotically distinguished John Forsythe face whenever he heard my looks complimented.

The "Smiling Mudderpucker" nickname was known only to close family for most of my life. Then, a few years after the Shriner Showdown, towards the end of the 1980s, Uncle Frank decided to give it a public debut that would define my reputation for years, and in some ways allow me to escape our family history and transcend it.

The occasion was happy—a Chicago Outfit funeral, a Mob funeral. Don't get me wrong, I liked the dead guy. Unlike most, he wasn't a greedy prick. Still, sometimes you can be sad that someone had to go but pleased by how they went. It was a Mafia send-off that didn't involve a bullet to the head or reporting to a prison or Witness Protection.

Good news! Hallelujah!

Though the FBI surveillance vans were parked within sight, the funeral attendees shared little nods and handshakes and pats on the shoulder like athletes congratulating each other on another good game played. Teamwork was the essence of our entire lives. Teamwork stretching over generations had contributed to this hard-fought victory: the old goombah in the expensive coffin had died free, rich, defiant, and completely silent. No one went to jail or to the morgue over the old fuck.

It was like winning the Sicilian Super Bowl.

As we said goodbye to old-what's-his-name with a sense of "job well done" for both the dead guy and those of us he left behind, there was something else in the air. Conspiracy. Drama. Tension. Deep politics. Deep-in-each-others'-pockets politics. The survivors were wasting no time jockeying for position after his death. You'd never see such fat fucking pieces on a chessboard.

You could tell who the important conspirators at the funeral were by how closely they stood together, off to the side of the coffin. With their black silk suits, white shirts, round bellies, short stature, and steaming cigars and cigarettes, they looked like penguins huddled for warmth.

As I approached the crowd, from a few paces away I began to hear the low, jumbled muttering of wiseguys whispering out of the corner of their mouths like master ventriloquists. Without ever looking at each other or moving their lips, they were having a spirited ten-sided conversation at a decibel level scarcely louder than a dove farting.

Like at all Mob funerals, the talk in the huddle was about underworld politics: which cousin had a murderous hard-on for another cousin, which old-timer was losing his shit, which intolerable motherfucker was about to get paroled and give everyone angina.

Since the Golden Age wiseguys who apprenticed under Al Capone and Paul Ricca were finally dying off, the real action was with the youthful veterans approaching social security age. Everyone was making moves, and the crowd was handicapping the contenders for the top spots like the degenerate gamblers they were.

"You know who I like?" muttered one little toadstool. "That guy with that thing on his face. He's real bona fide. The crew is strong. No one's going to say anything."

"Nah, you fuckin' kiddin' me, it's his cousin," mocked a George Constanza lookalike as he pretended to stifle a yawn. He cocked an eyebrow and let out a little snort of a laugh.

"Don't count out the funny guy at all," said a tall, Barney Fife wiseguy. "I wouldn't say shit to him."

In the middle of this nail salon gossip session stood Frank Fratto. Everyone gave him his space and tried to avoid direct eye contact. Uncle Frank wasn't their boss, and in fact some of them outranked him. But none of that leadership pyramid bullshit mattered when it came to Uncle Frank. All that mattered was that Frank would kill anyone for any reason and laugh about it at their funeral as he hit on the widow. In the Mob, they are two great equalizers: money and murder.

Instead of actually talking to him as a human, everyone who mattered in that Outfit crowd just slipped Frank Fratto envelopes of cash like offerings to a vengeful god. Those envelopes bought a reprieve from Uncle Frank's physical violence, but not his verbal poundings. He could hold back his fists if there was money to be made, but he could never hold his tongue.

Uncle Frank was rolling his eyes, sighing and casting disgusted looks at all of the Chatty Cathys surrounding him in the graveside huddle, hypothesizing and debating Mob politics. I could read his mind: *You dumb fucks realize this is supposed to be a secret society, right?*

Finally, Uncle Frank had heard enough sissy shit. He started mouthing prayers of deliverance to God in the sky as the chatter continued all around him. Then he let loose like a demolished dam of alcohol.

"Oh, shut the puck up, all of you!" he moaned so loud that the priest paused his prayer over the coffin. No corner-of-the-mouth ventriloquism for Uncle Frank. "You punks are all talk!" Everyone in the crowd was suddenly squirming and staring at their spit-shined shoes.

In Uncle Frank's mind, that was encouragement.

"D'ya know what the puckin' problem is with all you mudderpuckers?" Uncle Frank taunted. "You all think with your ears. You think talk means something. Your brain is connected right to your puckin' ears, you know-nothin' sons of whores. You keep lookin' for the guys who talk a big game and swing a big dick to make a move, but the loud ones are never the ones to worry about! You want to know who you should be worrying about?"

Everyone thought the same thing: *You, Frank. You're the one to worry about.* But Uncle Frank had a bigger threat in mind.

He lifted his right hand over their heads and pointed straight at me. I had been sitting peacefully as a schoolgirl, quietly observing the festivities from behind light blue sunglasses, bothering no one. I turned to see my uncle's finger pointing at me.

"*THAT SMILING MUDDERPUCKER!*" Uncle Frank cried. There went the priest's concentration. The eulogy was pucked.

"That smiling mudderpucker right over there...that goopy, joking, harmless-looking, smiling mudderpuckin' Johnny is the one you should be worrying about. The only reason you don't is because he keeps his real pucking thoughts to himself. And there's a reason he does: he's got a dangerous mind. *That* smiling mudderpucker has a *dangerous* mind! Trust me, I know what that smiling mudderpucker is thinking, and that's why I'm tellin' you he's the smiling mudderpucker to watch!"

Well, thanks, Uncle Frank. The funeral was a symphony of awkward titters and coughs, all desperately restrained by those nearby who knew what would happen if Frank thought *he* was being laughed at. Finally, the priest continued, and Uncle Prankie went back to muttering, or muddering, to himself.

But that conversation has never stopped paying dividends, and it has always resonated with me.

The funny thing is that Uncle Frank never understood me and didn't have the smallest clue what the fuck I was thinking. At the very moment that Uncle Frank was accusing me of concocting plans for underworld dominance, I was actually fantasizing about the nice plate of sausage I was going to grab after the service was over.

In general, however, Uncle Frank was right — my mind can be a terrifying weapon. I learned a great deal from him, silently observing the crazy old fucker as I smiled blankly. If I decided to give in to my true nature, I could draw on a bottomless reservoir of darkness and cruelty. I can be a hypnotic presence like Svengali or a woman with a high-caliber tit job. I can be Pavlov gone totally wrong, a mad street scientist. I can teach a grown man to be scared of the dark. I know just how to talk to make my words stalk and haunt my target like a demon.

Uncle Frank's endorsement of my mental sickness has saved me millions of dollars of trouble and thousands of hours of wiseguy drama since. The leadership of the Midwest Mob had heard the most ruthless killer in the history of Chicago call *me*, Johnny Lew Fratto, *terrifying*. What an Oprah book club selection does for books, an endorsement from Frank Fratto did for street cred. That's the sort of blurb you could build a career on in the Mafia.

But that life, The Life, wasn't for me. It's not for anybody anymore. Today, I sit under the California sun on the roof of my penthouse Beverly Hills apartment, tan and rich and indisputably not indicted. Somehow, despite decades of trying to do otherwise, I escaped my family's legacy and my rightful fate as a jailbird—while staying true to the life lessons taught to me by the great Lou Fratto, my father and my hero.

But which Lou?

In Catholic school, the nuns told me that there was good, and there was evil, and that was it. The traffic in souls went one way or the other. There was no middleman, no hedge betting. I knew better. I knew my dad.

Lou Fratto was the middleman of good and evil. Like Dr. Jekyll and Mr. Hyde, he had two separate identities: crime boss Lou Fratto, and admired pillar of the community "Lew Farrell." Between those two contradictory identities, Dad traveled along the moral spectrum as quickly as Chuck Berry slid up and down the neck of his guitar, and he never hit a false note.

If you listened to Dad, he was a good father, not a godfather; a wise guy, not a wiseguy; Lew Farrell, not Lou Fratto. You could accuse him of being a successor of his mentor Al Capone, but he would protest that his heart was guided by his beloved childhood nurse Mother Cabrini, a canonized saint, and by his friend Pope Pius XII. You threw indictments at him, and he'd toss back charity drives and church fundraisers.

Even as a Mob boss, Lou Fratto sincerely believed he was just a good-hearted slum kid who did what was necessary to thrive in a racist, violent, lawless country. Within the Mafia, Dad was a great civilizing influence, a peacemaker and diplomat who softened the edges. He was like a boy raised by wolves—a member of the pack, but no animal.

I am Lou's son. The credentials and the DNA are there. Identity crisis—that is the story of my life, just as it was the story of my Dad's life. That is the story of The Life. Am I, or am I not?

As a kid, I always related to vampires above all else. Vampires shared our dilemma—half man, half predator, forever in irresolvable conflict. Wolves were wolves, birds were birds, normal people were normal people; they absolutely inhabited their identities without a second thought. It was not even a question.

But vampires and me and my dad? We were forever caught in between. We can never see ourselves in the mirror. Our identity is a mystery, even to us.

Transylvania was closer to my childhood experiences than Andy Griffith's Mayberry any day. In my world, vampires were real, and they loved garlic. I was surrounded by them growing up—creatures of the night with black hair, black suits, black cars, and the power of looking at a man in a way that stole his will. These vampires preyed on many and corrupted a chosen few, remaking them in their image.

In my world, vampires were called gangsters, and my family was full of them. I was bit at birth without a choice in the matter, even though I grew up to be an artistic daydreamer who loves fashion—not a tough guy. This was the source of my identity crisis.

I would have been fine if only we Frattos eventually developed fangs. That was always my favorite part in the vampire movies: when the new recruit sees the fangs in the mirror and realizes that, as human as he will always feel, his ultimate essence is vampire.

I yearned for that moment. My life never had such resolution, such clarity. Most gangsters' lives don't; when I was growing up, they were generally devout Christians and family men who contradicted everything they held to be true on a daily basis. To be a gangster usually means to suffer from an identity crisis, since very few people are like my Uncle Frank and truly enjoy being *bad*, being *evil, hurting people professionally*.

On paper, I can look just like my Uncle Frank. You can look up my drug dealing charge, my weapons charge, the quotes from law enforcement agents speculating that I am a made man in the Mafia just like my dad . . . and my uncles . . . and my late older brother . . . and many of my cousins. There is a Fratto family legacy, and they say I am upholding it.

Nonetheless, if you ask me what I am, the answer you get will never be the same twice.

Sometimes, I think I am a boy raised by wolves—other times a human raised by vampires. Though I am deep down a normal person like my mom, I may display a lot of the characteristics of a gangster because I was *raised* by gangsters. That's why, every time a problem is brought to me, my response is always, "Let me think about it." I'm giving myself the time to let the evil pass and the good ideas, the humane ideas, to come through.

Maybe the identity is superficial, just a coat of black paint. After all, my mom was good; she was absolutely good. I have her in me too, and all of the many good parts of my father.

On the other hand, sometimes I think I'm like a domesticated animal, a wild predator that's spent too much time around people and lost my sense of identity. Sometimes, the feral streak may come through just enough to scare and unsettle me.

A tiger doesn't change his stripes, but some tigers kill water buffalo in the jungle—and other tigers do magic tricks with Siegfried & Roy. Those tigers doing a shuck and jive routine with the spray-tanned Austrians are still tigers, even though their behavior and surroundings no longer fit the identity.

My father, a much tougher man than me, died young without ever resolving who he really was. He handed down his confusion and his identity crisis to his son as a legacy. He left it to me to solve—and left me to figure out how to do it and die a free man like he did.

Luckily for you, I wouldn't have had allowed this book to be written if I hadn't found my answer, and discovered how to enjoy the perks of the life of a gangster without all of the many horrifying downsides.

It would just take the discovery of a human body being dismembered on a kitchen table in Skokie, Illinois for me to resolve our Identity Crisis, once and for all.

2

THE MONEY CHAIR

"Yet more than anything else, Lew wanted to be recognized as a person of respectability in Des Moines. To convince this author, he put a small son [Johnny Fratto]—who perhaps maybe five years old—up on a chair. The little fellow was impeccably dressed in brand new clothes. At his father's command, the lad recited flawlessly the Pledge of Allegiance, down to the last words, 'with liberty and justice for all.' The jubilant father exclaimed: 'See! That proves that I'm a patriotic American!'"

GEORGE MILLS
Looking in Windows

"On May 6, 1960, T-22 advised LEW FARRELL is trying to get the Teamsters Union to donate to various political groups, politicians, and campaign committees of various political candidates the sum of $250,000.00 to be used in promoting candidates during the coming national election. T-22 said the Teamsters Union...was to furnish campaign funds to candidates designated by FARRELL... it was estimated that approximately $100,000.00 of this money would eventually go to FARRELL...T-10 stated he had drawn the opinion that FARRELL and his Teamsters Union associates... primary interest was to stop KENNEDY...Omaha T-4...stated FARRELL is a close friend of ROBERT 'BARNEY' BAKER... Omaha T-19...advised that JAMES HOFFA, President of the

Teamsters Union, had personally informed him that LEW FAR-
RELL of DES MOINES was a good friend of his."

SPECIAL AGENT ROSSITER C. MULLANEY
Federal Bureau of Investigation
File OM 92-74

My earliest memory is of torturing Teamsters Union boss Jimmy Hoffa
in my family's living room. I was about four or five years old, and the weapon
was my mouth.

"Uncle Jimmy," I asked Hoffa, "who do you think would win in a fight,
Batman or Uncle Rocky?"

"Ugh, I think probably Marciano would take that one, kid," said Hoffa.
Exasperated, Hoffa cast a look of annoyance at his enforcer and bodyguard,
Robert "Barney" Baker, who was sitting by his side on the couch.

"I have to go with Marciano too, Little Lew," said Uncle Barney, who,
despite being called "Hoffa's Roving Ambassador of Violence" by Robert
Kennedy, was more like the Roving Ambassador of Kindness when it came to
me. I loved Uncle Barney.

"Uncle Jimmy," I continued, undeterred by Baker's attempt to distract me
from Hoffa. "Does Mickey Mouse know Superman?"

"Who knows? *Probably*, I'm sure them two get around," Hoffa charitably
guessed. That wasn't the end of Hoffa's begrudging charity, either. The snapping turtle leaned off the couch, plopped a $5 bill in my hand, patted me on the
shoulder, and forcefully patted me in the direction of someone else. "*Oh-kay*,
kid, run along."

I crumpled up the bill in my tiny hand and did just as Hoffa requested:
I disappeared, which is pretty fitting considering what happened to *him*.

With Hoffa taken care of, I pattered over to Sam Giancana, all sprawled
out on the loveseat, dangling an Italian loafer over the armrest. The party-
animal front man for the Chicago Outfit, the man the Family wanted the world
to think was the *real* boss, had family in our neighborhood, so Giancana was
always bopping around my house. I have countless memories of Sam charming
my mom with his hyperactive energy in between downing heaping mouthfuls
of her homemade Italian cooking. Giancana was a pleasure to do business with:
he tipped heavy and quickly, and he was happy to convince me that he hung
out with all of my cartoon pals back in Chicago.

"Uncle Sam, do you know Bugs Bunny?"

"Lemme think for a second, buster," Giancana teased. "Hmm, I've known a guy or two named Bugsy in my day...but I think I know who you mean. You talkin' about that guy with the ears?"

"Uh huh!"

"With the carrot?"

"Yeah, he's a bunny, silly!" I cried.

"Yeah, that's the guy I'm thinkin' about. He's a total rabbit. Yeah, I know the guy, a real smart-mouth if you ask me. But I'll give him your regards." With that, Giancana gently slipped a $10 bill into the front pocket of my tiny belted black slacks and pinched my cheek.

Next came Accardo, the *real* boss, the ultimate successor to Al Capone, the man who made it an empire. I've never met anyone who could be compared to Tony Accardo, and I don't think I ever will. Tony had a way of sitting on our couch like Genghis Khan would have sat on a throne. By the time I met him, Accardo was the most powerful Italian born since the fall of the Roman Empire: more powerful in his sleep than Mussolini ever was awake, more powerful than twenty John Gottis.

I was probably the last person in history to extort a tribute payment from old Joe Batters. A slice of just about every crime in the America committed in an organized fashion eventually made its way to Accardo—and right into little Johnny Lew Fratto's pajama pocket. Through Tony, I was getting tips direct from roulette wheels in Havana, heavyweight boxing matches in Madison Square Garden, labor union pension funds in Hollywood, and 10,000 gaming rooms in Chicago alone.

With Accardo, I didn't last long. No biker bar in Gary or Black P. Stone clubhouse on the south side of Chicago was frequented by a tougher caliber of bad motherfucker than our living room...but there was no one tougher than Tony Accardo. He and my Dad went way back—they were once next-door neighbors when they worked for Al Capone—and Lou Fratto never left any doubt that Accardo was the only person he'd put in the same category as his brother, Uncle Frank.

What category was that, you ask?

The category of "DON'T FUCK WITH UNDER ANY CIRCUM-STANCES."

Still, I gave it my best shot.

"Uncle Tony...do you know Jesus?" I asked the serious, somber man with the high hairline, the large nose, black eyebrows, and the beautiful Italian suit. Accardo was always deeply attentive, analyzing every new piece of information that came his way and working it into his running calculations. When he focused his dark, brilliant eyes on me, I remember even then feeling a little intimidated.

"Do I know *Jesus*?" he asked dryly, as if it were the most routine question I could have asked. "Not yet."

Absentmindedly, he offered me a rolled $20 bill as he turned away, subtly sending me along.

"Oh, don't do that, Sam!" Dad muttered in his raspy whisper from behind his desk, using the nickname for Accardo that only the highest levels of the Mafia used. "Sam" worked much better as a nickname than "Joe Batters" or the press-invented "Big Tuna" since, with dozens of high-profile Sams in the Outfit, including the fake boss Giancana, the last person a cop would think it referred to was Anthony Joseph Accardo. "Seriously, Sam, don't give him nuthin'!"

"Don't worry 'bout it, Golden Tongue," Accardo said with a slight nod, using his nickname for Dad. "The kid's fine. He's a chip off the old block."

I was the son of Golden Tongue. Though the press called Dad "Cock-Eyed Louis" and other wiseguys preferred "The Duke", only Accardo called him "Golden Tongue." That was Dad's value to Accardo; there were millions of guys who could bust noses and pull triggers, but only Dad had the class and intelligence to sweet-talk Popes and Presidents.

I left the rest of the various kingpins and vice lords in our living room to their conversation and conspiracy, making my way to my favorite piece of furniture in our house: The Money Chair.

Lou Fratto's Money Chair was renowned across the Midwest. Stuffed into the fold between the cushion and the armrest was an enormous envelope full of cash, refilled daily by anyone *but* Dad. If you visited our home and pleased him, he gestured for you to take a seat in the Money Chair. What you did while seated . . . well, it was between you and the Money Chair.

And the Money Chair never talked.

No one ever saw my father give a single payoff in his entire life in Iowa. The Money Chair was the only piece of furniture in our house that I don't think had a speck of my dad's DNA on it.

But it sure was covered with *my* DNA. I grabbed a few bills from the Money Chair to add to the rest of my haul. I ambled over to see Dad with a cabbage of cash that barely fit in my tiny hands.

I yanked on his tie like a mountaineering cord on my way up to his lap. With his patient help, I counted out the money into the soft, well-manicured hands that somehow once knocked out champion boxers. Most dads would be sickened by such a shameless display of greed—my older brother Frankie, named after Uncle Prankie, was positively nauseated by my antics—but Lou only smiled and pinched my cheek.

That was the greatest joy of all: seeing that love in my dad's big round face. That smile and the love that poured from it made me into a lifelong capitalist and entrepreneur.

Even a preschooler could see that the most effective way to gain Lou Fratto's respect and approval was to display an ability to make scratch. It was unmistakable; every discussion with his associates in our living room ended with a cash transaction or a promise of later payment and a smile from my father. At the age most kids are learning their ABCs, I was learning C.R.E.A.M.—Cash Rules Everything Around Me.

As soon as I saw how affectionately my father treated men known as "moneymakers," I resolved to impress him by showing that I could do the same. I learned my first cash racket from watching how my Uncle Frank talked to anyone and everyone. Uncle Frank was the only person allowed to be menacing in our living room since Dad always stood to benefit from it one way or another. At first, I just thought Uncle Frank was a grump for no reason, but gradually I started to notice people *rewarded* Uncle Frank for bad behavior with *money*.

I was at that real observant, sponge-like preschooler age when you learn how to process the world and pick up on patterns, so the mechanics of Uncle Frank's play quickly revealed themselves to me. Uncle Frank was a walking protection racket. You know that old chestnut—pay up and I'll protect you from *me*, you helpless motherfucker!

Impersonating Uncle Frank was easy. The only problem was that I couldn't be scary like my Uncle Frank; I was still at the age where my mom could dress me up in a sailor suit without it being creepy. However, I *definitely* could be annoying.

As soon as I learned how to walk and be obnoxious, I set about collecting tribute from the many visitors to our house by being a pain in the ass. Jimmy Hoffa, Barney Baker, Sam Giancana, and Tony Accardo knew I was annoying, but I'm pretty sure they didn't realize that *I* knew I was being annoying. It was an act, a con. My first racket was being obnoxious to crime bosses until they paid me to go away.

And there was no better hunting ground in America than the living room in our modest white house on Caulder Avenue in the suburbs of Des Moines,

Iowa. This living room with the golden Persian carpet and panoramic view of the golf course in our backyard was basically the United Nations of the underworld. Everyone who ever mattered in organized crime talked business on the luxurious couches under the prints of Michelangelo and the large stone tablet depicting a Roman villa scene.

That's because our suburban house was the headquarters of the Des Moines Mafia Family.

Yes, the Mafia had a Family in Iowa, and Dad was the boss. Yes, I said *Des Moines, Iowa*. In the Midwest underworld, Dad's name was as synonymous to corruption as John Deere was to tractors.

And please, go look all this up online so you realize I'm not running a con. I'll take a smoke break and wait for you.

See?

The mystery wasn't whether there was an Iowa Family run by my Dad—it's *why* did Lou Fratto give up Chicago to come to Iowa in the first place? It's a mystery none of Lou's kids knew the answer to until the writing of this book, and the revelation of what happened in Skokie, Illinois . . .

If the "why" was a mystery, the "how" and "when" are historical fact. The Family was started when Capone lieutenant Charles "Cherry Nose" Gioe came to Iowa to pacify the strategically important state and secure it as a Mafia territory. It was the reverse *Green Acres* scenario for Charley Gioe: farm living was not the life for him; he was more of penthouse view and city life sort of guy. After a few years, Cherry Nose left for Beverly Hills and gave the Family he created in Iowa to a man far better suited to the Heartland lifestyle: his protégé Lou Fratto.

Unlike me, Cherry Nose washed out in Beverly Hills and returned to the Midwest to reclaim his Family. Instead, he was shot to death on the day of my baptism. The top suspects were my uncle Frank and my godfather, Felix "Milwaukee Phil" Alderisio.

Cherry Nose's convenient death made my dad the undisputed boss of the Des Moines Family, which more than satisfied his ambition. To Lou Fratto, Iowa was the Promised Land of Milk and Honey. My dad saw in the sleepy towns and fertile cornfields of Iowa what Bugsy Siegel saw in the deserts of Las Vegas: unlimited opportunity. Iowa was a major distribution hub that bordered seven states and was bookended by the Mississippi River on one side and the Missouri on the other. The man who controlled the strategic bottleneck of Iowa controlled the distribution of illegal goods throughout upper Midwest.

Best of all, it was virgin territory, completely unclaimed and untouched. A smart gangster could walk into this gangland vacuum and make millions without drawing unwanted attention since there would be no resistance and no informed observers to see what was happening.

If you wanted to do serious business as a racketeer or influence peddler in the state of Iowa and certain parts of Nebraska, Indiana, and Illinois, then you first had to visit that little-known living room on Caulder Avenue and pay tribute to my father. During most visits in the late 1950s and early 1960s, you'd also end up paying tribute to a little rugrat named Johnny.

I spent my childhood around an endless parade of gangsters, racketeers, conmen, pimps, hitmen, dirty cops, and politicians. Dad invited some of the most vicious predators and killers in America history into the home he shared with his beloved family . . . and took *pride* in his ability to get away with it. This gamble perfectly reflected Lou's identity crisis: he did gangster shit, but only in the manner of *Father Knows Best*. His TV show would have been *Godfather Knows Best*.

I was born when Lou Fratto was already a 47-year-old homebody, very established and as mellow as a fat housecat. Lou had all the money he needed and didn't have any reason to hustle. All he wanted from his life by that point was good food, peaceful streets, and quality time with his family. He surrounded himself constantly with his wife and children and rarely left home without us. It appealed to Lou's self-image to have us kids around to soften him up and lessen his sense of guilt.

His loving family was evidence that Lou wasn't a "real" gangster like those animals he left behind in Chicago . . . those animals who visited our home and did Dad's dirty work, those savage apes who all-too-often were swinging from branches of our family tree.

From the beginning, I led a double life. At school, I was Johnny Farrell, the good Catholic schoolboy son of a prominent Iowa businessman and philanthropist. At home, I was Johnny Fratto—son of Luigi "Cock-Eyed Louis" Fratto, nephew of Frank "Frankie One-Ear" Fratto and Rudolph Fratto ("the garbage king of Rush Street"), cousin and godson of Felix "Milwaukee Phil" Alderisio, cousin of William "Willie Potatoes" Daddano and Albert "Obie" Frabotta—and on it goes.

As if this double life were not surreal and mind-warping enough for 1950s America, remember that some of the biggest stars alive at that time were Rocky Marciano, Frank Sinatra, and Dean Martin — and these were guys *I knew.* In Rocky's case, he wasn't even just a family friend—he was just family, our frequently live-in "uncle." Imagine how *that* played in school—to be a rich, well-connected, good-looking boy who could name-drop the most famous people on Earth without lying.

You may not realize it, but stardom is contagious. I know, because growing up in my family was like growing up a celebrity.

My fucked-up personality makes perfect sense: I was a child star.

LET ME TELL YOU A QUICK STORY...

WEEKEND AT DUNKY'S

When I was kid, Uncle Frank talked nuts, but he talked like a tough, *cool* nut. He didn't waste words. He mostly said cryptic, ominous Dirty Harry shit that didn't waste anyone's time.

If he wasn't drunk, of course.

When Uncle Frank would get into his booze, get a good brag going, and look at me with his soupy eyes, he'd decide that I needed to hear "man stories" so I would toughen up. My favorite story the old man told me was the story of Dunky's last night out on the town.

Back in the early 1930s, when Uncle Frank was just a teenage hood in a street gang called The 42 Gang, he was best friends with a little boozehound nicknamed Dunky. For years, Frank and Dunky left a snail trail of gore and vomit in their wake.

Another nickname for Dunky was "Javier la Cadaver"—you're about to find out why.

Well, one day during the course of business, Dunky was whacked by a couple mystery gunmen. Uncle Frank was still young enough to have "feelings" at that point and deeply mourned his lost friend. He coped with his grief by resolving to give Dunky the sendoff he would have wanted: one last night on the town.

So Uncle Frank and the 42 Gang broke into the morgue and stole Dunky's corpse. After dressing up the ragdoll body in Dunky's finest suit, they dragged him around town to all of his favorite bars, telling everyone that their comatose friend had "knocked back one too many."

When Uncle Frank first told me this preposterous story, I was hanging on every word since I could intuit it was actually true. Uncle Frank could tell I was enjoying his story, so he decided to pause and slowly get out a new cigarette to torture me. He took out his pack of smokes and slowly slapped the bottom of the package five times. Finally, he pulled out a cigarette with care, as if he could discriminate the good ones from the bad, lit it up, and leisurely saved a good, deep breath.

Then he laughed. Laughed like a maniac. First it was a low chuckle, then a guffaw, then a maniacal cackle, then a pants-wetting out-of-control laugh like Robert De Niro in *Cape Fear*.

"Uncle Frank, what's so funny?"

"Well, you see," he said as he rubbed his teary eyes on his sleeves since his booze and smokes were monopolizing his hands, "The party with Dunky got goin' real good, and pretty soon all of us guys with the dead guy were just about as pucked up as him.

"As the night wore on and I got drunker, something about Dunky started to get to me. I mean, it wasn't sitting right. He had this careless expression on his pace, like he no longer had a worry in the world, while I was still stuck in the shit . . . it pissed me right the puck off. I was puckin' jealous of the lucky pucker!

"So, I stumbled out of our booth at the restaurant and whipped out my revolver. You should've seen how quick my friends dived out of that booth, leaving poor Dunky all by himself. 'Listen up, Dunky!' I yelled loud enough for the entire bar to hear, 'I've had enough of your bullshit! Tonight is the night you die, mudderpucker!'"

Uncle Frank was so into the story he actually put down his glass so he could make a pistol with his free hand.

"Pow! Pow! Pow! I shot that dead mudderpucker three times, right in the chest! Since they hadn't embalmed the mudderpucker yet, blood and shit sprayed all over the restaurant. Women were screaming, men were running, tables were being knocked over . . . my friends were yanking me towards the door, half-scared and half laughing their balls off because they were in on the joke, see . . . they knew I hadn't hurt nobody."

Uncle Frank took a moment to swallow another screwdriver, swishing the last mouthful around a little bit to savor. "Y'know, I been to dozens of funerals since Dunky died, but I don't think anyone's ever been given a better sendoff than the one I gave Dunky.

"That crazy mudderpucker would have loved that shit . . . Especially when the cops found his puckin' body murdered for the second goddamn time that day."

3

TAKE YOUR LITTLE FUCKER TO WORK DAY

"Confidential Informant Omaha T-24 on May 14, 1958 . . . described FARRELL as a 'man of mystery' and stated that one thing was certain in whatever activity FARRELL might be involved in, and that was that FARRELL would be well back in the background, so concealed and hidden from view that it would be almost impossible to determine his connection with the business or activity."

SPECIAL AGENT ROSSITER C. MULLANEY
Federal Bureau of Investigation
File OM 92-74

"Hey, there goes your dad!" one of my friends at St. Anthony's Catholic School shouted during class.

I twisted my body in my desk to get a peek at the window. Cruising down the street was a garbage truck with Dad hanging off the back like Gene Kelly swinging on a lamppost in *Singing in the Rain*. This was all for show: in Lou's head, hitching a ride on the back of one of his sanitation company's trucks in a silk suit and gold jewelry made him look like a real blue collar guy. It also made me look like the son of an eccentric garbage man. But that was pretty much the point: at least I didn't look like the son of a gangster.

At the age of eight, I didn't appreciate the thinking behind Dad's mode of transportation. I was just embarrassed. I was blushing, though you couldn't tell on my brown skin. I was the spitting image of Mowgli from *The Jungle Book*, gangly and wild and dark. Nimble as a pickpocket, I made a break for it when my teacher turned her back to the chalkboard.

Once in the hallway, I went skulking around for nuns to spy on to distract myself from my embarrassment. I loved it when they caught me spying on them and shot me this paranoid look like I was Scooby Doo meddling in their conspiratorial plans. That look gave me a rush; I reveled in violating their privacy.

The Catholic Church: that was the secret society I wanted to penetrate as a little boy. What the Mafia was to American society, the nuns of St. Anthony's Catholic School were to me.

The bitches in black were soldiers in a shadowy organization that ruled the classrooms through intimidation and violence. The only way out for them was death or dishonor. They demanded "donations" from our families that they would kick up the ladder all the way back to the old *padre* back in Italy. You went to the nuns' boss to beg for forgiveness for your sins, and you humbly called him Father as you bowed and kissed his ring.

As a little kid, I seemed to be the only one who noticed how strange they were. In the middle of 1960s America, here was this secretive coven of single women in strange black costumes who summoned supernatural powers through spells spoken in a mysterious ancient language called Latin. I was going to be the one to uncover their mysteries.

I silently slid up to the door of the principal's office like the characters in *Mad Magazine*'s "Spy vs. Spy" comics. I could hear Sister Mary Esther, the boss witch of St. Anthony's Catholic School, gossiping with her sidekick.

"Oh, you know, I wonder about what they say about Johnny Farrell's dad," Sister Mary Esther said in her harsh Joe Pesci voice, referring to me, Johnny Fratto, son of Lou Fratto—only I was known at St. Anthony's as Johnny Farrell, son of Lew Farrell. Don't forget: I had good reason to see conspiracies everywhere!

"The horrible things they say about his dad, Lew, in the paper . . . I confess it's hard not to believe *some* of the bad things they say about Johnny's dad."

"Oh, Sister, I know," said the junior nun, who was like Sister Mary Esther's Barney Rubble. She looked like Barney, too. "You have to admit, though, when you hear the sort of evil deeds they blame on Mr. Farrell, it makes you think. It is *horrible* to think that the world outside of Iowa believes Mr. Farrell is a gangster!"

Gangster . . . this word could not mean what I thought it meant. In our household, the only definition of the word "gangster" I was ever taught was: *not* my dad. Whatever a gangster was, Dad wouldn't say besides categorically insisting it had nothing to do with him. The word was Kryptonite to Super Dad.

My tiny mind was in shock. I mean, didn't these nuns know who Dad *was*? He way outranked those old crones when it came to God. Dad was always reminding everyone about his nurse Mother Cabrini and his pal Pope Pius and his school buddy Walt Disney (whose embarrassing drawings of rodents Dad angrily tore out of his locker; didn't he realize rats were no good?) and his teenage lackey Studs Terkel, a nerd who only lived to become a famous writer because Dad protected him from the teenage gangs of Prohibition Chicago.

What could the nuns put up against all that?

Standing outside of Sister Mary Esther's office, I didn't know how to process my pain and outrage at the idea that these ungrateful nuns were slandering the man who bankrolled every mission, every charity drive, and every renovation at the church behind his broad back.

I was steaming, bouncing on my feet and balling my little frustrated fists. My eyes were stinging, squeezing out tears. I told myself I was going to kick down that door with my little brown foot and set those crusty old witches straight.

But let's be honest: I wasn't going to do that. Nuns in those days were bad motherfuckers. I backed off and drooped back to my class.

When I sat down in my tiny desk, I was so tense that I felt as old and stiff as Ed Sullivan. I tried to distract myself by listening to my teacher for once, but that turned out to be another mistake.

"Boys, remember President Kennedy and his brother Bobby in your prayers every night," my teacher prattled on. "Pray to God to deliver them from danger so that they can continue to lead our great nation with the wisdom and piety they receive from the Holy Mother Church!"

Judging by how those horny old nuns mooned over the Kennedy boys, you'd swear they ended their prayers with *In the Name of Joe, John, and Bobby, Amen!* Their pictures were prominently displayed over the chalkboard along with the Pope, the Virgin Mary, and the usual painting of Jesus if he were as blond as an Allman Brother. Those nuns were positive that the Kennedys were going to secretly stack the government deck in favor of the Church.

I normally didn't pay attention to the Kennedy prayers, but that day I listened with new ears. I remembered what Dad called the Kennedys—"deviants, degenerates, and dope addicts"—and what Robert Kennedy called Dad—"a racketeer" ... a bad word of ambiguous meaning.

I raised my hand.

"Yes, Johnny?" asked the nun, preparing for the worst.

"What's a racketeer?"

"That's a strange question, Johnny, but, to answer you, a racketeer is a gangster."

Oh shit.

"And what's a gangster?" I asked.

The nun, knowing my family, hesitated to answer. She opened her mouth, but no sound came out. She stuttered. Finally, she appealed to the crucifix on the wall and found the courage of her convictions.

"A gangster is a bad man, a criminal who preys on the weak and innocent. A gangster is not a good Christian. He will go to Hell."

That description sure as fuck fit Uncle Frank alright, but Dad? *Dad going to Hell?*

That was the moment I probably earned my first tiny silver hair somewhere on my scalp. I exhaled and rubbed my sweating forehead. Though I didn't know it then, I needed a fucking cigarette.

It was impossible for me to think of Lou as a bad person. I used to think the only people on Earth who can understand what it felt like to grow up around Dad in Iowa are *maybe* Paul McCartney's kids. The love and admiration Lou was given was *that* universal from my vantage point. When I was around him, it was like living in a world that consisted of nothing but one big, warm, joyful family reunion. Everyone wanted to be our friends, to be next to us.

That's why it was so easy to ignore all the evidence he was up to no good. Dad would just smile and say, "Just because there's smoke don't mean there's fire!"

And I believed him.

Of course, there was reason to be suspicious. Yes, Dad's name was really Luigi "Lou" Fratto, an Italian ex-boxer from the Chicago immigrant slum known as the Patch. Yes, the bull-necked, broad-shouldered Lou had acted as the doorman, bodyguard, and assistant to bootlegging king Al Capone, who gave him Canadian Ace Brewery in Des Moines.

Yes, Lou's younger brothers Rudy and Frank Fratto, his cousin Felix "Milwaukee Phil" Alderisio, his brother-in-law Albert "Obie" Frabotta, and his childhood best friends Sam "Teets" Battaglia and Marshall Caifano all became notorious criminals within Capone's "Outfit." And yes, every couple years Dad was called in front of Congress due to his suspected ties to organized crime.

But . . . all of that was just smoke. There was no fire. My good-hearted, devout dad had rejected the lifestyle and morality of his entire Chicago circle of friends and family by leaving town and accepting the chance offered by his old buddy, dearly departed "Hollywood producer" Charles Gioe: a fresh start as a legitimate businessman in Iowa.

To get as far away from his old Mafia connections as possible, Dad even adopted his old boxing name, Lew Farrell, and embarked upon his new life as a peerlessly honest businessman and philanthropist with a clean name, clean record, and a new godly wife, my mom Carmella.

I know what you're thinking after watching *The Sopranos*—not every wiseguy has a mom named Carmella, but I sure as fuck did. And I don't care how dago I sound; the woman really *was* an honest-to-God saint.

Carmella was Dad's secret weapon, his camouflage in Iowa. It was very hard to believe ill of Carmella Farrell's husband. She was the youngest daughter of Iowa's leading Italian family, the Randas. My grandmother ran the most popular restaurant in Des Moines, Aunt Jenny's Trattoria, which meant that everyone who mattered in the state had watched my mom grow up from a sugar-and-spice little girl into a plump, soft-spoken, gentle-natured woman with a tender bleeding heart for the less fortunate. There was no way the most devoutly Christian lady in the Midwest loved an unreformed gangster.

Sitting in my desk at St. Anthony's, what I *really* wanted to know was whether Carmella could give birth to and raise an unreformed gangster. I suddenly had the feeling I was destined in the same way that most people are imprisoned. Original Sin made a whole new load of sense to me. If Dad was a gangster, I didn't think I had it in me to become a stockbroker. After all, cats don't give birth to dogs.

If Dad was Hellbound, so was I. I fidgeted in my desk, fingered my sore eyes, and scanned the room suspiciously to see if anyone saw me for what I was: Evil. Damned.

I tried to calm myself down. I scrounged around my soul like I was searching for change hidden under couch cushions: was there any reason to believe I had evil inside of me?

Yes. I took account of the big sins my teachers were always stressing: lying, cheating, stealing, and dishonoring the Lord Jesus Christ. I flunked all four commandments. I lied when I said my name was Johnny Farrell, cheated on every test I could, and stole everything that fit into my tiny hands whenever I went shopping with my mad kleptomaniac aunt Babe.

The only sin I could even mount a credible defense against was the sin of godlessness. I tried to pray every night and *never* thought a disrespectful thought about the Virgin Mary, who reminded me exactly of my mother. I even made a point to tell Mom how good the Body of Christ tasted after communion every Sunday.

But there was also the little matter of my admiration for Satan. I mean, I loved Jesus, but I secretly thought to myself that the Devil was clearly *the shit*. He was off the fucking chain.

The snake, the apple, the tempting of Adam's naked girlfriend with the long Joan Baez hair *just* covering her creamy... all of that dark shit was just *everything* I wanted to be when I grew up. I kept telling myself I wanted to go to Heaven, but I would always daydream about hanging out in Hell with bad motherfuckers like Goliath and Jezebel and Cain... especially Cain. After all, I had too many brothers—we could've streamlined.

This was no joke to me. I was already paranoid because I was surrounded by Lucifer symbolism—my middle name was Lew and I was born with a birthmark in the shape of the number 667 on the top of my head. Shivering in my Catholic school desk, I was having visions of hellfire and torture by demons. A neurosis was spreading like fungus spores over my brain. If Adam's Original Sin thousands of years ago damned me as his descendant, surely my gangster Dad's sins doomed me rotten.

I was eight.

I unleashed my sudden, inexplicable identity crisis on my family at dinner that night. Arrayed around the table were the usual suspects:

LUIGI FRATTO, aka. "Louis Fratto", "Lew Fratto", "Dad."

CARMELLA RANDA FRATTO, aka. "Mom."

THOMAS JUDE FRATTO, aka. "Tommy", my oldest brother, a sixteen-year-old pathological womanizer.

FRANCIS CARMEN FRATTO, aka. "Frankie", an unstoppable 5'6", fifteen-year-old Terminator with an already legendary track record of straight-A report cards and sports accomplishments.

CARMEL LOU FRATTO, aka. "Carmie Lou", my eleven-year-old sister.

WILLIAM PIUS FRATTO, aka. "Willie", the saintly baby of the family.

And, of course, there was me—Johnny Fratto, nail-biting Hell-fearing pint-sized basketcase, and obviously the looker of the bunch.

I asked my poor family over and over and *over* to remind my needy ass that I was a good boy, that everyone thought I would turn out okay. Though Frankie replied with his usual venomous honesty that I was "frankly an annoying little brat", the rest of the family did their best to allay my fears... until I wore them out. Finally, Dad closed the subject by solemnly announcing that "Santa Claus is the ultimate decider of who is naughty and who is nice, so you're going to have to wait for December to find out."

Thanks Dad! It was fucking September!

I went to bed that night undecided if Lou and Johnny Fratto were evil gangsters or not.

I woke up the next morning still undecided.

I argued with myself over the next week and remained undecided.

I speculated away the next month, forever undecided.

I waited for the holidays to ask Santa. The Santa impersonator at the mall didn't know what to say when I told him all I wanted for Christmas was to know whether Lou Fratto was a gangster. I waited on Christmas Eve for the *real* Santa to tell me the truth—I stayed up *all night* waiting for that derelict jingle-bells-my-balls ass. I prayed for a Soviet MiG to shoot down his sleigh.

Finally, in the New Year, a letter came in the mail that promised to solve the only mystery that mattered to me in the universe.

The Fratto family was sitting at the kitchen table for breakfast. Lou was the picture of middle-aged elegance in a silk suit, beautiful gold watch, and reading glasses. Tommy was already out the door so he could drive some girl to school, and Frankie was grimly drinking a glass of eggs and eating a T-bone steak to pack on the protein for baseball. I was sitting next to Willie, kicking him in the shin under the table and munching on cereal.

My mom had just taken a seat after getting everyone's breakfast ready when she began to absentmindedly flip through the morning mail. I could see her posture change and her eyes light up.

"Lou, how exciting! This letter from Johnny's school says next Monday is Take Your Son to Work Day. What a great opportunity for you to spend some quality time with Johnny!"

Dad rustled his newspapers—an involuntary spasm of nerves. He spoke lightly from behind the cover of the papers. "Oh, Carm, you know I work from home most days, and Johnny could use some time in the classroom."

"Don't be silly, Lou," Carmella said with her self-satisfied, setting-the-world-straight-for-all-the-helpless-men mom voice. "You could make your rounds that day and take Johnny along. I'm sure Johnny..."

"DAD DAD DAD DAD PLEASE PLEASE PLEASE!" my mouth Tommy-gunned, spraying Dad's heart full of holes. He let his newspaper sag so I could see his friendly cartoon grandfather clock face. He squinted his eyes at me, letting me know he was wise to the fact that I just wanted to skip school.

"Alright, alright you two. Give a man his peace in the morning."

The next day, Dad opened up my eyes for the first time to The Life.

It began first thing in the morning as I watched Dad dress. Dad loved clothes. He was always dressed beautifully in a tailored silk suit and tie—which, considering he worked from home, made me think he was fucking nuts! Who dresses up in a $1000 suit to go sit on your own living room couch?

It was only that morning that I realized Dad had two separate closets: one for Iowa, and one for everywhere else. No matter how elegant Dad looked in his handmade suits, Italian leather shoes, silk ties, perfectly crumpled hand-kerchiefs, and European watches from brands that Iowans could not even hope to pronounce, he never showed Des Moines the clothes from the second closet: The A-Wardrobe. The clothes in this closet were so nice, so *fine,* that he only let himself wear them on visits to places like Chicago or New York—places where a gangster could be flamboyant without fear of being bothered.

As we left that morning, Dad didn't subject me to a day spent hanging from one of his fleet of garbage trucks. Instead, we traveled in a plain white pickup truck . . . which was considerably less impressive than the chauffeured limo or Cadillac we drove during visits to Chicago. That wouldn't fly in Iowa. It would make him look conspicuous.

That was Dad's challenge: to be an organized criminal in an area where respect for that profession had never been established. In Chicago, you could walk around and blatantly be a *gangster*; not only would you not be bothered, but you would be feared, worshipped, flattered. Those people knew the mean-ing of respect.

In Iowa, if you acted like a gangster, some redneck would just shoot you. They just didn't know any better. Dad's challenge was being the godfather of a state that had no idea what that concept meant and would have immediately killed him if it did.

And he succeeded in hiding his true nature from Iowa society at large. No more than a handful of Iowa's farmers, businessmen, and pastors ever sus-pected that they were living in one of the most locked-down pieces of Mafia real estate in the country. I know dozens of law-abiding Des Moines residents who *to this day* refuse to believe that "good ole Lew" was an *invader* sent from a shadowy Chicago underworld to secretly take over their neighborhoods. We didn't get *those types* in nice Christian places like Iowa.

The All-American appearance of everyday life in Iowa was like a great big Norman Rockwell painting that Dad hung up to hide the massive, smoke-spew-ing, black-steel Fratto political machine that actually ran the state. Behind the scenes, Lou Fratto was pulling the levers and greasing the wheels, getting his hands dirty, quietly enforcing the unspoken rules that kept Midwest society and its secret black market economy running profitably and smoothly... but only a handful of people saw behind the scenes.

On the morning of Take Your Son to Work Day, my dad pulled aside the curtain for the first time and showed me his *real* job.

That day, the Fratto family white pickup truck visited everyone in Des Moines who would kiss Dad's ring, call him Don Luigi, and offer him tribute in cash or in kind. We stopped by every bookmaker, every betting parlor, every hookered-up lounge, every go-go joint, every smoky labor union hall, and even the girlie show at the Iowa State Fair. Dad never explained who we were seeing, or why we were seeing them, or why some of the women had their titties out—he believed in my ability to observe and figure things out.

I was transfixed by the hulking, scarred, dark-eyed comic book villains we met and how they groveled in front of Dad. I was in awe of how Dad ordered these big, tough goons around with nothing more than a grunt or a whisper.

I was thinking to myself the entire time: *this is the answer. We are gangsters.* I was like a vampire that finally felt those fangs take the elevator down into my mouth. I knew—for that moment at least—Lou was Dad at home, but he was The Boss everywhere else.

I was eerily quiet when I came home that day. Mom kept asking me if I had fun, but I just nodded and ran up to my room to decompress from being so close to the power Dad held. I knew that one day that power would be mine. And with it, my soul would probably belong to the Devil.

For once, I settled down to do my homework: explain your dad's job as you observed it during Take Your Son to Work Day. I guess it helped me come to terms with what I had seen.

That night, Frankie caught on pretty quick that something was wrong with his most troublesome little brother: I was quietly doing my own homework and not annoying anyone. This obviously meant I was up to some serious shit.

"Hey, twerp," he said as he flicked one of my ears with his strong finger, "what are you writing there?"

Without a word, I lifted the piece of paper up with the hand that wasn't rubbing my throbbing ear. I wanted Frankie to read and see that *I knew* Dad's job was to be Don Luigi and collect money from bad men in smoky rooms and naked women in tents at the Fair. The impression he was supposed to get was that we were on the same level, two peers within a secret brotherhood.

The impression Frankie actually got was that I was a bonehead and Dad wasn't much better. "Ah, for fuck's sake, Johnny!" Frankie snarled as he looked down with a mixture of confusion and disgust.

With that, Frankie walked out of the room with my homework assignment and marched off to talk to Dad in the living room. I heard one sentence—"Take a look at what Johnny is writing for class!"—followed by the rarest sound in my universe: our living room door being slammed shut.

My heart sank; I hated when I was responsible for Dad getting lectured by Frankie. I hated it both for Dad's sake and because I disliked giving Frankie the pleasure of lording it over everyone else how smart and responsible he was.

The next morning, I came down for breakfast and was told by Dad that I had been called in sick for school. "Why? What did I do wrong?"

"Nothing, nothing," Lou said, putting his hand on my shoulder and smiling. He knew I was expecting a reaming. "Don't worry. I just enjoyed Take Your Son to Work Day so much that I wanted to have another. Besides, there are some jobs today that you can help me with."

Daydreams of me in a pinstripe suit blasting a Tommy gun out the window of our white pickup truck flashed through my mind.

My day was nothing like my daydream or my first Father/Son Day with Dad. Instead of gogo joints and betting parlors, Dad drove me to all of his legitimate business interests: the family friendly Hymie's Family Drive-In Restaurant, The Gas Light Lounge, The High Flyer Bar, his contracting company Empire Builders, his garbage company Sanitary Disposal, and various breweries whose product he distributed through his Manhattan Brewing Company.

Instead of standing beside my dad like an enforcer as he picked up envelopes of cash and had his ring kissed, this time I felt like a personal assistant to a major CEO. All day long was spent negotiating business deals, looking at blueprints, dropping off bags of receipts at the accountant's office, signing contracts, writing checks, and paying friendly visits to other Iowan business and political leaders. It was boring.

Between each meeting, Dad would take me aside and make sure I understood what I was witnessing.

"See, Johnny? I always get what I want, and I never have to be mean or violent. And Johnny, how do I get what I want? Simple: I pour a little sugar everywhere I go. That's how you get your way in life: you make people like you, happy to see you, and happy to make you happy. If a little money is needed, don't hesitate to give 'em a little money. Just pour a little sugar everywhere, and you find your problems will disappear. That's all business is."

Whenever my 5'2" rhino of a father hopped out of his pickup truck in his beautiful silk suit, he landed on the ground with a Hollywood megawatt smile already lit. Whoever encountered Dad was met with a smile that told them that running into them was the most pleasant surprise in the world, as if his secret wish during the entire day had been to see *you*—whoever the fuck you were.

It didn't matter. Dad was always smiling, always ready with a compliment, a joke, and a kind word for your family, whose individual names he always instantly remembered. Lou Fratto's life in civilian Iowa was a campaign of sunshine. Whenever my dad left the house on civilian business, he concentrated every single second on finding as many people as possible to make happy and feel good about themselves and "good ole Lew Farrell."

At the end of the day, we returned to our home, and Dad told me to go to my room and rewrite the homework assignment Frankie had shown him using that day's experience instead of the first.

"Remember what you saw today, Johnny, and remember . . . *always* remember, no matter what anyone says, your Dad is no gangster. He is just a businessman!"

"But isn't Chicago a better place to be a businessman? There's a lot more money there!"

He tousled my hair. It was the end of our conversation. He never told me why he left for Iowa.

In my room, I didn't waste my time doing schoolwork. I was too busy weighing matters of good and evil. The first day with Dad had convinced me that he was a remorseless gangster, and the second day with Dad convinced me that he was an extremely kind, generous, and saintly pillar of the community. The Lou Fratto from Monday and the Lew Farrell from Wednesday were opposites . . . like Jesus and the Devil.

Lou Fratto was a double man, a Dr. Jekyll who rationalized away the existence of Mr. Hyde. He never accepted that he was a gangster; he would turn red with self-righteous outrage at the thought that *anyone* could belittle his accomplishments with that word. This wasn't for show: the man would argue with *other gangsters* over his identity.

As a child, I had no idea which was the real man. He had a good act, whichever one it was. Thanks to him, I had no idea who he was or who I was destined to be. Heaven and Hell seemed like equally probable destinations for the two of us. I was confused, profoundly confused.

My entire childhood would be colored with speculation over whether my heart pumped poisoned blood.

LET ME TELL YOU A QUICK STORY...

ABOUT BILL OATES AND JON FAIRCHILD

Dad was sold on Bill Oates. Very few people understood why. He was just a small potatoes bookmaker and gambler, yet Dad regularly invited him over to our house for priceless face-to-face time.

I knew why Dad loved Bill Oates: his fucking chimp. Bill had a pet chimpanzee that accompanied him everywhere dressed up in human clothes. This made Bill a valuable tool in winning over our affection. Dad was taught by organ grinders and 1950s variety show hosts like Milton Berle that monkeys were rambunctious, fun-loving little slapstick comedians who would make the perfect playmates for his rascally young sons.

Me and Willie loved Dad too much to take away his delusion that the gift of a jungle animal in a minstrel suit made him Dad of the Year 1962. Whenever Bill came over, we'd glumly walk outside holding the chimp's hand as he squeezed just hard enough to let us know he could crush our bones into dust.

Once out of the view of the adults, we immediately began to cower and beg the evil primate for mercy. No luck. The chimp would smile, grab our hands, spin in a circle as fast as he could, and launch us through the air like Frisbees. We'd land five or six feet away, and the chimp would start clapping. We hated that abusive ape.

We were downright excited when Dad told us one afternoon that the chimp had been taken away from Bill. I didn't know anything about animal maintenance and care, but I had a feeling that anyone who daily dressed up a chimpanzee in a tuxedo wasn't a qualified caretaker for a wild animal.

We weren't so happy when we happened to see Bill again and noticed that all of the fingers on one of his hands had been torn clean off! I couldn't sleep for weeks. I had come very close to losing my ability to wear diamond rings! How different my future would have been!

The story of Bill Oates brings me to an important point. People are always telling me how the Mob is dead in the 21st century, how it has lost its power.

If you're talking about the Mafia as an organization that levies street taxes and sets down rules for other criminals, yeah, that's been fucked for decades.

But the Mob wasn't only a criminal organization; it was also an international social and business community. They did favors for each other, played together, made money together, conspired together, intermarried with each other, and acted as godparents to each other's children. This was called the Network. Though the criminal element of the Mob shrunk, The Network has only gotten bigger.

Scarcely a week goes by when I don't randomly encounter either an old criminal associate from the Mob or his kid, nephew, ex-wife, business partner, protégé, attorney, in-law, or good friend. They are often in positions of power and have no compulsion using that power on my behalf *solely* because of our tenuous tie within the Network.

Bill Oates is a great example.

One day as legitimate adult businessmen, my brother Tommy and I were being introduced to well-dressed powerbrokers in a lavish conference room. I immediately zeroed in on one old gentleman who was unmistakably familiar. At first, I thought he might be some politician or banker that I used to see at Gibson's Steakhouse in Chicago. Cursing myself for forgetting this powerful man's name, I faked a smile and offered my hand. He shifted uncomfortably and twisted his body to present me with his other hand.

I looked down. His right hand was a misshapen lump of knuckles. No wonder I recognized him; it was Fingerless Bill Oates!

Stuttering, Bill Oates introduced himself as "Jon Fairchild"—he really overcompensated with *that* bullshit name. Jon Fairchild! It just screams "con-man trying to pass himself off as a trustworthy businessman." I was about to bust his balls and call him his old name, but Tommy's elbow landed on my ribcage just in time.

Then I understood: Fingerless Bill Oates was the "in" on this business deal. The 1960s wiseguy organ grinder was now a powerful businessman with connections and credibility to exploit. And he was just as honored to do business with Tommy and Johnny Fratto as he had been to do business with Lou Fratto.

That's how the Network works.

4

THE ROCKET RACKET

"As stated above, subject's wife is CARMELLA FARRELL, nee RANDA. On August 30, 1960, during the interview referred to above, FARRELL advised he had five minor children whom he identified as 'TOMMIE, FRANKIE, JOHNNY, WILLIE, and CARMIE-LOU.'"

SPECIAL AGENT ROSSITER C. MULLANEY
Federal Bureau of Investigation
File OM 92-74

Dad was an energetic, sweet-tempered man in his fifties when I was a kid. Though he still had an imposingly muscular 50-inch back and trim 32-inch waist, Dad didn't let any of his tough guy show around us kids. He carried himself with gentleness and lightness. He never showed us his strength, never spanked or yelled, rarely even frowned. He only made us happy.

Lou felt he had a role to play with us. Deep down, I think he felt guilty for having some of his children so late in life since he knew he wouldn't be there for us as long as we might need him.

So Dad spoiled us. Lou Fratto was a wild, wasteful, carefree, and extravagantly generous father. He knew damn well that he was spoiling us until it was just *sick*, and he loved it. He took pride in the idea of his little privileged rich kids.

When combined with my deeply felt belief that I was likely predestined for Hell, the surreal upbringing given to me by Lou Fratto distorted my handle on reality beyond any hope of repair. If you listen to my ex-girlfriends and ex-wife, Dad ruined me and made me a pathological narcissist with a deranged sense of entitlement. If you ask my siblings, I never left the dreamy fantasy land of wish-fulfillment Dad created for me to join the rest of mankind in the grim, disappointing real world.

That's probably why I did well in Hollywood. That's probably why I'm so much more ambitious and daring than the rest of my family. Dad taught me I could get absolutely *anything* I wanted.

When family talk about Dad's spoiling of me, there is one story that always comes up, and for good reason: Dad risked going to jail for high treason to grant a wish of mine that any other parent in America would have instantly dismissed as ridiculous. I'm talking about the infamous story of how my father stole a NASA spacecraft and installed it in our living room to fulfill my dreams of becoming an astronaut.

The story begins at Camp Dodge, a military base outside of Des Moines that included a park for families to swim and play. My mom drove my little brother Willie and I to Camp Dodge for the weekend to raise hell far away from Dad's important meetings at home.

While we were walking around Camp Dodge, I casually stumbled upon a Mercury Project space capsule just sitting on the grass. Now, I know that may seem a bit strange—I assume there are no spaceships decorating your local park, but it's the truth. In 1962, the Treasury Department was taking Mercury-7 space capsules on tours across America to raise funds for treasury bonds, and Camp Dodge was just another stop on the intergalactic tour.

Like most eight-year-old boys in 1962, I was positive that I would one day become an astronaut like John Glenn. My family encouraged my wacky dreams since I certainly seemed better suited to Mars than Iowa. Once I saw that space capsule, I saw my ticket to life as a *Jetson*. This was a couple years before *Lost in Space* taught little boys to fear outer space, where intergalactic predators like Dr. Smith were on the prowl for succulent young meat.

So I was tripping pretty hard on astronaut fantasies as I marveled at this 12-foot-tall, 6-foot-wide, bullet-shaped black lawn ornament. I really let my mom have it—a spoiled kid like me didn't wanna hear that you couldn't just buy the Mercury-7 spaceship and take it home. As my mom always said, the squeaky wheel gets the oil, and I was squeakier than a buttfucked pig.

Nonetheless, my mom wasn't about to steal a spacecraft for me. She was the very picture of hefty, rosy-cheeked, ever-patient Italian motherhood.

"Ma, I want that spaceship!"

"Sorry, it's not for sale, Johnny."

"*Ma-ah*, then just take it!"

"That's stealing; that would be a sin, Johnny." My mom was so religious that she would pray to St. Bernard when our dog got sick. She loved me, but sinning on my behalf was out of the question. Like Meatloaf, she would do anything for me—but she wouldn't do that.

"Fine, I'm taking it up with dad!" Lou had never turned me down before, so I had no reason to doubt that the spaceship catalogue would soon be delivered to our home.

As soon as we got home that weekend, I hauled ass through our house, flailing my limbs like a goofball, and busted into the living room where Dad was conducting a meeting discussing life and death matters with his cronies.

Outfit business could wait. This was an emergency. I let him have it with the "Daddy! Daddy! Daddy!" and "You shoulda *seen* it!" routine.

Dad spoke in a whisper—he made Don Corleone look like Sam Kinison—but I got the *LOUD* genes. After a few minutes of my deafening, lightning-fast yammering, Lou turned to the wiseguys watching with bemusement and said, "Well, you heard 'im. If the kids wants it, we gotta go get it!"

Three days later, on Wednesday afternoon, I came home to find a gigantic cardboard box and a Home Juice semi-truck in our backyard. Home Juice was the fruit juice company of Detroit mobster Anthony "Tony Jack" Giacalone, the man later accused of clipping our friend Jimmy Hoffa. At first, I figured Tony Jack was just sending us a truly fucking *huge* shipment of orange juice. This wasn't that odd: Tony Jack had *plenty* of juice.

Get it?

When I went inside, Dad had this sly smile on this face. "Look at our new refrigerator in the backyard," he said. Considering that this fucking cardboard box was 13 or 14 feet tall, that would be one excessively roomy refrigerator. Maybe Mom had bought a *Flintstones* cookbook and needed a fridge that could fit brontosaurus ribs.

The Cardboard Box of Mystery disappeared for a few days, and I didn't think about it again. That Saturday morning, I got my brother Willie up and we ran down to stairs to play. As we were rappelling down the stairs, we encountered our dad on the way up. He waved us in to come really close, like he was sharing a secret.

"Listen, I got somethin' for you kids," Dad said in his usual whisper. "You can't keep it, but you can play with it for a little while. But you gotta keep your mouths shut!" As he said this, he bulged out his eyes and zipped his lips with his finger and threw away the key. We made the same gesture to him and ran down to the living room to see what our dad had bought for us.

And there it was! A spacecraft that weighed 2500 pounds when operational was sitting in our living room, scraping at the ceiling. I could not fathom how they got this thing inside. Frankly, I didn't give even half of a space-traveling fuck; I trampled Willie like we were in a Calcutta breadline to get at this thing. I wanted to be the first one to fire the engines and take it out for a test drive.

Minutes later, Dad hustled back into the room, worried that he had forgotten something. He tossed Willie and I out of the spacecraft so he could crawl inside.

"Hey dad, no fair! I thought you said *we* could play with it!" I whined.

"I ain't playin' in this thing, you nuts?" Dad wheezed. "I forgot to take the key out of the ignition. I don't want you kids to blast away the entire house."

"Daddy, don't take the key, I wanna fly to school tomorrow so everyone can see!" I screeched, dreaming of arriving in a full spacesuit, a hero to all the kids of Des Moines. You *know* I wasn't going to miss the opportunity to fly this motherfucker. I was fully prepared to jimmy the ignition if Dad took the key. Dad rolled his eyes at me.

"You ain't flyin' this thing nowhere!" Dad continued to rifle around, frustrated that he couldn't find the key and the ignition for the space car.

"Where the hell is this thing... How do you turn this dang thing on? *Oh shit!*" Dad shouted as he recoiled from the controls. He had touched a button that immediately lit up part of the console; he thought he was about to launch his ass to the moon.

Once he satisfied himself that there was no way for us to create a "Des Moines, we have a problem!" scenario in his living room, Dad handed over the capsule to Willie and I. Over the next few days, we went wild playing out our every space travel and astronaut fantasy. When we got bored, Dad invited over some of our cousins who came from good families.

That's code for *they could keep their mouths shut.* Willie and I became intrepid space warriors defending our craft against our alien invader cousins. We were like those angry old white guys who camp out on the Rio Grande with rifles and binoculars looking for Mexican border-jumpers. I don't think I've ever had so much fun outside of a bedroom.

Before you get the wrong idea, I had no delusions about what my dad had done, and neither did Willie. We were not thinking, "Wow, our wonderful daddy did something great for us!" We were thinking, "Holy shit! Dad stole a fucking spaceship! Dad's a fucking gangster!"

Still, you gotta admit: this was one *cool* thing for a dad to do. It was heart-warming; my dad was committing an enormous national security breach for no reason better than making his little boy Johnny smile.

On the other hand, my much older brother Frankie, who was a very self-important pain-in-the-ass teenager, was not a real indulgent sort of guy. Frankie was just about the most uptight, stick-up-the-shitbox teenager you could ever meet: straight A's in school, superstar athlete in baseball and bas-ketball, and formally dressed apprentice Mob boss at home. Frankie was not like my other older brother, Tommy, who was too concerned with partying and getting laid to ever worry about what gifts the babies of the family were getting. Tommy was getting *pussy*—we could keep our spaceships.

Instead, Frankie was the sort of big brother who would take us to the batting cages and make us stand in front of the pitching machines as it Gat-ling-gunned baseballs at our heads at 90-miles-per-hour until we learned how to catch or were concussed. Like most teenage big brothers, Frankie was firmly in the "cut the little rugrats no slack" school of parenting, and he had no fear letting Dad know it.

"Dad," Frankie lectured as he stood dumbfounded before the spacecraft in our living room. "These fucking kids, dad...you *gotta* stop. Really, this is the end. It can't get worse. It literally *cannot* possibly get worse in any way!" Frankie was craning his head back and forth in amazement as he watched his little brothers ransacking a Mercury-7. "This really is beyond parody, dad."

Like a big kid, Dad would laugh and tell Frankie to lighten up, but even-tually my big brother would wear him down. Killjoy Frankie Fratto won out when rumors started to appear locally that the military had "misplaced" a Mercury-7 capsule.

When we came down to play Saturday morning, we knew there was trou-ble before we even entered the living room: the room was too bright. The cur-tains looking out onto the golf course in our backyard had to have been open. If they were open, that meant there was no spaceship on display.

Sure enough, the Fratto family intergalactic cruiser was dismantled into a million pieces on our backyard lawn. A bunch of knockaround guys were painstakingly repackaging the thing into the giant cardboard box; Tony Jack's Home Juice truck was waiting to cart it away.

Dad was standing on the porch pulling his nine-mile-long phone cord be-hind him, supervising the job. I'd like to say I was above begging to keep my

Johnny-7 spaceship, but that would be a horrible lie. I begged and begged Dad, just *groveled*, but all I won in the end was the concession that we would drive behind the Home Juice truck as it took away my favorite toy.

I remember that "Walk Like a Man" by the Four Seasons was playing on the FM radio as we followed the Home Juice truck to the Des Moines Fairgrounds. I didn't take the hint and kept whining like a kid.

If you think that stealing a spaceship would be hard, imagine how difficult it is to *return* a stolen spaceship. No real subtle way to do that, right? My dad's solution was so lazy and reckless that it reminds me of me. I guess you can't be too surprised that a man crazy enough to steal a space capsule from a military base would be a little cocky about returning it.

The next day, the police found a Mercury spaceship parked in an empty parking lot across the street from the Fairgrounds. I would have loved to see the look on that patrolman's face—*Um, I'd like to call for backup, there appears to be a fucking UFO parked across the street from the horse track!*

Since it was common knowledge that Dad was the gambling boss of Des Moines, it's hard to exaggerate how arrogant it was for him to park that spaceship right next door to the Fairgrounds. It would be as if the Hamburglar stole the goddamn thing and then left it in a McDonald's parking lot to be found.

As we were driving home, Dad saw me pouting and tried to cheer me up. "Johnny," he said in his soft voice, "did you learn anything from this?"

"Not to get excited about gifts because Frankie will make you take them back?" I responded.

"No-*o*," Dad said, shaking his big full-moon face side to side. "I'm serious. What you need to learn is this: anytime someone tells you can't do something...*don't*...*listen*...*to*...*them*. Prove them wrong. You can do anything!"

Knowing what I know about Dad now, it's clear what happened. My joy wasn't his only motivation.

When he said in one of his living room summits that he should get me that spaceship to play with, his cronies laughed and told him it was impossible to steal something like that from the federal government and get away with it. As soon as Dad heard the word "impossible", it was fucking *on*.

"Impossible" is like a showboating matador with a smarmy grin waving a big red flag to a Fratto. From that moment, Lou Fratto knew for damn sure his son was going to get that spaceship. It took about three days.

I got Dad's message loud and crystal fucking clear: the rules didn't apply to the Fratto family. We did anything we wanted, and we got away with it.

LET ME TELL YOU A QUICK STORY...

ABOUT MY CROSS TO BEAR

Right around my eighth or ninth birthday, it became clear that my little brother Willie was a baseball prodigy just like the golden-boy Frankie. For a helplessly lazy and unathletic pretty boy like me, the idea that I would be living my entire life sandwiched between two super-athletes was an intolerable injustice.

Since my dad made his way out of the ghettos of Chicago through his skill as a boxer, sports definitely mattered in our household. I felt like a total zero, especially when I overheard my father brag to his buddies that Willie would be "the next Mickey Mantle."

So what? I couldn't play baseball, but I knew there had to be something in the world that a 1960s Italian-American gentleman of taste thought was more admirable than athletic skill.

"Dad, you say Willie's gonna be the next Mickey Mantle, right?" I asked, as I pulled on his tie and played with one of the buttons on his shirt. "There must be someone who's a bigger star than Mickey Mantle, right?"

My dad looked around the living room to all of his cronies and started chuckling. "Yes, Johnny, there is a star bigger than Mickey Mantle," my dad said with a teasing tone, "and his name is Jesus Christ!" The room resounded with the wheezing, coughing, boozy laughter of half a dozen wiseguys.

I was not laughing. I was no longer even in the room. I was on a mission.

Next door to our home was a house under construction. I walked right inside the frame of that half-built house and stole a hammer, some nails, and some planks of wood. I then grabbed a pillowcase and a pair of scissors.

Less than twenty minutes after my dad made his Mickey Mantle crack and embarrassed me in front of his wiseguy cronies, Lou Fratto's copper-skinned boy with long black hair reemerged in the living room dressed in a makeshift white tunic and shouldering the burden of a life-sized cross.

My dad blinked. Slowly, one eyebrow lifted itself an inch above the other.

Finally, my dad laughed...and laughed...and laughed. "You gotta fuckin' love this kid's moxie!" Lou wheezed as he clapped his hands together.

Frankie and Willie may have had incredible athletic talent, but they had nothing on me when it came to the shamelessness of my hustle.

My dad loved my Jesus impersonation as a one-time gag, but its charm wore out quickly with him. To his horror, he would be talking with Tony Accardo or Jimmy Hoffa in the living room when, suddenly, I would stumble into view in the backyard dressed as the Messiah. My dad's peers would stand up and look through the living room window in shock as Lou Fratto's son lugged a cross around the yard while little boys in Ben Hur Halloween costumes beat him with makeshift whips and exploded ketchup packets on his head to simulate blood.

Long before Mel Gibson dialed up the violence in *The Passion*, I was stirring up controversy across Des Moines by rewriting the Stations of the Cross so that the itinerary included roughly seventy beatings, a hundred falls, and ten or twenty gruesome crucifixions. By the time sundown sent me home to get resurrected, I was so exhausted that I'd just dump the cross in the driveway. This once sent Dad into a rare tirade when he accidentally ran over it with his pickup truck.

"FOR GOD'S FUCKING SAKE JOHNNY!" he screamed, straining his worn-out vocal cords to the point of a tear.

"Aren't you taking the Lord's name in vain, my son?" I asked in my sleepy-voiced Jesus impression.

Dad was just about to ban me from dressing up like Jesus for all of eternity...until I reminded him we were scheduled to go visit Uncle Frank and Aunt Kay. Blasphemy or not, Dad wasn't going to let such an incredible opportunity to wind up his little brother pass him by.

Dad had me carry the cross through Des Moines Airport and take it on the plane as my carry-on. The driver who picked us up at O'Hare Airport in Chicago reverently tied it to the roof of his cab. At Uncle Frank's palatial home in the suburbs, my dad told the other kids to go in first and distract Uncle Frank while he helped me get into my robes and untie the cross from the roof of the cab. After a few minutes, we made our grand entrance together.

The moment was epic. The only time you ever saw Uncle Frank really smile and show love on his face was when he saw my father. Let's just say I've never seen a more drastic and quick descent from a look of joy and admiration to a look of rage and disgust than when I followed my dad into Uncle Frank's house dressed as Jesus lugging a cross.

"Oh, this little devil worshipper is SICK, Lou! Don't you see it?!"

As I said earlier, Uncle Frank sometimes had a point when it came to me. He knew me at my worst.

5

ZAPPY STARDUST & HIS SICILIANS FROM MARS

While the police were still swarming around the space capsule with drawn service weapons and flashlights like something out of *The Day the Earth Stood Still*, I was already seeking my next method of space exploration.

My first plan was quaintly conventional by Fratto standards: I would become an honest-to-God astronaut through the normal and legal channels. This delusion lasted one hour before Frankie flicked my ear and told me, "Hey, dummy, you actually have to be *good* at math *and* science to become an astronaut." To this day, the only sort of math I can do involves loans and gambling.

So I dumped the astronaut idea. Besides, I had been told those guys have to wear diapers, and that didn't exactly appeal to a kid who just got over wetting his bed. With my dad out of the space exploration business and NASA in the shitting-your-pants business, I was left with only one option when it came to leaving planet Earth: alien abduction. And this didn't sound too bad, since the whole "anal probe" phenomenon had not yet made its way into UFO abduction lore.

I bought every single pulp magazine that even hinted at containing the tiniest tidbit of information on aliens and getting abducted by them. I was especially obsessed with the descriptions of the little green men themselves: child-size off-color creatures with enormous heads, slanted eyes, emaciated bodies, and strange, inhuman speech patterns. Just about every night I dreamed that one of these tiny space travelers would beam me out of bed and take me on an intergalactic version of the joyrides around Des Moines my eldest brother Tommy sometimes took me on in his "pussy wagon."

One day, I woke after an especially intense and evocative dream about an alien abduction feeling a little out of sorts. Had I been abducted and suppressed the memory? Maybe. Anything is possible, especially in my life.

In class that morning, I sat down in the desk closest to the back corner door so I could slip out and snoop around the school unnoticed. Shortly after the lessons started, however, a small group of adults gathered by the doorway, and the nun excused herself to chat with them in the hall.

I could hear strange, reedy sounds coming from the hall, like a small songbird having its dick squeezed. I knew the nuns were into some conspiratorial shit, and I smelled another cover-up. I heard shoes scuffling and old bags sighing.

After a moment, our teacher returned with a new friend. Without the slightest hesitation, our teacher escorted a little alien from my dream into our room. *Ho-lee shit! They're coming for me in broad daylight!*

"Class, I have to introduce you to a new student. Please meet...um," the nun began to blush and looked down uncomfortably at the visitor. "How do you say it, again?"

The little alien was too advanced a spiritual being to be offended by her primitive humanoid rudeness. He had a serene, peaceful air to him, like a hippie on a real warm Quaaludes high. The creature lifted his antlike head up to the teacher, lightly blinked his low lids over his oil black eyes, and emitted an incomprehensible series of sounds like a rusty rattled bell.

"Oh, uh, *okay*," the poor nun said, "I guess, class...um, let's call our new classmate Zap. Say hello to Zap, class."

"HELLO ZAP!"

A smile of immense satisfaction came across Zap's face. I knew that look. I had seen Dad give it to the big muscular guys who kissed his hand and begged to do favors for him. *Oh fuck, this fucker thinks we are declaring our homage!* Pleased with our submission, our tiny intergalactic ruler bowed his head and klucked at us in his moon language.

"Okay, Zap, please take a... *seat*," this note of disappointment appeared in the nun's voice as she noticed that the only free desk was directly to the left of mine in the educational deadzone at the back of the classroom. Nonetheless, she motioned for the space emperor to enthrone himself in the seat next to me.

The little Yoda creature floated over to my seat with a serene, glowing smile. Zap hovered into the seat next to me and nodded his head with imperial grace. There was no doubt in my mind that the creature sitting beside me radiating peace and knowledge like a Martian Buddha was the alien from my dream. Physically, he was a dead match: the slanted eyes, the globular head, the body like a collapsed tent, the black hole eyes, the off-color skin, and the strange all-gray uniform with huge sleeves and choking tight collar.

Clearly, he had come for me. He quacked something at me in a high-pitched, scratchy space voice than sounded older than the Pyramids.

DANGER DANGER JOHNNY FRATTO!

I was out of that fucking room at top speed. I ran out of that fucking class-room like it was the possessed menstrual flow hallway from *The Shining* and sprinted all the way home. My limbs were flailing like a kid's cheap wooden puppet, and I was hyperventilating and lightheaded, but I could not stop. My life depended on it.

Lou Fratto was the only person on Earth I trusted to protect me from an alien invasion—I'm sure he could pull some strings on Mars and arrange for this Zap cocksucker to get recalled and sent on plunger duty to the sewer system on Saturn.

Given the fact that it was the middle of the school day, Dad was pretty nonchalant about my sudden panicked arrival at home. He was sitting with Jimmy Hoffa's gigantic brick shithouse bonebreaker Barney Baker. In addition to playing Barney Rubble to Hoffa's Fred Flintstone, Mr. Baker was definitely the sort of guy you wanted on your side in an intergalactic street fight.

"*Dad, they got a alien in my classroom!*"

Dad squinted at me with a look of mild confusion and motioned for me to jump on his lap. "Johnny, calm down, calm down. Describe the alien for me."

"He's named Zap..."

"Are you sure they didn't call him 'Zip'?" Dad asked sedately. He didn't seem surprised, just a little curious. My skin went so pale and my eyes blew up so big that I must have looked like a snowy owl. Did my dad *know* these creatures?

"No, I think it was Zap..."

"Was he big, dark, have a mustache? Did he talk like the people from the 'Old Country?'"

What was this *Lord of the Rings* fairyland shit? I wasn't talking about Zips from the Old Country; I was talking about motherfucking space aliens.

"Dad, no! LISTEN! Why won't you listen? Jeez. He's a little yellow insect with big black eyes with slanty lids, black hair, a tiny body..."

"Whew!" Dad exhaled and laughed. "Boy, you had me scared. My aliens don't come through New Orleans until next week. I thought they had gotten here early. I'm sending them to St. Anthony's..."

HO!...LEE!...SHIT! Even Dad was in on this conspiracy. I had no protection, no safe haven. If Lou was importing aliens from outer space and sending them to St. Anthony's, was he engaging in some sort of cultural exchange program? Would he have to send *one of his own* to the planet of the Zaps? Would he send... *me?*

"AAAAAAAAAAAAAAAAH!" I exploded right in Dad's face like the famous screaming batboy on the cover of *National Enquirer.* I was howling like a fire truck as I fled the room, waving my hands in the air in terror. "You go on, boy!" called a laughing Barney Baker from the couch. Being surrounded by Teamsters all day, Barney was completely used to such excitable behavior.

My hysterical stampede through my house made a crash landing against my mom's warm, cushioned figure. "Johnny, what on Earth are you doing home?"

"Mom...MOM!" I cried, breaking into tears. Here, at last, was my one safe haven from the intergalactic conspiracy. Here was the one person completely immune to any sort of suspicious, clandestine, or crooked impulse.

"Baby, what could possibly make you this upset?"

"The nuns brought an alien into my class room, and dad said he is importing aliens through New Orleans, and but they are going to steal me and smell funny and look like ants and..."

"Johnny, don't be silly. You are completely overreacting." My mom pulled me to her bosom. "Listen, here's something you should know. *Everyone* in America is descended from an alien!"

My blood chilled to the temperature and consistency of a daiquiri.

"Even our families are descended from aliens. You are descended from aliens! In fact, the government is trying to send some of your dad's friends — like Dad's friend Carlos in New Orleans—*back home...*"

I backed away and collapsed. I was already operating at full capacity when it came to psychological strain. I could not handle a third dimension to my identity crisis: gangster, good boy, and alien from outer space subject to deportation.

I took to my bed for a week, a shivery ice-blue mess. I was cracking up. In Victorian days, they would have said I was suffering from a bad case of "the vapours" and whipped out the leeches and smelling salts.

My only consolation and entertainment in my bedroom were those very same boys' UFO magazines. At first, I kept away from those magazines like they were platters of cooties. Eventually, boredom kicked in and I began browsing through one of the magazines with the morbid curiosity of a death row inmate reading *Electric Chair Monthly.*

One article caught my eye: a contest promising a $1 million prize to anyone who can lead the magazine to a living alien on planet Earth. *One . . . million . . . dollars.*

Sorry, dad; I became the first Fratto in history to rat. For the good of the rest of mankind—and to give myself the resources to possibly escape—I laid out the entire conspiracy on a pad of paper and had my mom send it to the magazine. I resolved to wait in my bedroom until the information reached the authorities and they sent someone to rescue me.

Well, playing sick lasted a couple days until my big brother Frankie prescribed a daily dosage of calling me a "fag" and bullied me into going back to school. He told me that if Dad and Mom were in on the conspiracy, then the magazine editors were probably part of the plot, too, so I might as well face my fate.

I was a dead boy walking down the squeaky, shiny, lemon-antiseptic-smelling hallway of St. Anthony's. I was in no rush, but I grimly continued on my way like a half-ass gunslinger too proud to back out of a standoff with Wyatt Earp. By the time I entered my classroom, everyone was already seated and class had started.

"*Oh,* welcome back, Johnny," said the nun with a look of disappointment and resignation on her face. *Thanks, sister. Motherfuck you too.* "Well, there's only one seat left, so take your place quickly."

I scanned to the back of the room and there was the empty seat in the back row, second nearest to the door. My seat in the far corner was now occupied by the self-important little space ant Zap, who nodded at me like a smug executioner looking forward to his job. I dwelled on Zap, the terror of my waking nightmares over the past week, for a moment. Then I noticed that, on the other side of the seat, were two other strangers: large, greasy, hairy, mustachioed humanoids dressed like medieval villagers.

On sight, I knew what these old Geraldo creatures were: the alien "zips" my father had sent to St. Anthony's. Of course, it made perfect sense. The Great Gazoo-sized Zap would never dirty his hands subduing a far larger creature such as me. Of course, he would have muscle. These two thugs were the kidnappers who were going to straightjacket me and take me to my space slavery . . .

"Johnny Farrell, sit down this instant!" barked the nun. "You're holding up the class!"

A great, phlegmy, gurgling commotion rose up in the back of the classroom. It was the two new aliens. I couldn't understand anything they were saying besides, "*Farrell . . . Fratto . . . Farrell . . . Fratto!*"

One of them looked at me with the whites of his eyes glowing, pointed his finger, and asked, "*You-a . . . Don Luigi boy?*"

Don Luigi . . . my dad! Oh god, they were coming for me right now. My time had come. Like a prisoner facing a firing squad, this moment called for bravery.

"Yes, Don Luigi boy," I said with all the composure and dignity of Sidney Poitier facing racist persecutors. "I am him."

The two space thugs screeched out of their desks and charged at me bent low and compact. Each grabbed a wrist; I waited for the spacecuffs.

Instead, both of the swarthy aliens fell to the ground and proceeded to gently kiss my hand. "*Don Giovanni! Don Giovanni!*" I had seen this act before with Dad. It meant one thing: I was their boss. Actually, it meant two things: I was the boss . . . and little Zap was motherfucked.

I felt my blood warm, my mind clear and my posture correct itself. *It's on, you little cocksucker.* I gave little Zap my best sulfurous antichrist look and pointed my little kid's finger at him. "Amiche . . . *him! WATCH HIM!*"

The two stubbly aliens swung their heads in tiny Zap's direction and began to babble venomously at him and spit on the floor and place curses on his family unto the ninth generation. Understanding that he was in danger, Zap leaned back in his chair and began to scream in his moon dialect, begging for mercy.

This farcical intergalactic *West Side Story* showdown came as a bit of surprise to the rest of the classroom. All four of the alien combatants were immediately ushered to the principal's office.

On the way to Sister Mary Esther's cave, my high spirits were slightly dampened with guilt: how could I have doubted Dad's intentions? Of course he would arrange for goons from outer space to protect his son from being annihilated by a star-hopping hitman. This was Lou Fratto, after all.

There wasn't much of a summit in Sister Mary Esther's office since we were the only two people in the room who spoke English. So it didn't take too long for Sister Mary Esther to correct my inaccurate read of the situation. I had made a few observational errors: the word "alien" also meant humans from foreign countries; Zap was not a Martian in a spacesuit, but a Chinese immigrant in a Mao-style uniform who spoke no English; my two servant aliens were Sicilians ("zips") that my dad had smuggled through the port of New Orleans and arranged to send to St. Anthony's for a semester so they could pick up English through osmosis; and I wouldn't get my million dollars.

6

CLIMBING POLES FOR FUN & PROFIT

And I don't mean hot blondes from Warsaw—though fun, that came later, and it definitely hasn't turned a profit for me.

I discovered a new cash racket while trying to cherry-bomb a bird's nest in my backyard. To get to my target, I tucked the cherry bomb and match-book into my overall pockets and wrapped all four limbs around my mom's clothesline pole. As I slowly scooched upwards, I felt my thoughts of blowing innocent little hatchlings to smithereens slowly evaporate. In fact, my ability to think about *anything* just melted away.

I had entered a universe of sensation that I had never suspected existed. Sliding my crotch slowly up this pole was the best feeling in the entire world. And the best part about it was that I was too young to finish, slide down, and smoke a candy cigarette. No, I could slide up and down that pole for *hours*, and it kept feeling good.

You should have seen the strange looks those birds were giving me as I hung from this laundry pole with my eyes rolled back in my head like a de-ranged zombie. From my vantage point atop the pole, I caught sight of an even stranger sight: a black man in a white car full of white women! And he was pulling up to our driveway!

This was newsworthy. In Des Moines, I never met any black people besides the occasional boxers like Sonny Liston who came to pay their very humble re-spects to my father. As far as I knew, black people were not a separate race so much as boxers who got beaten so black and blue that they never regained their color. When I saw guys like Fats Domino or Chubby Checker on TV, I thought to myself, *Wow, those guys must be pretty tough.*

I sensually slid down from the clothesline pole and ran into the house to meet this new and strange boxer. The moment I saw him up close, I could tell that I would have to rethink my theory of how black people came to be: this guy was no boxer. He was maybe 6'2" and 120 pounds of well-moisturized black skin over bone. He was dressed so pretty and walked so fine that I was positive he had never fought a day in his life.

I was introduced to Eddie "The Treetop" Tree, an apparent good old friend of Dad's. Treetop's clothing was delicate and immaculate, hanging just right on his fashion model skinny frame.

"Mr. Treetop, what kinda outfit are you wearing?" I asked.

"Oh, check this out, lil' playa," he told me in a whispery, hopping, rhythmic voice that was Snoop Dogg before Snoop Dogg was born. "What you see here is a $250 mohair, continental-to-the-bone hustler's suit, the finest alligator shoes $250 can buy, a straight-up wool worsted scarf, a diamond stick pin on the lapel, the finest silk socks ever spun by a worm, and what we call a stingy-brim hat on my head placed *just* so."

"Why doesn't your hat fit, Mr. Treetop?"

"Listen 'ere, lil' playa, it fit just right: sittin' right on top my head ever so gently, I mean *just* so, lil' man. I don't want it all tight up on my crown because what you see here..."

Treetop flicked his tiny-brimmed hat in the air, caught it with the other hand, and leaned down to show me a glowing James Brown perm.

"...is a bona fide eight dollar doo that I ain't plannin' on *un*-doin' any time soon, you feel me? If I push down on this here hat, then there goes this here doo, and there went my eight dollars!"

This made perfect sense to me; if I had plastic action figure hair like Mr. Treetop, I'd go out of my way to protect it, too. "Mr. Treetop, what about your car? I've never seen one like that."

"That, my man, ain't no car. That, lil' playa, is what you call a *hog*, or, if you prefer its trade name, a Cadillac. If you want to be exact about a hustler's ride, that is a straight-up, brand-new Cadillac convertible, colored white on white on *white!* It matches the three white women who drive in it with me, so you could say, lil' playa, that what you saw was a bona fide *white on white on white on white on white on white* hog, because that's just how Treetop do!"

Clearly, I was speaking to a very wise man. His words had the sound of prophecy to me; I had never heard language so crazy except when the priest or nuns read from the Book of Revelations. I thought back to my bible teachings, and I recalled that one of the Three Wise Men was colored just like Mr. Treetop—a sign from Heaven. When Dad uncharacteristically told me to scram and leave him to talk with Mr. Treetop, I did not wonder why; it made perfect sense for Dad to want to consult privately with such a learned sage.

As Dad conferred with Mr. Treetop, I looked out of the front windows and studied his "three white women." I wondered if they were like his Three Wise Men. They didn't seem too bright, patiently filing their nails and twirling their big, curly, Nashville hairdos in his hog. I asked my mom if I should invite them inside to play, but, surprisingly, she turned me down. She was normally so polite to visitors.

After a few minutes, Treetop sauntered from the living room to the front door and gave me my first ever hustler handshake. As he said goodbye with a tip of his stingy-brim hat, I thought to myself that I had just met the most remarkable man in the world.

Still, I was confused about his three white women and their purpose, so I ran over to the living room to ask Dad, who was sitting with his apprentice, my teenage brother Frankie.

"Dad, why do The Three White Women follow Mr. Treetop around?" I asked with all the innocence and sincerity of an altar boy.

"Uhh . . . well, uhh," Dad couldn't help but stutter. "Well, you see, Johnny, Mr. Treetop is those women's agent."

My brother Frankie sighed loud, shooting Dad a disapproving look that only he could get away with. Frankie lived to bust balls and enforce the rules, and he'd take Dad to task for being dishonest just as quickly as he would his little brothers.

"Dad, don't fill Johnny's head up with nonsense; there's too much up there as is," he reprimanded before turning his intense eyes on me. "Johnny, Treetop is not an agent . . . he is a pleasure salesman. He sells something that feels *really* good."

Any other day, Frankie's explanation wouldn't have made a big impact on me at all. But today was no regular day; this was the day I had discovered the clothesline pole. This was the day I discovered *pleasure*. When I heard how Frankie said "*really* good", I knew exactly the type of sensation he was talking about.

It didn't take me long to realize what I needed to do. If selling pleasure got Mr. Treetop an awesome plastic haircut, a white on white on white Cadillac, and three women to follow him around, then Johnny Fratto needed to get into the pleasure-selling business to make enough money to earn his dad's affection. Luckily, I had a bottomless supply of product: the neighborhood clothesline poles.

I got my little friends together the next afternoon and paid them all a quarter to sell the rights in perpetuity to their family's laundry poles. These marks looked at me like I was crazy —what good was a laundry pole to a little boy?

"Just you wait and see, lil' playas," I said to them in my best slithery impression of Mr. Treetop.

Once I had secured a monopoly on all the clothesline poles, I gathered all the local boys in my backyard and invited them to take a free shimmy up the Fratto family pole, one at a time. These little boys didn't know what was coming: they scooched up that pole real fast, but they slid down *real* slow. Soon, boys were paying me a quarter-per-ride to climb up the clothesline poles in their own backyards.

Business was booming, but I wasn't satisfied. I kept thinking of new ways to increase the profit margin. My greatest innovation was naming each pole and giving them their own sales rap. My elite model was the pole in my Aunt Mary's backyard, which I named Bertha because it was the biggest and blackest pole in the neighborhood. This fucking pole had a lot of love to give.

"Now, if you want pleasure," I'd tell my customers, "any of my poles will take care of you, but if you want *the best*, then you gotta go with Bertha. She's got the length; she's got the girth; and she's got the track record. You ask around about Bertha, and you'll hear that she's worth the dollar!"

After a few days, I had a roll of $1 bills the size of a cheese wheel and a sack of quarters too heavy to carry even if I got Willie's help. Any day, I'd have enough scratch to get me my three white women and my white-on-white-on-white hog.

Let's just say Frankie was unimpressed when he came home early from baseball practice one afternoon to find the entire neighborhood overrun by hysterical little boys humping clothesline poles. Once he saw me counting my money, he figured out what was happening.

Frankie didn't need to consult the adults. *He* was the authority in this neighborhood. First, Frankie picked up his baseball bat . . . but then he thought better of it and went inside our house to borrow my mom's broom. Within minutes, Frankie had beaten off . . . I mean, whacked off . . . I mean, hit every little boy with that broomstick until they fell down and ran away.

After Frankie had delivered a couple whacks with that broom on my head, he confiscated my ill-gotten money and told me to cut the shit and stop embarrassing Dad. I was chastened. I had learned an important lesson: never sell pleasure when anti-pleasure crusader Frankie was around.

I went up to my mom all sweet and innocent and asked for Frankie's baseball practice schedule so I could go watch "my hero" play ball in the afternoon. From that day forward, pole pimping began ten minutes after Frankie's practice started and came to a close ten minutes before it ended.

I was well on my way to purchasing my first $250 continental-to-the-bone mohair hustler's suit when Frankie's coach unexpectedly cancelled practice. Instead of grabbing the broom, this time my brother smartened up and did the same thing all cops do when they need to rein in the sex trade: he went to the local crime boss.

"Dad!" Frankie called through the house while still in his baseball uniform. "You need to come outside right away! Johnny is being a little pimp!"

"Oh, Frankie," Lou sighed. "Don't you think you're exaggerating?"

"Why don't you come outside and judge for yourself," Frankie insisted, standing nose-to-nose with Dad. It was typical of Dad never to stare down or humble Frankie, both because he was too laid back and because he *wanted* Frankie to be a dominant little shit so that he could succeed to the throne.

Dad came outside in his beautiful suit smiling and laughing, figuring my brother was overreacting as usual. One look around the neighborhood convinced him otherwise. It was like a panorama of Caligula's Rome: in every yard was a little boy writhing on a pole with a look of ecstasy on his face like a cheesy stripper.

This was some sick shit! Though Dad hated to admit it, Frankie was right. "Don't you worry, Frankie," Dad said in his raspy whisper, "leave this to me. I'll take care of it."

The next day, Dad told me that Frankie was going out of town on Saturday morning for a prolonged baseball tournament. I picked up my tin can on a string and sent out word through my network that we would be in business all weekend, starting first thing Saturday morning.

When I went outside Saturday morning with all the cockiness of Tom Cruise in *Risky Business*, I discovered that my rackets had been eliminated. Every clothesline pole in the neighborhood had disappeared. Distraught little boys were standing gape-mouthed in their yards, on the verge of tears. I could feel my balls learning how to go blue.

Driving slowly down the block came a large Sears delivery truck followed by my bicycling brother Frankie, who was supposed to be out of town. I saw Frankie glide up to a neighbor's door, knock, and politely usher a team of Sears movers carrying a brand new washer and dryer set into the home. The whole operation barely took three minutes. After that neighbor's house, they went one house over and did the same thing.

On one sunny Saturday morning in 1963, Lou Fratto bought our entire neighborhood new electric washers and dryers. All Dad asked for in return was that each family hand over their old clothesline poles, which Frankie delivered to the dump at the end of day.

That was the end of my pimping days.

I will say this, however. I just saw a news story about how environmentalists are bringing back the clothesline since it doesn't use electricity. So far, this trend has not reached Beverly Hills, but I'm going to bide my time until it does. I'm going to wait until it won't be suspicious in the least for me to install two clothesline poles on the roof of my penthouse condo.

And let me tell you something, these are going to be the two fattest, tallest clotheslines in history.

7

BLINKY CAN'T BLINK

There was only thing Dad could not give me as a kid: my own identity.

Fratto genes are strong. We all have that Fratto look and Fratto stubbornness. Going to Fratto family get-togethers was like visiting a hall of funhouse mirrors. Each of my male relatives with the Fratto face and larger-than-life Fratto personality was just one more slightly distorted version of me, of what I would become.

I felt so insignificant and small in comparison to the family legend that it seemed arrogant for me to raise my little voice and claim an identity separate from something as important and respected as the Fratto family. I was an irrelevant appendage—like an eleventh toe hanging uselessly onto a family that included Iowa godfather Lou Fratto, a half-dozen Chicago Outfit *capos* and street bosses, and the local sports heroes Frankie and Willie.

I was not a star; I was just an extra.

The best I could hope for was to do a half-ass job of not letting down Dad's legacy. That's why Dad's identity crisis mattered so much to me: his reputation, his identity, his life were ultimately going to be my own. You know the Catholic rap—the sins of the father are visited upon the son.

My first heartbreak was a product of Dad's sins. My best friend, Billy, lived next door with his extremely religious family. They were one of those special breeds of Christian that love Jesus so much that the guys dress up like Abraham Lincoln and the women like *Doctor Quinn, Medicine Woman* to honor him.

One day, Billy's parents read a Chicago newspaper and came away with the notion that notorious gangster Luigi Fratto was a bad influence on children. From that day on, their innocent angel Billy was no longer allowed to play with the gangster's kids. I lost my best friend.

I did my best to prove Billy's parents wrong and involve Billy in all of our after-school playtime regardless of the fact that he wasn't allowed to leave his yard. I would bring all of my toys and set them out next to Billy's fence, and I played with him through the big holes in the fence for hours at a time. After a while, Dad joked that Billy should be given the wiseguy nickname "Billy Behind-The-Fence" since I only saw him behind his fence, and it stuck.

Dad was inconsolably disturbed by the idea that his reputation was causing me to be rejected by my peers. This struck him at his most vulnerable part: his belief that his business interests in no way interfered with his ability to be a caring and wonderful father. When Dad found himself unable to convince Billy Behind-The-Fence's parents to let their kid play with us, he tried to console me by buying tickets for the family to see the famous Harlem Globetrotters.

I loved the Globetrotters. What's not to love about the Harlem Globetrotters: a basketball team of giant black men who perform comedy routines and circus stunts while pretending to embarrass a gang of white ringers? For a moment, I forgot about poor Billy and dreamed of nothing besides watching the great Globetrotters perform slam dunks from mid-court.

On the big day, I was playing in the backyard when I stepped on an exposed nail. Feeling a little punchdrunk and queasy, I dragged my gory, bleeding foot into the house. On sight, my mom announced that I was not going to the game and would instead have to go to the doctor's office to get a shot to prevent an infection.

This was an unmitigated disaster. I was now a friendless, one-footed kid who went from spending the day doing the most exciting thing in the world (watching the Harlem Globetrotters) to doing the worst (going to the doctor's office). I filibustered as best as I could, screaming and yelling and crying, but Dad took a hard stance for once and forcibly lifted me up and brought me out to the station wagon.

He was followed by my much older cousin Sammy, a gofer for the local wiseguys who went by the nickname of "Blinky." After tossing me in the backseat, Dad told Blinky to watch me and prevent an escape while he ran inside to make a quick phone call. Two minutes later, all three of us were on our way to the doctor's office.

In the office parking lot, I waited until Dad and Blinky had gotten out of the car to leap to the front and push down the locks for all of the doors. "Ha ha! I told you I wasn't getting a shot!"

"C'mon, Johnny, knock this shit off!" Dad sighed, looking around the parking lot in fear of being embarrassed.

"Nuh-uh. I ain't getting no shot, and there's nothing you can do about it!"

Well, turns out there was something Dad could do about it. Within seconds, Dad displayed a heretofore unknown talent for breaking into cars. I was yanked out of the car and carried like a kidnapped child through the waiting room and directly into an empty examination room. One of the perks of being a boss was that Dad never tolerated the idea of a waiting room.

A waiting room was where other people waited for *our* family to be done.

Blinky brought the doctor into the examination room. A minute later, he was joined by a nurse carrying a syringe. I had a deadly fear of needles and begged Dad not to have me held down and stabbed against my will.

"C'mon Johnny, what's the big deal? It's just a needle."

"Needles are just skinny knives, Dad. It will hurt."

"No, it doesn't hurt. Look, Blinky, show Johnny it doesn't hurt." I could see the hesitation in Blinky's rapidly blinking eyes. I could tell he didn't like needles either, but he wasn't going to ignore an order from Dad. Neither was the nurse, for that matter: without a question, she dutifully injected whatever was in the kid-sized syringe into Blinky. He mustered a smile.

"See, Johnny? No big deal!"

I let the nurse give me my shot. Afterwards, the doctor bandaged my foot, and we made our way home.

I spent the entire ride pouting against the cold, wet glass of the backseat passenger's side window, daydreaming about all the awesome stunts I would miss at the Globetrotters game. I considered finding a nail at home and stabbing Willie in the foot to keep things fair in the Fratto household.

As I gingerly stepped into our driveway, I heard an instantly recognizable tune emanating from our backyard: "Sweet Georgia Brown", the theme song of the Harlem Globetrotters. It was obvious who the culprit was. "*Hey, unfair! Da-ad!* Go tell Frankie to turn that off and stop torturing me!"

"Y'know what, Johnny?" Dad said as he shook his head. "You're right. It's unfair to rub it in. Blinky, pick up Johnny and take him to the backyard so he can help me set Frankie straight."

Blinky's hands were sweaty and cold, and to be honest his face looked discomfited, a little bit like he was fighting off a batch of the squirts. I wasn't too eager to be picked up by this goof, but my foot hurt, and the idea of seeing Frankie getting verbally reamed by Dad made any intervening indignity seem irrelevant.

When we reached the backyard, I found that my suspicions were justified: Frankie *was* in the backyard, sitting next to our basketball half-court beside the record player spinning "Sweet Georgia Brown." To my surprise, he was surrounded by dozens of acquaintances and the roster of the Harlem motherfucking Globetrotters.

THE HARLEM GLOBETROTTERS WERE IN MY BACKYARD!

"Hey, listen up! It's the guest of honor!" called out Dad.

"Hey Johnny!" bellowed one 10-foot-tall Globetrotter in his red, white, and blue uniform.

"What's happenin', lil' man?" crowed another.

"Hey man, make way for Johnny, he's the guest of honor!" said the littlest Globetrotter.

I was enthroned in the Lawn Chair of Honor surrounded by all of my friends and family, and the skyscraping Globetrotters gathered around to shake my hand, pat me on the shoulder, and congratulate me on my courageous trip to the doctor. "See, Johnny?" asked Dad with this triumphant look on his face, "this is what happens when little boys are good."

"The Harlem Globetrotters visit them?" Whenever people tell me I'm a jaded, impossible-to-impress goofball with delusions of grandeur for myself, I think to myself, "What do they expect?" I grew up being taught that a normal present was a NASA space capsule, and a personal visit from the world famous Harlem Globetrotters was a just reward for pouting through a visit to the doctor's office.

For that day at least, I was a good boy to the core. Why be bad if being good got you rewarded like *this*? For the next hour, the Harlem Globetrotters played a pickup game in our backyard, making sure to come to me whenever they had an audience participation stunt to perform—spinning the basketball on my finger, passing the ball behind my head, that sort of trick.

Everyone in the crowd was having a wonderful time...I mean, besides Blinky. His face looked like a baboon's inflamed ass—swollen, wet, and hot red. "Dad, what's wrong with Blinky?"

"Oh? Nothing, no big deal," Dad said convincingly. "It turns out he's allergic to the shot they gave him. Don't worry. If it wasn't for you, Blinky never would have known about his allergy, and, when he *did* find out, it would have been through a full adult dosage of the drug. Since they only gave him a kid dosage, he'll be fine! You really did Blinky a favor! Ain't that right, Blinks?"

Dad turned expectantly to the man with a melting glob of strawberry ice cream for a face.

"That's . . ." Blinky paused to catch his wheezing, shallow breath,". . .right, Lou. You . . .[*wheeze, phlegm gargle, cough*] . . .saved my life . . .[*cough, phlegm gargle*] . . .Johnny."

"See, Johnny? Saved your first life."

"Cool!"

I was having the time of my life watching the Globetrotters' performance when suddenly my happiness was interrupted. I realized that not *all* of my friends were in our backyard. One was missing, the most important of all: Billy Behind-The-Fence.

That exception made all the difference. Though I was supposed to be a good boy enjoying my just rewards, I felt at that moment like nothing less than a despised, shunned gangster getting punished for his crimes.

Sitting in my lawn chair of honor, I thought about what a shame it was that Billy Behind-The-Fence was missing this unforgettable moment. I wondered if he was listening to "Sweet Georgia Brown" in the distance and squinting through the cracks in his fence to make out the action.

Shortly after that game, Billy Behind-The-Fence's family moved their precious choirboy far away from bad influences like Lou and Johnny Fratto. I never saw him again . . .

But I sure as fuck heard about him. Without any input from me, my old buddy became an infamous cross-country bankrobber. It turns out the Billy Behind-The-Fence nickname was a prophecy: the motherfucker still lives behind a fence in prison. I guess his parents weren't such good influences, huh?

If the kid was going to be a burglar, he could've stuck with me and never got caught . . . just like *I* never got caught.

If he had stuck with me, Billy Behind-The-Fence would have ended up Billy Behind-The-Wheel-of-a-Brand-New-Mercedes-SL500.

LET ME TELL YOU A QUICK STORY...

ABOUT THE HIGHWAY TO AN ASSKICKING

"[Name redacted] had taken a bus load of Indian children to Des Moines, Iowa where they appeared in a parade; he stated that FARRELL appeared to be in charge of the festivities."

SPECIAL AGENT ROSSITER C. MULLANEY
Federal Bureau of Investigation
File OM 92-74

Dad made Iowa seem like the center of the planet. He could pick up the phone and get any singer, comedian, celebrity, athlete, or traveling attraction on Earth to come to Des Moines on short notice. That's one reason I've always been attracted to Hollywood: only Los Angeles could compare to the star power, excitement, and glamour I grew up around.

That's also one reason I've never been impressed by celebrity. Celebrities were nothing more than humble jesters to Frattos. Entertainers took direction for a living; wiseguys *gave* direction for a living.

That's why it was no surprise to me when Dad announced he had arranged for the entire cast of the TV show *Bonanza* to fly to Des Moines for a fundraiser to pay off St. Anthony's mortgage. To everyone else in Des Moines, the announcement was a jaw-dropping display of Dad's power.

You can gauge the maturity of a man by his relationship with *Bonanza*. Anyone who is too young to remember what a big fucking deal that TV show was is too young to be trusted with any important non-athletic job. *Bonanza* somehow got away with being a series set in the Wild West that had almost no action, violence, or anything else a red-blooded Fratto could enjoy. The entire show revolved around the relationships between the widower Cartwright and his three sons on this big fuck-off farm. The dad looked about 50 and the two oldest sons not a day under 47, a big bunch of hairpieces.

Even though *Bonanza* was a boring Old West sausage party, something like 40% of American TVs tuned into his stupid show every week at its peak. So the idea of the entire cast coming to Des Moines was a cultural event akin to Dad booking the Super Bowl at Kinnick Stadium in Iowa City.

Since my big brothers thought *Bonanza* was a bit gay, Dad let Willie and me accompany him to watch the preparations at the Holiday Inn where the fundraiser would be held. I always got a kick out of watching Dad stage-manage an event. He'd put on these absurdly huge glasses, grab a pen and notebook, and strain his weak voice to be heard as he checked things off his to-do list.

The biggest star of all was Michael Landon, *Bonanza*'s lone young heartthrob. Before the Beatles debuted, *no one* in America got stickier fan mail than Michael Landon. The kid was a rock star.

When he walked into the suite in his sunglasses and stone cool Hollywood clothes, I could tell Mr. Hot Shit was in Iowa only under extreme protest. As soon as Landon walked in the room, Dad shouted him down. "Hey, Landon, over here!" He might as well have been calling the coat check boy.

Dad was used to Frank Sinatra kissing his ass and Pope Pius sending Christmas cards—he figured this little pretty boy should be starstruck to meet *him*. To be honest, Landon really did miss an opportunity; Dad made movie stars with one fucking phone call. He did that shit all day long. If Landon had charmed Dad, he would have gone on to be Steve McQueen instead of a middle-rung actor with a life sentence on TV.

So Dad, with his giant reading glasses and clipboard, began talking to Landon like a wedding planner instructing a busboy. Willie and I were quietly sitting against the wall, watching in awe as Dad acted like a drill sergeant working over these celebrities.

"Listen up, pay attention since I've only got time to say this once," Dad continued, talking down to Landon because of his youth. "The schedule goes like this . . . this afternoon, you're gonna to do a meet 'n' greet with some very close friends of mine. You'll sign some autographs, kiss some babies, be charming, get it? Tonight is the fundraiser dinner; you'll get up, say a little something about 'helping a good cause', and sit back down and smile. Afterwards, you'll shake hands and take photos with all the attendees."

Landon's face was responding to each new item on the itinerary like it was a turd being squeezed out of a Great Dane's ass right in front of his face. He kept trying to talk, but Dad wouldn't give him the air to break in. ". . . And finally, tomorrow, you're gonna ride in the parade we're throwin' down the center of . . ."

"Listen!" Landon finally interjected, loudly. I instinctually threw my arm over Willie to protect him and pressed our backs against the wall as if waiting for a grenade to explode. I had never seen anyone say a single word to Dad in that tone. Tony Accardo and Vito Genovese and Jimmy Hoffa didn't talk to Dad like that.

"Let's get one thing straight," Landon continued, his head cocked to the side and a pissy look on his face. "I *ain't* ridin' in no fuckin' parade."

Silence. One beat, two beats, three beats. For a creepily long time, Dad just stood still as a wax sculpture, not even blinking. I instinctually knew Michael Landon was speeding down the *Highway to Heaven* with no seatbelt.

Finally, Dad moved. One finger. He lifted his right index finger to the rim of his huge glasses and dragged them down the bridge of his nose so Landon could see his eyes unobstructed. He cocked his eyebrow.

Then *it happened*. Dad blinked, and when his eyes came back into the view, they were giving the most chilling death stare I have *ever* encountered. I used to run into Mike Tyson at his absolute peak, and, for all his hype, Iron Mike *never* gave off the menace Dad's eyes mustered at that moment.

"*Li-sten*," Dad said through a locked jaw, "no cursin' in front of the children." Those words speak for themselves, but Dad's delivery carried an entirely different meaning: *I am going to kill you, motherfucker!* One look had communicated Dad's entire rapsheet and background.

"*AND . . . YOU . . . WILL . . . RIDE . . . IN . . . THAT . . . PARADE.*" Each word was slammed down by Dad's tongue like a jackhammer. He wasn't yelling; in fact his voice was even quieter than normal. It was all in the emphasis. This motherfucker meant *every* syllable.

Slowly, *very* slowly, Dad's right hand traveled up to Michael Landon's throat as the pretty boy's terrified, crossed eyes followed its approach. There was nothing he could do. Dad's hand took its time getting there to rub that point in.

As soon as that big fighter's mitt reached Landon's throat, it took a turn and grabbed hold of the heartthrob's chin. And *squeezed*. HARD. As tears welled up in Landon's eyes, Dad slowly but forcefully made that chin go up and down like a puppet. Landon was nodding "yes" to Dad's orders.

"When I want your opinion," Dad said, "I'll give it to you."

Not until that motorcade made its way through Dealey Plaza in Dallas did I ever see someone look more uncomfortable riding in a parade than Michael Landon.

8

THE RUGRAT PACK

"Omaha T-6 on October 29, 1959, advised that he talked further...about FARRELL's new motel in Des Moines and was now of the opinion that subject had references to an architect who built the Sands Motel in Chicago and also the Lake Tower Motel in Chicago. T-6 stated that FARRELL had also claimed that his brother, [name redacted] of Chicago, had a piece of singers SAMMY DAVIS and FRANK SINATRA and because of his connection, FARRELL planned to have one or both of these singers at the opening of his motel in Des Moines."

SPECIAL AGENT ROSSITER C. MULLANEY
Federal Bureau of Investigation
File OM 92-74

Of all the formative influences in my life, none was more damaging to my sanity than my own good luck and good looks. I was born the rich, beautiful son of a pathologically generous Mob boss. When you begin life surrounded by this much power, luxury, and glamour, it's not easy to moonwalk back to being a well-balanced, centered, humble individual.

I basically *had* to grow up to be a spoiled, conceited, lazy motherfucker with a royal disconnect with reality. I was just *fucked* by luck.

It didn't help my mental health that all six hundred of my aunts had to mention how gorgeous I was every time they saw me. Even Uncle Frank pointed out "what a handsome little shit" I was whenever he came around.

It didn't take long for an opportunistic little fucker like me to learn to play on my looks. It was just one more hustle, one more game of manipulation I learned from my Dad. I quickly learned how batting my eyes and hugging, teasing, and shamelessly flattering women turned them into pushovers. I didn't know what the word "no" even meant—not because I never heard it, but because there was no such thing as a "no" that I couldn't flip like a pancake into a "yes!"

That was, of course, until I started trying to get my way with girls around my own age. Like most men, my first heartbreaking dose of rejection came from the first pair of tits that ever caught my attention. The tits in question belonged to one of my big sister Carmie's friends, this 14-year-old blond who had been on the business end of a visit from puberty before any other girl I knew. These cans weren't training bra booblets; these were serious *gazongas*, big life-giving woman *breasts*. I was entranced.

I was only ten years old. When a girl is a pubescent fourteen and you're a prepubescent ten, looks don't even mater. You might as well be a puppy hitting on dolphin; you're an entirely different species. This girl wouldn't even acknowledge that we spoke the same language.

I was devastated. It wasn't so much heartbreak—more a childish tantrum at not getting my way. Who did this fourteen-year-old think she was? I was a fucking Fratto!

"Dad, can you make a girl be my girlfriend?" I asked Lou in the living room after he hung up an important phone call. He was nonplussed; labor union bosses and Mob kingpins asked him for girlfriends all the time when they visited Iowa.

"What kind a question is that?" he said without too much emotion. "I guess it depends on the girl, Johnny, if you really want the answer."

"Dad, do you know Carmie's friend with the HUGE BOOBS?"

My dad did a bit of a double-take, as he hadn't yet realized that I had been infected.

"Yes…yes I do, Johnny," Dad said with a raised eyebrow that told me he definitely knew which friend I was talking about. I'm telling you—you had to work hard *not* to notice her.

"Dad, she won't be my girlfriend. Can you make *her*?"

"Sorry, Johnny. She's not the kind of girl I can help you with."

"Oh come on, if you don't know how to get this girl to like me, do you know anyone who does?"

Dad thought for a moment, theatrically rubbing his chin to illustrate to me that he was taking this question seriously. Then, a crazy thought occurred to him, and he began to chuckle. "Yes, son, in fact I do know two guys who can help you if *anyone* can help you."

We took a flight to Chicago where Frank and Dean were performing at Sam Giancana's Villa Venice. For once, my big brother Frankie was jealous of *me*—unlike me and just about every other kid his age, Frankie pretended to idolize the Rat Pack. It was part of his quest to fit in with the Mob old timers. This would have been a great opportunity for him to score points in front of Dad's Outfit cronies.

Me? I could take or leave the music, but I loved the titties I saw bouncing up and down in the crowd at the Villa Venice. It boded very well for my quest to seduce Carmie's friend and her tits. Dad and I were sitting in the front row, surrounded by all these broads *roaring* in sexual frustration. The crowd sounded like a cannonade of girls exploding all over themselves.

After the show, Dad took me backstage. The man was greeted like the President of the United States at a campaign rally; all the big shots backstage stopped paying attention to the supposed "stars" and fought for position around Dad. I saw numerous famous comedians, musicians, politicians, and gangsters fawn over Dad like he was giving out tickets to Blowjob Night at Ann Margret's house.

At the back of the line of well-wishers and grovelers was a little sweaty red elf with a torn-open collar and big blue puppet eyes. It was Frank Sinatra, looking forlorn and awkward now that he had to do a little ass-kissing of his own. When he made his way to Dad, he kept his eyes low and mumbled, "Hey Lou, great to see you! Hope you enjoyed the show!"

Dad gave him this weird, hesitant look and then slapped him on the shoulder like an old friend. "Nice gig, Frank! Great job!" I could tell that Dad wasn't exactly overflowing with sincerity.

I didn't know it then, but there was considerable tension between the Frattos and Sinatra . . . and all of it was coming from us. Uncle Frank remorselessly bullied Sinatra every time he saw him for being an effeminate little poseur who fronted like a tough guy when he was really "a fucking lounge singer for teenage girls." Just to keep him in place, Uncle Frank treated Sinatra to little reminders of "the pecking order." One famous example was when Uncle Frank followed Sinatra to the men's room during one of Sinatra's birthday dinners and picked the urinal next to where the "Chairman" was relieving himself. Sinatra was startled a moment later to discover Uncle Frank pissing on his designer shoes while nonchalantly staring at him

Dad tolerated Sinatra, but he too cultivated an immense dislike for the singer after Sinatra influenced Accardo and Giancana in Chicago to back his pussy-chasing pal Kennedy instead of Dad's boy Nixon.

Dad never again gave Ol' Blue Eyes even a little play.

For that reason, Sinatra shuffled away before Dad could ask him how to seduce a teenage girl . . . a task for which Sintatra was very qualified, Dad begrudgingly admitted. Lucky for us, Dean Martin had managed to stay in the good graces of the Frattos, primarily because he stayed out of politics and was just about the only person on Earth besides Mickey Mantle willing to go drink for drink with Uncle Frank.

While Sinatra came off like a squirmy, bitter little shit when I met him, Dean Martin swaggered over like Italian Elvis and immediately impressed me as the coolest motherfucker on Earth. The man was so tan, relaxed, and effortlessly cool that it seemed like he just floated from place to place without even bothering to move a muscle. He was just sopping wet with sweat, and his disheveled hair was a swirling black tornado, but Dean couldn't have looked more like a celebrity. The man had more charisma than anyone I've ever met.

Dean sloshed right over in a cloud of cologne with a glass of booze in his jeweled fingers and gave Dad a hug and Italian kiss on the cheek that Lou returned. "Dino, the best as always! Great show!" Dad said with a wink.

Unlike that conceited Jersey Shore prick Sinatra, Dino Crocetti was just like Dad: the son of Italian immigrants in the Midwest who came into the wrong crowd as a teenage boxer and bootlegger. They ended up in different professions, but Dad and Dino shared the same social circle and values.

"Ahh, thanks Lou. I was performing just for you. And . . ." Dean swung his hooded gaze to me. "Who are you, short stuff?"

"I'm . . . *his* son," I said, leaning into Dad. I was starstruck for perhaps the only time in my life.

"Johnny, don't be shy. Ask Dean the question you wanted to ask him."

With my beloved's tits in mind, I gained courage. "Dino, I got this problem."

"Well, tell me little man. Maybe Uncle Dino can help."

"I got this girl who won't give me the time of day. How do you make all the women fall in love with you?"

"Well, that's easy, killer," Dean said with a chuckle. "You think those girls out there like me for my *personality?* The secret to getting girls is to sing . . . and dressin' nice don't hurt. Your old man should be able to help you there!" Dean slurred as he gave Dad a playful punch in the shoulder.

I had a new idol. Before leaving Chicago, Dad took me shopping and got me a haircut. He got Dean Martin's tailor in town to make an exact replica of one of his tuxedos, and my long wild hair was cut, sculpted, and curled into an exaggerated Dino pompadour.

When Carmie brought her friend to our home the next day for a sleepover, there was a surprise waiting in her bedroom: her ten-year-old little brother in a tuxedo with a glass of apple juice on the rocks and a flower. "Baby, this is for you," I said in my most chill, suave voice as I handed the flower to Carmie's friend. "And here's a little number I'll think you'll like . . ."

Before the stunned girls even had a chance to laugh, I sucked in all the air in the room and bellowed out with all of the passion in my tiny chest: "WHEN . . . THE . . . MOON HITS THE SKY LIKE A BIG PIZZA PIE . . . *THAT'S* AMOORRRRR-RRAAAAAY!"

Needless to say, this girl had to change her panties after I was done crooning to her.

No, really, I swear!

She had to change those big, white, cotton 1960s panties . . . because she pissed herself laughing at me!

Well, ain't that a kick in the head, I thought to myself. Refusing to believe that my singing could be the problem, I figured I must have made a misstep with the song choice. I insisted "You're Nobody Until Somebody Loves You", reminded her "Everyone Loves Somebody Sometimes", and even tried to convince her of whatever the fuck "Volare" is saying. All I managed to do was send my sister into hysterics and chase this poor girl from our house.

As I pouted afterward in my bed just as sweaty, disheveled, and grumpy as Sinatra the previous night, Carmie came into my room to "console" me. Putting her arm around my shoulder, she whispered to me, "Johnny, don't give up. Let me tell you a little secret: my friend is just *shy*. She is too shy to admit she loves you. If you serenade her after school tomorrow, then I think she'll break and be yours."

This lifted my spirits. To make sure I didn't miss my opportunity, first thing in the morning I dressed up in my Dean outfit—complete with apple juice on the rocks—and insisted that my mom let me go to St. Anthony's in a tuxedo with gelled hair. Since I apparently learned nothing from my escapades dressed as Jesus with a life-sized cross, my mom figured that maybe I'd learn a lesson if I embarrassed myself.

It turns out I didn't embarrass myself at all. I was too cute to be embarrassed. The nuns all thought I was "just darling." That's the problem with being handsome: you don't realize when you're being a jackass until you're an old, washed-up motherfucker set in his jackass ways.

But to my friends, I was the coolest motherfucker on the planet. I managed to convince my parents to buy me an exact replica of Dean Martin's tuxedo, let me wear it to school, and somehow get praised by the nuns for impersonating a drunken pussyhound. With my confidence in the fucking stratosphere, I was *positive* that those fourteen-year-old titties would be mine within minutes of Carmie and her friend arriving at the Fratto household.

Sadly, it was not to be. The previous day, my crooner act had been hilarious. On this day, it had lost its novelty and was simply obnoxious. I waltzed into Carmie's room as debonair and chill as old Dino, winking and doing a little jive dance before singing "Evree-body, needs sum-bodee, sumtimes!" Carmie's friend jiggled over to me and shoved me out of the room, slamming the door.

The next day, I stopped giving a shit about The Rat Pack and Carmie's friend. The Beatles were on Ed Sullivan, and my life had a new meaning.

Within two weeks, I had my own pointy black boots and charcoal gray mod suit with aNehru jacket—all special-ordered at enormous expense from London. A couple months later and I had perfect Paul McCartney hair.

As Dean Martin, I was a zero with girls. As Paul McCartney, I was no longer a virgin. Shining through the prism of Beatlemania, my looks were irresistible to Baby Boomer girls. And that was just the start. I got what I wanted from women for the next forty years.

And it's not that my charms ever stopped working. I just got worn out!

Back in 1964, I had finally worn out Frankie's patience. My decision to dress up like the Beatles and speak with a fake English accent made my uptight jock brother psycho. This wasn't just mere "faggot shit" to Frankie. This was "*total* fucking faggot shit."

Frankie couldn't stop me from dressing like Paul McCartney and affecting an English accent, but he could punish me in innumerable other ways: noogies, Indian burns, stealthy smacks upside the head. His ultimate revenge came the next year, on the release day for the Beatles movie *A Hard Day's Night*.

My mom promised me and my three fellow Beatlemaniac friends a ride to the debut at the Holiday Theater across town. However, after my friends' parents had dropped them off at our house early on Saturday morning, my mother made a surprise announcement, "Kids, I won't be driving you to the theater today. Frankie volunteered to take you."

I was horrified, too scared to say anything. My mom left the kitchen, and Frankie emerged from a dark corner with an evil smirk on his face. He leaned over the kitchen table where the four of us sat in our Nehru jackets eating breakfast.

"Listen up, you little shits," Frankie hissed, venom dripping from his teeth. "If you want to watch your faggot shit movie, you're going to have to walk . . . and guess what, you little shitbirds? It's a long walk to the Holiday. I'd get going now if you want to make it and be the only supposed men in a crowd full of crying little girls."

My friends and I were trapped between two horrendous choices: missing the Beatles cinematic debut, or walking unaccompanied all the way to the Holiday Theater. My brother knew my greatest fear was all of the untethered, unleashed, unsupervised big dogs who prowled our suburban neighborhood. Since Iowans in those days still thought they lived in the countryside and needed guard dogs to roam around the perimeter of their city lot "homesteads," Iowa kids spent their formative years watching milkmen and mailmen get mauled.

We were terrified of the local dogs, but, as Beatles fanatics, we had no choice. We snuck out into the morning sunlight in our Beatles suits and tiptoed the countless blocks to the Holiday, sprinting at the tiniest hint of a bark. We were lucky on the way over; there were no serious run-ins with the canine population.

After the show, I was on a high. Never had I seen such an inspiring, hilarious, exciting movie. It was just kinetic.

One of the things I liked best about the Beatles was that, being a profoundly goofy and silly motherfucker by nature and upbringing myself, they were the first people who I ever saw make it *cool* and *sexy* to be funny in a self-deprecating, playful way. Paul McCartney could be a slapstick spaz and still cause riots of horny girls.

Without the Beatles, I would never have been able to be myself as an adult. They loosened up American culture so profoundly that it allowed me to be a stylish, big-haired, self-deprecating, wise-cracking, silly goofball even within the Mafia subculture. Without the Beatles, I would have had to portray a stick-up-my-ass tough guy like Frankie to ever have a chance of fitting in around Dad's world. So blame The Beatles; they are responsible for all of my horseshit since 1964.

On the walk home, the four aspiring Merseybeat gangsters of Iowa were not so lucky. Within seconds of entering our suburban neighborhood, the dogs appeared on the prowl.

Notice I said *dogs*. I'm talking about a fucking wolfpack, like half a dozen local dogs. And, in those days, a redneck state like Iowa didn't even know what a small dog looked like; we're talking Dobermans, German Shepherds, Great Danes—*beasts*. And they started chasing us, barking and snapping their teeth at our heels.

My three other friends were terrified. So was I at first. Then my imagination took over. The creative, fantastical side of me—which I would have had to suppress if not for the Beatles —protected me from the danger I was in.

As I started to run, the mob of wild, slobbering, growling dogs panting on my heels transformed into hyperactive, crying, shrieking teenage girls giving chase. My three friends were no longer pants-shitting little kids; they were John, George, and Ringo. And I became Paul McCartney, laughing and smiling as my jacket flapped fashionably in the wind, barely escaping my pursuers.

9

LOU LOSES A FINGER

"As previously reported, subject received a cut on his hand during an argument in the Silver Dollar Tavern, Des Moines, Iowa...records of the Wildon Osteopathic Hospital...reflect that subject appeared there...with a cut tendon in the palm of his right hand, which subject explained as having been caused from a fall off the curb of a sidewalk...infection had sent in...his right index finger was amputated on October 25, 1959...[Name redacted], who was involved with FARRELL in the tavern brawl at the Silver Dollar Tavern, stated that the fracas was one of those things that developed when too much liquor is being consumed. He stated his [redacted] who drinks too much, made a few playful remarks to a girl in the tavern and that FARELLL, who was accompanied by his brother from Chicago...intervened."

SPECIAL AGENT ROSSITER C. MULLANEY
Federal Bureau of Investigation
File OM 92-74

Right before my bedtime, I heard the door open and shut...lightly, as if the person entering wanted no one to hear. This was so unusual that it had the opposite effect: Tommy, Frankie, and I all heard that door creak closed as if it were loud as a gunshot and came rushing to see what was up.

It was our dad, his beautiful suit drenched in blood and his right hand wrapped in gory napkins. His face was shining, sparkling with a coating of sweat. I had never seen him look disheveled. Ever. The man lived *turned out*.

He signaled for quiet with his left hand and cocked his head to the left so we would follow him into the living room.

"Shhh, I don't want to scare your mom," he whispered as he squeezed down on the napkins to apply pressure.

"Dad, what the hell happened?" Frankie asked, speaking for his two shellshocked brothers. Only Frankie was strong enough to confront an image as unusual and scary as wounded and bleeding Lou Fratto. It was like seeing Superman on crutches.

"It's fuckin' stupid, a fluke!" Lou said with an irritated, exasperated voice. He looked like he *wanted* to share how bad his luck was so we could feel sorry for him. "Your uncle Frank went with me to pick up some cash from a bar. Uncle Frank, of course, had to stop to get a drink or twenty at the bar. As we're waiting, this big drunken prick, Junie Coppola, starts calling himself 'The Tarzan of Des Moines' and bragging how he can kick Uncle Frank's ass..."

"Oh Jesus!" said Frankie.

"Is he really Tarzan?" I asked, completely missing the point.

"No, he's a fuckin' idiot, Johnny. So, the last thing I need right now is a fight at one of my bars with my own brother, so I keep Uncle Frank calm and beg this Junie to shut up. I try to tell the bartender to escort the shithead out. *BUT*...Junie keeps talking, keeps yapping in Frank's good ear, calling him a pussy so loud that the entire place hears. I can just see Frank's face going red, his hands start to clench, but I'm *begging* my brother not to cause me problems in my own backyard...but..."

"But it's Uncle Frank," said Frankie.

"Exactly," sighed Dad.

"So, Uncle Frank killed him?" Frankie asked, as if the question was a mere formality.

"No...*almost*, but no. He just beat the everliving fuck out of him. Broke every rib in his body and every bone in his face."

"Wait..." Frankie said, cocking his head to the side and leaning towards Dad. "There's no way Uncle Frank needed your help. How on Earth did *you* get hurt?"

"*That's* the thing," Dad said with new frustration, walking in place and shaking his head. "That's why it's so fucking stupid. Frank dumps this guy's carcass onto the bar after he's done. I look around the destruction and think of all the money we lost, and how the cops will be called, and all the possible repercussions...and I just lose my temper. I grabbed the nearest shot glass and smacked Junie right in his fucking head!"

"And . . ." Frankie said, following the thread to its end like a detective, "the glass broke in your hand!"

"And severed my fucking finger!"

"SEVERED YOUR FINGER?" I yelped. I was not traumatized. In fact, I could not have been more excited barring an in-home acoustic performance from the Beatles. "THAT'S SO COOL!"

"Shut up, you dummy," hissed Frankie as he shoved me in the head. "Which finger?"

"Pointer finger," Dad said, flinching at the thought. Dad was going to be detached from the finger that I had seen him use to nearly puncture the chest of every wiseass he had ever lectured in our living room.

"Dad! Dad! Dad! Can I have the finger?"

"Johnny, I'm going to rip off your fucking fingers if you don't shut up," said Frankie, in that quiet scream Italians can pull off when they don't want the neighbors or Mom to hear. "Dad, are you going to go to the hospital?"

"Yeah. Or a surgeon I know. Either way, I'm going to lose this finger. When I come back, I may only have nine!"

"DAD! DAD! DAD!" I said as I squirmed out of Frankie's range. "WILL YOU . . ."

"Yes, Johnny, I'll bring you back the finger," he said, a look of bemused indulgence coming to his clammy face. Looking up to my brothers, he smiled and winked, "See, I promised I'd give your little brother the finger!"

It took a while, but eventually an infection set in, and Dad lost his finger. Using the hands of four-fingered cartoon characters as his blueprint, the surgeon removed the severed finger and shaved part of the hand so that it curved down to the thumb more naturally. Like my buddy Fred Flintstone, Dad benefited from an optical illusion that made the missing finger almost invisible. Almost no one noticed that he had lost a finger without being told outright.

I, however, was troubled. Not by Dad's grievous injury—no, I was troubled because he never gave me the finger!

I'd make Frankie and Tommy laugh by yelling back and forth across the house "Dad, give me the finger! Dad, give me the finger! Dad, give me the finger!" Frankie assured me that *he* was giving me the finger all the time, but I couldn't take *Frankie's* finger to show-and-tell since it was still attached.

Finally, Dad bought me off with a goldfish. To compensate for the disappointment of the friends who I had promised a peek at the dismembered finger, I had my friend Mike Tenini arrange a corpse viewing at midnight on

Halloween at his dad's mortuary. Basking in the glory of *that* stunt, I forgot about the finger and Dad's troubles for a while.

I can't believe how blind I was. Here was indisputable proof that Dad was a mortal, fallible, flesh-and-blood man . . . not an invincible superhero. He was just a man, a man showing distinct signs of being in trouble.

The unflappably calm, in-control Lou Fratto I had known in my childhood would never have hit a man in the head with a shot glass, and especially in public! Something was wrong. The pressure of being the target of RFK's Justice Department had started to really get to him. He was getting jumpy, paranoid.

And things only got worse after JFK's assassination.

Weeks after the murder of John F. Kennedy, a meeting was held in Chicago that changed the history of the American underworld. Tony Accardo called the Chicago wing of my family to a closed-off restaurant on the Westside suburbs for a "conclave." When Tony arrived, he was attended by thunderclouds, lightning bolts, and a murder of ravens.

It was time to cut the shit. Tony was fed up with his emissary on the streets, his "pope"—front boss Sam Giancana—and had called a meeting of the Outfit leadership to decide his fate. Giancana had fucked up by throwing the Outfit's weight behind the backstabbing Kennedys, falling in love with famous singer Phyllis MacGuire, and carrying himself like Hugh Hefner. Tony didn't want a celebrity; he wanted an all-business, down-low administrator like Lou Fratto.

Either Giancana would be deposed, demoted, and sent off to the gangland equivalent of a monastery . . . or Giancana would be murdered. Even though Dad was not present at the meeting, Sam Giancana's fate was in the hands of the Fratto family.

I don't say that out of any sort of Fratto family boosterism. It was just a fact. Besides Accardo and fellow "elder statesman" Paul Ricca, all of the cardinals at the conclave were actual or honorary Frattos: Dad's brothers Frank and Rudy, his cousin Felix "Milwaukee Phil" Alderisio, Fratto family in-laws William "Willie Potatoes" Daddano and Albert "Obie" Frabotta, and Dad's childhood "blood brothers" Marshall Caifano and former next door neighbor Sam "Teets" Battaglia.

Dad technically could not attend the meeting since he had become, in title, the leader of an "independent" family in Iowa. Lou loved the security, stability, safety, and anonymity that came from peacefully leading his own small organization in Iowa, but he also knew his position could only be maintained with the backing of the Outfit's muscle. He could never turn his back on Chicago—

one weary eye was always pointed back home. To protect his position, Dad needed to ensure that a bloody civil war was averted and another "safe pair of hands" was installed in Chicago.

Calling in every favor he had accrued in Chicago, Dad achieved a great diplomatic victory in that Westside suburban restaurant: his friend Giancana was allowed to keep his life, and Iowa's most reliable ally in Chicago, Teets Battaglia, became Accardo's new front boss.

Dad got everything he wanted out of that meeting except for the most important thing—secrecy. Someone tipped off the police to the time, whereabouts, and results of that meeting, and the police broke all the rules of Chicago pay-as-you-go politics by leaking to the press. Less than a month later, the details of that winter meeting in the Westside suburbs were published in *The Chicago Sun-Times*.

One of the headlines in the huge article was **BROTHERS OF LEW FARRELL**, an in-depth dissection of the ties of Des Moines "racket boss" Lou Fratto and his incredible web of Outfit family ties. Someone with inside information had made a point to shoehorn Dad into the article and make him one of its focal points . . . even though he was in a different state at the time of the meeting!

Seemingly random, unrelated asides in newspapers stories about the Mafia are never random and unrelated. Almost always, they are planted in cooperative newspapers by FBI agents and U.S. Attorneys looking to raise the profile of their targets and artificially increase the amount of fawning press they will receive when the inevitable indictment is handed down.

It's a fix: they build'em up to knock'em down. History is nothing more than the press releases issued by the winner before and after they take their fallen opponents for a perp walk for the cameras.

Look at John Gotti. When U.S. Attorney Rudy Giuliani first encountered Gotti, he knew he had met his prize guido. This guy was a state's attorney's dream: a swaggering, well-dressed, loudmouth goofball prone to impulsive acts of violence and saying self-incriminating things like "You tell this punk, I—me, John Gotti—will sever his motherfuckin' head off!" on wiretaps. Rudy proceeded to make Gotti a star so he could achieve stardom imprisoning him.

The press leaks started coming quick, and before you knew it, a previously anonymous neighborhood wiseguy was being hailed as the "New York's Top Crime Boss." This was hilarious since everyone in the underworld knew Gotti was nothing compared to Lucchese Family boss Anthony "Tony Ducks"

Carollo and was outright fucking terrified of Genovese Family boss Vincent "The Chin" Gigante. That was ridiculous enough, but then Giuliani began calling Gotti the most powerful gangster *in all of America.*

Sorry New Yorkers, there has *never* been *any* New York godfather who was the most powerful crime boss in America. New York is one over-policed, over-reported city whose rackets are divided up between five ruthlessly competitive, infighting Mafia families. In comparison, the Outfit was a monolithic dictatorship that ruled *all* of Chicago, *all* of Illinois, and held sway over thousands of square miles of territory in the Midwest, Nevada, and California. In my Dad's era, the godfathers of New Orleans and Kansas City and Tampa were usually more powerful than New York bosses since they discreetly controlled entire *states.*

Gotti especially was a *nobody* on the national stage. He was one of these New York guidos who never traveled and rarely even left his Queens social club. Gotti had no connections and no credibility outside of his home territory; he couldn't have bribed his way into a single meeting with Frank Fratto, let alone Tony Accardo.

Yet Gotti's gone down in history as the most powerful gangster since Al Capone. Thanks to a great PR campaign, Gotti became a great villain worthy of being slain by a great public defender, the heroic Sir Rudy Giuliani. Both of them were complete hype jobs, but that's how politics and pro wrestling work.

That's how it always worked. Way back in the 1960s, when some FBI prick decided to make his career on arresting my Dad, he resorted to the same sort of fantastic exaggeration. Dad had been accused of being a labor racketeer, Iowa crime boss, and Capone protégé for decades, but now the leaks became constant and the charges preposterous. The most damaging *Sun-Times* article quoted anonymous FBI agents as saying that Dad was "the #1 target" of the government's plan to clean up the Midwest underworld.

I can't begin to describe how shocking and scandalous a statement like that was. It simply did not compute. How could little old "Lew Farrell" in sleepy, conflict-free Iowa be considered a bigger public enemy than the worst mass murderers from gangland warzones like Chicago, Detroit, Kansas City, or Cleveland?

It was one thing for the locals to blow off claims that Dad was involved in shady labor deals, but it was hard for even the most naïve Iowan to think Lou was completely clean when federal agents were calling him the worst criminal in the entire Midwest. Though most still thought of him as a "good" man, the illusion of perfection was gone.

This was a catastrophe for Dad. Dad no longer thought of himself as Luigi Fratto, the slum kid and gangster from Chicago, but as Lew Farrell, the clean-cut Heartland businessman and father.

The bad press was forcing him to wear a name and identity that he no longer felt was his own. As Luigi Fratto, he had been hunted, a constantly endangered target of Elliot Ness and rival bootlegging syndicates. As Lew Farrell, he had been loved and respected by everyone. Though he was still Lew Farrell to most of the outside world, in his own head he was being shoved back into the body of Luigi Fratto . . . and all the miserable fear and insecurity that came with it.

As his reputation suffered, Dad's persecution complex intensified. He began to rant and rave about the "fucking liars" who made him out to be "some kind of gangster" on an hourly basis. He justified himself compulsively, giving longwinded lawyerly defenses of the most innocuous family decisions. Above his always-easy smile were eyes that had a newfound hurt and suspicion.

Lou felt persecuted, as if the rules of American society had been arbitrarily changed on him. The criminal activities that had once drawn a wink and a pat on the back from the authorities suddenly began to be met with demonic bad press, suffocating police surveillance, and constant threats of imprisonment. In the town where he once was greeted only by affectionate smiles and groveling flattery, Dad began to see out of the corner of his eyes judgmental looks, shaking heads, and gossipy whispers.

Was he suffering from paranoia?

Absolutely.

As far as I could tell, Dad still enjoyed the almost universal esteem of Iowa. In his heart, however, he didn't believe this to be true. He felt like he had spent the three decades since Al Capone's imprisonment painstakingly scrubbing his name and soul clean of blood—only for the feds to undo all that work in a moment by dumping a vat of gore over his head.

Every time he saw the FBI in their surveillance vans and Mormon missionary suits shadowing his life, Lou was reminded that the time he had left as our blameless, beloved father was short. He knew that the hour when he would be transformed from the hero of his children into the cause of their public shame and humiliation was approaching. He knew his secret would be exposed soon.

He knew *both* of his secrets would be exposed soon. The question was, which one would be revealed first?

His true identity or his terminal illness?

10

ONE OBLIVIOUS BANANA SMOKER

"When Alan Rosenberg, the 235-pound con man and 'scam' operator, threatened Iowa's No. 1 Mafia boss, Louis (Cockeyed Louis) Fratto, he may have sentenced himself to death. [...] One investigator told *The Sun-Times* 'How could Rosenberg expect to have remained living after all that?'"

CHICAGO SUN-TIMES
July 1, 1967

I wasn't exactly Newton sitting under the apple tree in junior high school. My powers of perception were not particularly sharp. I was a bit distracted.

I had discovered rock 'n' roll and the girls who loved rock 'n' roll. I was enthralled with The Beatles, The Rolling Stones, The Jimi Hendrix Experience, and the little hippie teenage girls that loved them. Every thirteen-year-old with any sense nowadays wishes he had come of age in 1967, the year of the Summer of Love and *Sgt. Pepper's Lonely Heart Clubs Band*, but I lived that dream.

Every week a new sound, song, or album was released that sounded like something leaked by a really hip scientist from the Roswell UFO crash site. Every week a new drug hit the streets that, when consumed while huddled around your turntable, allowed you to actually *visit* those alien planets. It was so intoxicating just to be young in 1967 that it was hard to pay attention to what the adults were doing.

They seemed so boring.

So I never really noticed how sick Dad truly was. I was too self-obsessed to bother noticing.

My family was honest about the diagnosis but spectacularly dishonest about the prognosis. I know the older brothers were told the truth, but the story Willie and I were fed beginning in 1965 was that Dad had been diagnosed with a mild case of colon cancer. Dad's struggle against this weak batch of cancer was supposedly a foregone conclusion: he would get better real soon.

As far as Willie and I knew, Dad was developing new and ingenious ways of kicking the everliving fuck out of cancer up to the day he died. His rapid weight loss was only a sign of him "getting in shape." If he almost never left home and abandoned his formal suit-and-tie wardrobe for crisp silk robes, that was because he was "pooling his strength to finish the cancer off." If our brother Frankie dropped out of college at Arizona State University, where he was a baseball star with his buddy, future Major League Baseball Hall of Famer Reggie Jackson, it was only "to give Dad that extra little help that will put him over the top."

This is why I love Dad. He gave me as much of my childhood, as much of my innocence and happiness as he possibly could. He spent two years putting on a ridiculous act, never showing his pain, his despair, his fear—just to relieve his two youngest sons and his wife from preemptive misery.

There would be plenty of time for us to cry and miss him when he was gone.

Lou Fratto spent his last months on Earth doing things like paying barbers ridiculous amounts of money to reproduce the *exact* right haircut from the cover of the Beatles *Revolver* with forensic accuracy and detail. In his sickbed, he was making international calls to England, favor-trading with friends of friends of friends to get referrals to the hottest rock 'n' roll fashion designers in London.

In 1966, a swarthy 15-year-old Indian kid with carbon black hair named Sajid Khan became a short-lived teen heartthrob in America. Sajid Khan looked *identical* to me. The same clothing shop in London that sent me my Beatlemania gear and mod getups began to import costumes from Bollywood so I could dress *exactly* like Sajid in his starring role on TV's *Maya*. I was every girl's dream: the boy from *Tiger Beat* that lived next door.

When Sajid became passé, I had the misfortune of meeting a stuck-up little 14-year-old hippie blond at the public pool who wanted nothing to do with an innocent little Bollywood prince. So, I had Dad order me some bellbottoms and a medieval-style hemp vest, and I got one of my dirtbag friends to teach me how to smoke banana peels.

Yes, smoking bananas. It didn't get you high, but back in the day it let you pretend to girls more naïve than you that you could "turn them on." I peeled off the banana peels, put them under the broiler in our oven until they burned, threw them outside to dry under the sunlight, chopped up the dried-out peels, and rolled them in paper like joints.

One look at my new Jefferson Airplane outfit, one hit off my magic banana joint, and I *owned* that teenage hippy pussy.

I was one oblivious banana smoker as Dad slipped away. Dad didn't want to arouse my suspicion by sitting me down and saying goodbye. Instead, he'd try to drop a little wisdom on me here and there in the course of our conversations that he hoped I would have the sense to recall and process when I was older.

Whenever I fucked up, he'd immediately "forgive" me for whatever and start dissecting how I "played my hand" wrong and how to redo everything "the right way" the next time around. It was confusing to me at the time, because Dad would start off by telling me that what I did was wrong ... and then give me instructions on how to get away with it next time!

He was planting the seeds and hoping they took root and grew in his absence. This is no idle guess; I know from my older brothers that he was more worried about me than anyone besides our mom.

I baffled Dad. I was a helplessly silly daydreamer who loved fashion, smoking bananas, listening to "faggy English music", and waltzing around Iowa in tiny leather pants, a pirate shirt, and heeled boots like Jim Morrison.

Some days, Dad must have thought he had raised a fucking drag queen.

Nonetheless, Lou Fratto loved me, and he tried to have faith that I wouldn't turn out to be "a degenerate fruitcake" like my Uncle Frank always predicted. Lou comforted himself with the idea that he would almost subliminally teach me everything I needed to know before he died, and, in due time, those half-forgotten lessons would make an impact on my psyche.

One side effect of Dad trying to impart his wisdom to me was that he tried to keep me around him whenever he felt up to talking and doing business during his final months.

That's the reason I happened to be in the living room with him and Frankie on a fateful night in March of 1967.

I was lying on the floor of the living room, reading a *Mad* magazine as Lou and Frankie talked business. At the time, the Family in Iowa was in disarray due to Dad's prolonged absence and obvious vulnerability. Frankie was intensely interrogating Dad about various Iowa underworld figures, getting the dirt on them, what they owed the family, and how they operated. Lou knew exactly what my brother was planning to do when he was gone—and he was proud of it. Chip off the old block and all of that bullshit.

The phone rang. Dad sighed and picked up. He was never in the mood for business any more.

"Hello, Alan, how's it goin'?" he rasped. He spoke in a whisper even in the prime of his life, but by this point his voice was so low and frail that it was almost inaudible. At that point, I would have thought it impossible for Lou to raise his voice even if provoked.

Alan Rosenberg was a 6'4", 325-pound behemoth who looked the part of the well-dressed, well-coifed, lumpy-knuckled, big-nosed Chicago gangster. As a street kid, he impressed our cousin Milwaukee Phil with his toughness and smarts—so Milwaukee Phil referred him to Dad, who was a recognized expert at making the most of the talents of non-Italian criminals.

Dad liked the look and smarts of Alan, so he placed him in his Chicago crew, which was run by a brilliant Jewish gangster named Nimrod "Timmy" Solomon. Timmy's specialties were crazy *Mission Impossible*-style burglaries and complex white-collar crimes. Timmy's crew was like one of them from the *Ocean's 11* movies, a crack squad of ethnically diverse badasses.

Alan fit right in with this gang, and pretty soon he was making millions of dollars a year for Timmy, Dad, and the Outfit. Alan Rosenberg was ahead of his time: he would open up huge warehouse-style discount department stores similar to a Target under a shell corporation, buy all the inventory on credit from the wholesalers, sell and steal everything he could, and then file for bankruptcy and disappear. This scam was the Outfit's biggest ATM for a year or two.

Becoming an overnight millionaire did bad things to Alan, who was just a simple thug. He was a perfect example of a man killed by quick success. He went straight from being a neighborhood nobody to being flattered by underworld leaders like Lou Fratto and Milwaukee Phil.

He didn't realize that, though guys like that flattered *anyone* who made money, their flattery did not translate to respect or power. At the end of the day, Alan was just a comparatively young Jewish crook with a short record and limited connections; he didn't get that he was just another white guy in Timmy Solomon's crew to Lou and Phil, who had seen hundreds of moneymakers come and go.

Alan began to think that Dad was yesterday's news: a fatally ill, effectively retired old has-been in Des Moines. In comparison, Alan was this young, tough prodigy with moneymaking potential for decades. Alan became convinced that he was the future.

It turns out Alan was about to become the past.

I could only hear one side of Lou and Alan's phone conversation, and at first I wasn't paying attention. I first took notice when I heard Dad uncharac-teristically raise his voice. He wasn't anywhere near screaming, but you had to violently enrage Dad to get the tiniest decibel increase out of him.

"You must not be hearin' me, Alan," Dad said in an exasperated tone. "It just won't do. Your guys are young, they got short records, I got all the heat I can take. They'll do the time and get out. It ain't worth sticking my neck out over."

Though I was dropping in mid-conversation, this told me everything I needed to know. Some of Alan's underlings had been pinched, and he was insisting that Dad use his juice with a judge or police officer or politician to spring them. This was a prime example of both Alan's inflated view of his own importance and his criminal inexperience. Dad would never waste important favors on the non-Italian associates of an associate of an associate—and he would certainly never do a favor for *anyone* who called our tapped home phone line and discussed it openly.

Alan didn't understand any of that.

I didn't hear whatever Alan said next, but I could tell it must have been fucking epic. For the first time in years, I heard my dad scream; in fact, I had never heard Dad scream with such intensity ever before. This was a blinding, uncontrollable rage of a sort I was used to seeing out of Uncle Frank, but never my docile old pops.

"LISTEN 'ERE, YOU MOTHERFUCKER YOU!" Dad roared, stab-bing the air with his remaining index finger as his sunken eyes bulged and his powdery white face seared red. "FUCK YOU! YOU 'EAR ME? YOU'RE FUCKED, MOTHERFUCKER!"

Looking back, the most incredible thing about that moment was that Frankie and I started laughing uncontrollably. I mean wheezing, knee-slapping laughter. To us, Dad's tough guy act was about as convincing as an old James Cagney gangster movie.

It was just an example of our dad being silly, of Lou letting some nobody wear so heavily on his already frayed nerves that he showed the Chicago guido core of his personality he worked so hard to disguise. It was comedic.

There was a short pause as Dad panted and tried to catch his breath. Frankie and I could hear wild barking from the receiver; apparently, Rosenberg was as mad as Dad. And whatever he said made Lou shoot up to his feet like a gymnast. Frankie and I stared in disbelief as our dad began to violently shake as if he were being electrocuted.

"OH REALLY, TOUGH GUY?" he screamed in a voice hoarse and wild. "YOU THINK YOU'RE GOING TO THREATEN *MY* KIDS?"

This caused Frankie and I to nearly die of suffocation...not from fear, just hilarity. We couldn't believe Alan would ever say something so silly. This big oaf was not a threat to us; Alan was practically family. His wife babysat us, and we played with his kids all the time. We thought Alan had to be like Uncle Frank, one of those harmless guys who will threaten to kill family when they get agitated without meaning anything by it.

We didn't realize the only person who could threaten a Fratto was a Fratto.

Dad seemed to be acting just as hotheaded and silly. "GUESS WHAT, MOTHERFUCKER?" he shrieked, losing his breath. "I'M GONNA HAVE SOMEBODY CUT YOUR FUCKING HEAD OFF TOMORROW!"

Dad slammed down the receiver, ripped the phone out of the wall, and threw it across the room. Showing no sign of any illness, he began to walk briskly right out of the house. Frankie and I ran behind him, following him into the station wagon. He could not be spoken to. All he did was shake and mutter under his breath.

There was no doubt where we were going: the airport. For the Outfit, the airport was the disposable cellphone of 1967. They all thought it was illegal for the feds to tap a busy public phone.

Without saying a word, Frankie and I knew who Dad was calling: Milwaukee Phil, the "rabbi" who vouched for Alan to be in Dad's presence. Technically, Alan Rosenberg was Milwaukee Phil's responsibility, so it was up to him to get him in line and solve Dad's problem. I didn't know at the time that Milwaukee Phil was another sort of problem solver: he was Uncle Frank's most reliable partner on murder contracts.

Just ask Charlie Gioe!

The phone call was short and sweet: "PHIL! CHOP THAT MOTHER-FUCKER ROSENBERG'S HEAD OFF!" Two seconds after arriving at the Des Moines Airport's row of public telephones, we were on our way back home.

Naturally, Frankie and I both thought Dad was being figurative; there was no way he would blatantly order one of our cousins to decapitate a family friend on a public phone in front of his two kids. Dad didn't seem like the decapitating type, and Alan was just one of the guys. This was just some silly, over-the-top squabble between a temperamental old Italian and a cheap Jew who wanted to keep the money rolling in. The problem would pass real quickly.

He passed, all right. Two days later, I walked into the living room, stretching out my sticky scrotum skin under my underwear and yawning from a good night's sleep. I happened to catch the headline on one of the Chicago papers that Dad had delivered every morning. The newspaper was hard to miss: all by itself on a clean table, neatly folded to showcase a single article.

It turns out that the body of Alan Rosenberg was found in the trunk of a car parked at 3712 W. Ainslie Street in the Albany Park neighborhood on the North Side. He was found handcuffed, pumped full of bullets, and physically abused in every way imaginable.

In the lingo of Uncle Frank, Alan wasn't killed; he was *overkilled*. He was transformed from a human being into an example. That's why he was left somewhere he would be found instead of just disappearing. They wanted everyone to know this is what happened when you crossed the Outfit.

Though I had literally witnessed my father order his death, not for one second that morning did I think Dad had been responsible for Alan Rosenberg's death.

Really!

I mean, the friends Dad had over to our house got killed all the time, and Uncle Frank would get into his booze and tip us off most of the time that this or that motherfucker in Chicago was responsible. It never had anything to do with Dad as far as we could tell. As far as I was concerned, all Dad's anger at Alan proved was that this was an unlikable, out-of-control guy who probably pissed *everyone* off, including guys who were much quicker to draw blood than Dad.

Any doubt lingering in my pubescent brain was erased by the visit from two FBI agents that morning. I was sitting with Dad in his office. He was behind his desk, looking so frail, meek, and drained that it was incredible to think he had mustered such energy a couple days before. When scowling, fist-balling Frankie escorted the two G-men into the living room, Dad turned to me, nodded, and smirked. He could have ordered me out, but he wanted to show me he had nothing to hide.

The feds didn't fuck around. "Did you do it, Lou?" the much bigger agent asked. This fucking moose with a buzzcut looked like he played left tackle at Nebraska.

"Did what?" Lou asked with upturned palms and a blank expression.

"Did you kill Alan Rosenberg?"

"I was at home, so obviously I didn't kill him," Dad said as if he were talking to a couple of "helmeted retards," as they said in those days.

"Lou, you know what we mean. Did you have him killed?"

"Well, you can answer that question."

"Not yet, that's why we're asking you."

"Ok, well, let me help you guys figure it out. Was his head chopped off?"

"No."

"Okay, well then you know it wasn't me. Trust me, if I had anything to do with it, that motherfucker would have been decapitated!" Lou said with a spark of joy in his eyes. He motioned to the door. "Frankie, escort these men out."

Within a few months, Dad was indicted for fraud charges relating to Rosenberg's racket. When announcing the indictments, the feds basically told the press that Lou Fratto was responsible for Al Rosenberg's murder and to expect an indictment for capital murder imminently.

So much for Dad's reputation.

11

JOHNNY LOSES HIS FATHER

"Jim Arpy ... finds the following two items in a Chicago paper:

'Louis Fratto...will never be forgotten. For how can anyone forget a great man? Des Moines, Iowa...will always remember that on Sept. 13, 1946, it was Louis Fratto who through his never-tiring efforts gave a charity bazaar that not only paid the mortgage on the church, but left a tidy sum in the church treasury. A humanitarian, Lou never stopped helping people...'

The second item in the same paper stated:

'Louis (Cockeyed Louie) Fratto, 60, crime syndicate boss of Des Moines, Iowa ... had used the alias Lew Farrell since the early 1940s when he was to assume the duties of racket boss and beer baron in Iowa.'

Now this, dear reader, illustrates the vast gulf between news and advertising."

CEDAR RAPIDS CITIZEN TIMES
December 20, 1967

My last memory of my father was our trip to Farmington, New Mexico to watch the Connie Mack World Series. He might never get to see Frankie and Willie play in the Majors, but this was a great opportunity to enjoy a few days at the park watching championship-caliber high school baseball with his kids.

Speaking of the majors, one of the most distinguished spectators at that Connie Mack World Series was Hall of Fame pitcher Warren Spahn.

How do I know?

Because we almost stole his 1957 Milwaukee Braves World Series ring.

We didn't do it intentionally. I just accidentally picked up the wrong suitcase at the baggage claim at the airport in Farmington. When Frankie was unpacking the bags, he noticed the error when he read what appeared to be love letters to Warren Spahn. Frankie had every intention of returning the bag to Mr. Spahn . . . until he found $5000 in cash and the World Series ring.

To Frankie, a World Series Ring was like that other ring to the Gollum guy in *Lord of the Rings*. It was the ultimate goal of his existence, his dream, his Grail. He tried it on; posed with it; had his brothers in hysterics as he took swings with an imaginable bat with it on his fingers. There was nothing he wanted to do more than keep that ring.

But it was also incriminating evidence. The gangster won out over the baseball nut, but not completely. Since Frankie kept the cash, the right thing to do if he wasn't going to keep the ring would be to toss it into the desert surrounding Farmington and eliminate it as evidence. But Frankie couldn't bring himself to disrespect Spahn and the game—it would have been like our mom destroying a priceless Catholic relic.

So instead, Frankie hid the suitcase the one place no one would dare look for it: under my dad's bed at the hotel. When Lou ordered the hotel locked down and organized a room-by-room search for the stolen suitcase that afternoon, guess which room was the one that wasn't searched?

Afterwards Frankie made sure Spahn got his ring. I had Randazzo, the writer on this book, confirm it with Spahn's kid . . . just to make sure Frankie hadn't pulled a fast one on his own brothers and palmed the ring.

Actually, now that I think about it, the very last memory I have of my father was a day at the movies. Lou took Frankie, Tommy, and me to see *The St. Valentine's Day Massacre*, a movie about Al Capone's most infamous murders. The film was *supposed to be* a gritty, bloody drama, but that's not how Dad took it. He was laughing through the whole movie like it was a comedy. "Oh my god!" he'd whisper through his giggles, "these fuckin' guys are too much! Where did they get this shit? If only they knew!"

I don't think Dad ever had a better time at the movies. I never would have guessed he only had weeks to live.

Even when Dad left for an admittedly "prolonged" stay at the Cancer Research Hospital during the Summer of Love, I was not troubled. I didn't even worry when my mom and Frankie suddenly dropped off Willie and me at our Aunt Lizzie's home in Des Moines and took the next flight to Madison. All Frankie said was that "Dad is getting homesick and wants some visitors."

I loved staying with Aunt Lizzie. She was a one-woman fried chicken franchise. You couldn't pass Aunt Lizzie's window without being dragged inside and stuffed full of the best deep-friend Southern chicken ever made by an Italian broad in Iowa. Willie and I were sucking on some chicken bones in the living room, carefree as Teamsters on break, when Aunt Lizzie softly padded up next to the couch where we were sitting.

"Boys, I have some bad news," she said with admirable calm and a note of sweetness that I can't imagine how she put into her voice. "I just got off the phone, and your father is not going to make it through the day. He's too sick. I'm sorry, boys. I'm really sorry."

Dad had been suffering from cancer for two years by this point, and I had never once seriously considered the possibility he would die until Aunt Lizzie told me he was basically already dead. It was pure shock, the total eclipse of everything—darkness and chaos.

To me, Lou Fratto was like God presiding over a well-ordered universe. He was in charge and oversaw everything, protected everyone from the repercussions that normally come with living. To be told that he no longer existed... I cannot describe how incomprehensible that thought was to me. It seemed as if the entire world should stop working without Dad, would veer out of control like a car whose driver dies. I felt immediately in danger, and helpless.

What can I say? What is a guy like me supposed to say when he talks about something like this? That I cried? That I panicked and screamed and called out for Dad to come back?

Yeah, all of that shit happened.

Dad may have been a gangster in *The Chicago Sun-Times*, but to me he was just a man who made me feel safe and loved and special every second of his time with me on Earth. The world as I knew it ended that moment at Aunt Lizzie's house. I can only compare it to dying and waking up in Hell.

And I wasn't alone. Hundreds of people—innocent people, nuns and charity workers and elderly invalids and countless down-on-their-luck Italian families—counted on Dad for emotional and financial support. In certain quarters of American society, this may have been seen as a bad man dying—but in our family and social circle, it honestly felt like a catastrophe, our own personal JFK assassination.

Even the Outfit was traumatized. They knew Lou was always the peacemaker, the cool head who for decades chilled out Angels of Death like Uncle Frank and Obie Frabotta and Milwaukee Phil. Without Dad around to talk the various factions out of going to war, the Midwest was closer to a Capone-style bloodbath than it had been in over thirty years.

Incredibly, the panic across my world only lasted about 48 hours. The grief was still terrible, but a return to stability was quickly enforced by Frankie. When he returned with my mom and Dad's body from the hospital in Madison, Wisconsin, he came through the door of our home with a look of fearless, Napoleonic determination in his black eyes. There were no tears on his cheeks, and no whining in his voice. Frankie was as hard, and as rigid, and as proud as a Roman statue.

My brother was Michael Corleone before Mario Puzo had written the name on paper.

He was finally in charge. Frankie was a 20-year-old college sports star with Major League Baseball ambitions when he dropped out of college to come home to support his widow mother and young siblings. Though Tommy was formally Dad's heir as the eldest child, everyone knew that Tommy idolized his little brother Frankie and looked to him as our family's obvious born-leader. It was Frankie's time, the time he had been preparing for his entire life.

Frankie knew the credibility challenge he would immediately face: would Lew Farrell's old associates respect and fear him enough to continue to pay our family what we were owed? The only way to secure our family's future was to ensure our Dad's extensive interests in legitimate businesses and outstanding debts with slippery debtors were acknowledged and honored—regardless if they were handshake deals or on paper. This required Frankie to carry himself like a man who demanded, and would compel, respect. He had to carry himself like a boss, which came naturally to Frankie.

Frankie was the boss of our family—the Fratto Family of Iowa—if not necessarily any associated criminal organization.

Given what happened to my brother, I want to be clear: I'm not going to speculate over what Frankie did or didn't do regarding assuming an official role within the Mafia, the Chicago Outfit, or the Iowa Family. I definitely wasn't his confidant at that young age, and I don't think it would be fair to him or his memory to publish other family members' secondhand insights on the issue.

As the son of a boss, tradition in Chicago allowed Frankie to become a "made guy" just by claiming it—though putting the "button" on your own chest was dangerous because, by not consulting with any of the old men, their only way to veto your decision was to kill you. There was no doubt that Uncle Frank and the rest of our Chicago relatives would have backed and defended Frankie, the adored family golden boy, if he chose to claim the mantle of Boss of the Iowa Family.

Regardless, Frankie would have to carry himself like a boss to deter any potential Alan Rosenbergs who might seek to fleece our family. When you are immersed in that culture, you can communicate your position and rank simply by how you make eye contact, in what order you enter or leave a room, how you shake a man's hand and kiss his cheek, how you introduce yourself, what tone you use in conversations, how tall you stand and where you sit a table, and how quickly you make requests or get angry. It might as well have been a beehive or ant colony for all the talk I ever heard about serious matters.

And what Frankie communicated with his body language after getting back from Wisconsin was very simple: he would not tolerate anyone fucking with him or his family, no matter who they were or who they were with . . . period.

Once he got home, Frankie grabbed me with a firm grip on my shoulders and walked me up to my bedroom for a talk. "Listen, Johnny," he said, his voice strong but not harsh, "nothing's changed. I am taking over for Dad. You are safe. No one is going to fuck with you.

"You hear me?" he said with a little growl in his voice, forcing me to pay attention. "No one is going to fuck with you *at all* with me around. Dad is in a better place, and I will do anything he would have done for you. Everything's the same; I've just graduated into Dad's spot."

Frankie was staring right into my eyes without blinking, his dark Rasputin eyes almost hypnotizing me. Like a vampire, he was exerting his own will over mine. He repeated himself, over and over until he saw my eyes blindly reflecting his fortitude back at him. Finally, I nodded and hugged him hard. I realized I needed him.

Like a lot of people, I didn't know how to exist without a Lou Fratto in the world, and Frankie wanted to do the best he could to fill that role for me and everyone else. With that hug, order was restored. Frankie replaced Lou. Consequences for my actions disappeared again. I missed Dad, but I was not in danger. I was a kid again. I could go smoke bananas, listen to the Beatles, and torture nuns in class.

To my surprise, Frankie continued talking, daring to confide in me a little bit, giving me far more respect and trust than he ever had before. Frankie was staring off at the wall as if it were a movie screen, no longer making eye contact. I could see that he was living out his glorious future in his mind. "Listen, things in Iowa have gotten out of hand without Dad being around. I'm going to set things straight."

Frankie had never, ever failed at anything he focused on accomplishing. Just like he became the best baseball and basketball player in Iowa, just like he scored a perfect 4.0 grade point average through high school and his time in college, Frankie would fulfill his destiny as Lew's successor. Who could stop Frankie with his talent, our family name, and our family's connections? He was destined to bring Lew's legacy to the next level.

What form that legacy would have taken over the years, we couldn't have guessed at that time—it was always easier for me to imagine my older brother as a sports star and corporate CEO than any type of wiseguy. He seemed too smart to be a cliché.

Regardless, I was relieved Frankie was taking up Dad's legacy and thereby freeing me from having to confront it. Our survival, our lifestyle, required at least one of us to fill Dad's role, and I'm sure Tommy was just as grateful as me that Frankie was hellbent on being the guy to risk his life on our behalf. As Frankie got up, he looked back in my direction, this time without raising his face all the way up to mine. "By the way," he said with a little rasp of emotion in his voice, "if you see mom crying, or hurting, just remind her Dad is in Heaven. Just remind her she believes in God, and that God would always protect her Lou. Just tell her Dad's no longer in pain, and he's in Heaven, looking down on her and telling her to be happy."

"Yes, Frankie," I said.

I was so in the thrall of Frankie's power that I unthinkingly followed him when he told me we were going to Dad's wake. I was too shellshocked to realize the nightmare I was walking into.

Upon entering the funeral home, Frankie detached himself from us and walked to the front of the room. Dad's longtime friend, retired heavyweight boxing champion Rocky Marciano, appeared out of nowhere and joined Uncle Frank in walking up to Frankie. As if choreographed, Uncle Frank and Rocky assumed positions behind Frankie on either side. Like God, he was flanked by two lesser manifestations of his own power. That's how great Frankie's charisma was: Uncle Frank flocked to his side.

At first, I stayed to the back to watch the scene unfold. I didn't go anywhere near that coffin in the far end of the room, focusing so intently on Frankie so as not to even look in its direction. One after another, the most powerful gangsters in America walked into that funeral parlor: New York godfather Joe Colombo, New England godfather Raymond Patriarca, Kansas City godfather Nick Civella, and, of course, the imperial Tony Accardo.

When those grim old men walked up to pay 20-year-old Frankie their respects, I watched in gape-mouthed disbelief as they treated him *exactly* as they would have my father: the same body language, the same tone, the same everything. They gave him standing and deference they did not give to Uncle Frank, a multimillionaire mass-murdering capo with thirty years under his belt, or Rocky Marciano, the foremost hero in all of Italian-American history.

The King is dead. Long Live the King. Frankie was no longer a kid, no longer even a man; he was now an office, the head of our family. And the office commanded respect.

It was incredible to see nearly everyone at that wake give Frankie outsized respect. If they didn't, he demanded it, and he also demanded the payments owed to Dad that had fallen into arrears. That's right, right next to the freshly cold body of Dad, Frankie eyeballed Lou's former lieutenants and business partners and told them *exactly down to the cent* how much they owed, *exactly down to the day* how late they were in paying it, and *exactly down to the decimal point* how much interest he was going to charge them.

I heard him say, over and over, "Time to shape up."

There was no grace period, no mourning, no mercy. Our family needed to pay the bills.

One after another, I saw crooks who had been freelancing and gorging themselves on Dad's rightful share shrink before Frankie's glance and, after a microsecond-long look at Uncle Frank's terrifying face looming over my brother's shoulder, nod and walk away trembling and pale. I could see Tony Accardo watching Frankie, and though I'm not going to lie and say that I could even begin to read what a sphinx like him was thinking, I couldn't help but assume he was impressed.

I was yanked out of observing Frankie and Joe Batters with a tug on my arm. Tommy was dragging me up to the coffin to say goodbye to Dad along with Willie, Mom, and Carmie. I didn't know what to do; I felt seasick and lightheaded. Before I could process what was happening, I was standing next to the coffin. Inside it was a tiny, frail, bone-white insect that looked nothing like Dad. At first, I didn't think it was him. It couldn't be. It didn't even look human, just 60 pounds of skeleton and the thinnest wax paper layer of flesh.

It was only when I looked at the hands, the nine-fingered hands with his watch and rings, that I knew it was Dad.

And I don't remember anything else from that night. The next thing I remember I was screaming and crying the next morning, threatening to jump out of the window to my death before I would attend the funeral. My older cousins Jojo and Sammy Cataldo had been babysitting me ever since Dad died, so Frankie called on another Cataldo, Georgie, to take one for the team and stay home with me during the funeral. Frankie hugged me, told me to calm down, not to worry, and to rest up. And then he left.

This surprised me more than anything else in the past few days. I had never thrown a tantrum without Frankie acting ashamed at my girliness and screaming at me to "ACT LIKE A MAN!" like Don Corleone ridiculing Johnny Fontane in *The Godfather*. In my heart, I knew Frankie wanted to kick my ass and toughen me up like a big brother should.

But Frankie's role wasn't to be my big brother anymore. He was kind enough to understand that I needed him to restore my support system by being just like Lou, so he comforted me and let me suffer without added embarrassment.

Sitting at home with Georgie, I thought about Frankie's behavior, and I decided that I would be okay. I was thirteen years old after all, a bona fide teenager. I was practically an adult. My parents weren't supposed to matter to me anymore, more like background noise or the fuddy-duddy neighbors that drop in for a couple jokes once an episode on a sitcom.

Dad had passed from my world. My identity had been almost completely eclipsed as long as he had been alive ... and I had no intention of emerging from the shadows any time soon. I went from being a bit player in Lou Fratto's story to a bit player in Frankie Fratto's story.

That served me fine. I was happy to hide. I was happy to shirk all responsibility and expectations. I wasn't ready to be a man—men in my family had to act like Frankie.

I was going to be a kid. I hadn't lost a dad; I had lost a big brother. What I did not realize was that, as Frankie replaced Dad, I was going to get a new big brother. Two of them, in fact.

One appearance at a wake hadn't won Frankie control over Lew's assets across the state of Iowa. He would need muscle. He would need credibility.

He would need Uncle Frank and Rocky Marciano.

12

EVERY TIME A MUDDERPUCKER DRINKS, AN ANGEL GETS ITS WINGS

"On April 14, 1967, OM T-1 further advised that LEW FARRELL had been a member of the 'outfit' for 40 years. For a period of approximately ten years, FARRELL was doing 'heavy work' for the 'outfit.' During that time FARRELL worked principally with three men…and that the above-mentioned four men were considered the 'roughest, roughest' men in the business at the time… OM T-1 pointed out, however, that the reputation made by FARRELL in the 'outfit' during that period served FARRELL well to the present time and has enabled him to lean on people when he needed to do so."

SPECIAL AGENT DANIEL H. HOWARD, JR.
Federal Bureau of Investigation
File OM 92-265

Just after my father passed, my Aunt Geri invited my mother and the kids to Chicago to take a little vacation. I was always excited to visit my Uncle Mike and Aunt Geri in Elmwood Park, the beautiful little suburb where all of the Chicago Mafia kingpins relocated during the "white flight" from the city during the turbulent 1960s. Aunt Geri was Mom's closest confidante and her sweetest-tempered, most docile sister within our otherwise crazy family, and Geri's son Gill was every bit as close to me as my own brothers.

A weekend with Geri, Mike, and Gill seemed like a perfect opportunity for our family to recuperate and relax after the loss of Dad. Unfortunately, there was no way we could relax in Chicago.

Why? Because that's where Uncle Frank lived.

My mom had hoped this trip to Chicago would be calmer than usual since, without Dad with us, she didn't feel it was necessary to stay with Uncle Frank and Auntie Kay: two chain-smoking, two-fisted drinkers with the social style of pirates. My mom would never forgive Frank and Kay for the time that my cousin Gill and I got shitfaced from caramel apples that Auntie Kay made using liquor-spiked caramel.

My mom wasn't in the mood to nurse another underage hangover. Unfortunately, her wishes were not going to be fulfilled.

Minutes after we arrived at Aunt Geri's clean, smoke-free, booze-free home, the phone rang. Everyone in our family got tense the moment we heard Aunt Geri say the words "Frank, don't upset her!"

My mom got on the phone, meekly whispering, "Well, Frank, Geri and Mike invited me and the kids, and they are having so much fun here with Geri's kids. So I think it's better we just stay here . . ."

I didn't even need to hear the other half of this conversation. I knew Uncle Frank would be beyond pissed at what he saw as a sign of disrespect. I also knew Uncle Frank would lose his temper and start verbally hitting my mom below the belt as he did with anyone he couldn't violently assault. His attitude towards conflict resolution could be boiled down to his favorite catchphrase: "If I put you in the trunk of a car, it's not to sneak you into a drive-in movie!"

I never could have guessed the strange turn his verbal offensive would take against my mom.

"Carmella," I could hear Frank screaming from the receiver, "your puckin' husband Louie couldn't even puckin' kill anybody, I had to do all the puckin' killin'! If it wasn't por me, he couldn't have been the puckin' boss cuz he couldn't even kill people!"

This was certainly an interesting indictment of Lou Fratto.

For a moment, my mom stood there with this solemn, lip-licking expression on her face and then, without saying a word, hung up the phone. After my apparently hard-of-hearing Aunt Geri asked what our horrible Uncle Frank had said, my mom smiled the most beautiful, serene smile I had ever seen.

"Frank said my Lou didn't kill anybody," Carmella said with mounting excitement. "You know what this means? Do you know what this *means*, Geri?

This means he committed no mortal sins that would stop him from going to Heaven. My Lou's in Heaven with my parents and all the people he loved! He's in Heaven waiting for me! So, when I die, I will be with Lou!"

My mom hugged Aunt Geri until Geri was turning blue and sucking wind.

This was the best moment of my Catholic mom's life: her one great fear—that Dad had committed some sin in his wild, desperate youth in the slums of Chicago that would prevent them from spending eternity together—had been eliminated. This one conversation with my Uncle Frank did more to dispel my mom's grief and restore her spirits than a thousand years of vacation with Aunt Geri could ever do.

A moment later, the phone rang. Aunt Geri answered.

"Frank, don't you upset Carmella again!" Aunt Geri chided. "If you are going to yell, I'm not going to put her on...You promise you won't yell?" Aunt Geri turned a skeptical eye to my mom, who was still flying in the clouds. "Okay, Carm, Frank promised he's not gonna yell."

"Hell-o Frank?" said my mom, her voice cracking with joy.

"Carmella, I'm sorry," Uncle Frank said, just drunk enough to still be audible over the phone without yelling. "I didn't mean to upset you with what I said...Louie killed *a lot* of guys. *A lot*. I wasn't giving him the puckin' credit he deserved."

My dad once told me I would get a knot in my stomach whenever anyone said something about him that was a lie. That knot would get all twisted sometimes when I read articles about Dad being a gangster...but it did *not* wind itself all up when Uncle Frank said he had killed people. Just like Dad said, I knew it in my gut. I suddenly saw the truth that was right in front of my eyes the entire time: Dad *had* killed Alan Rosenberg.

Dad could not have gone more out of his way to showcase his guilt for me. Dad had taken me to the airport to witness a phone call in which he ordered my cousin to murder another human being. When the FBI arrived shortly after the body was discovered, Dad insisted that I witness his defiance of them. He smiled and winked at me during their interrogation.

Lou Fratto wanted me to remember what he did so that one day, when I was older, I could understand he was proud of the sin that resulted in him dying while under investigation for Murder One. He was almost like Jesus—making sure everyone saw him crawl onto the cross to show that the blood he shed had been for them.

Dad had murdered to protect the children that Alan Rosenberg had threatened. Dad had murdered to protect me. He wanted me to know this.

This was a moment of truth. This was where a guy like me gets melted down to his core elements.

If goodhearted, gentle Willie had overheard what Uncle Frank had said—he hadn't—and taken it seriously, my little brother would have yelled and screamed and probably puked on the floor in horror. If he had learned that our beloved dad had murdered another human being to protect *him*, to save *his* life, Willie would *still* be agonized with guilt.

I was not Willie.

Why?

Because I didn't cry, didn't recoil in horror, didn't feel my stomach twist into a motherfucker of a knot. None of that happened. The realization went down quick and easy like a gulp of chocolate milk.

All that happened was a smile.

The thought slithered out from the depths of mind psyche and announced itself, "Good for Dad, that motherfucker Rosenberg deserved it!"

Willie definitely wouldn't have thought what Dad did to Alan Rosenberg was *cool*.

I thought what Dad did to Alan Rosenberg was *cool*.

I put out my hands and made the shape of a pistol. I imagined that the giant conman who had bullied Dad and threatened my life was standing before me. *POW!* The sound effect came from my mouth.

I saw Rosenberg tumble backwards in a spray of blood.

I saw my future before my eyes.

Meanwhile, my mom was crying by the telephone. She was convinced her husband was in Hell. Though I was beginning to feel my oats as the son of a murderous gangster, I wasn't so euphoric that I deluded myself into thinking I could avenge the pain my Uncle Frank needlessly caused my Mom. I was just a kid; that was a job that called for a man.

Luckily, my cousin Gill was prematurely mature.

Gill was a lot like my brother Tommy: a cool, fun hustler of a teenager with a pussywagon he drove all around town. Though he was four years older than me, Gill was cool enough to let me tag along everywhere he went, even though I was just a little pimple-faced shit. We would cruise around Elmwood Park, listening to the radio and watching all the wiseguys in their convertibles with their trophy girlfriends. They all knew Gill, and he made sure they knew me. It was a huge buzz.

Though Gill had plenty of love for his "lil' cuz," he was even closer to Carmella. We visited each other so often that Gill officially adopted my mom as his "second mom." Though I was too selfish and immature to let myself get depressed by how much Uncle Frank had hurt my mom, Gill took it personally and decided to get even ... as much as a non-suicidal seventeen-year-old could ... when it came to Uncle Frank.

We were sitting at Uncle Frank's place with Frank and Gill's brother-in-law Joey T. After a few minutes, Gill whispered to me without warning, "Keep him busy!" I had no idea what was going on and panicked.

I was left alone with Uncle Frank as Gill and Joey rummaged around in the kitchen, doing Lord knows what. This was a terrifying scenario: it was impossible for an un-athletic thirteen-year-old wannabe hippie to make small talk with Uncle Frank when he was so sober that he actually expected me to talk. There was just no common ground *at all*. Besides, the man already hated me.

Uncle Frank and I had a more antagonistic and juvenile relationship than I ever did with my brothers. It was a real sick situation, a child enduring a sibling rivalry with a Mafia killer in his fifties. Uncle Frank was so touchy that I could reduce him to the mentality of a kindergartener with just one look over the dinner table.

Whenever Uncle Frank visited our home when my Dad was still around, I went on the offensive—guerilla warfare style. The dinner table was my battlefield. First, I would lick my hand and very stealthily start touching his hand, his plate, his food, his face whenever Dad wasn't looking. By the time Frank was whining, "Lou-oo!" I was off minding my own business with a fork in my hand.

Dad would play right along. As the sneaky and stealthy older brother, he found infinite pleasure in my torture of Uncle Frank.

"Frank, stop being paranoid, he's just a kid. He ain't doin' nothin'," he'd say with a chuckle, trying to suppress the gigantic big brother smile spreading across his face. Whenever Dad would catch my glance when no one else was paying attention, he'd wink at me to tell me to keep going. At that point, I'd spill my milk on Uncle Frank's $500 suit or ball up a little piece of bread dough to throw at his bad ear.

This teasing would send Uncle Frank into high-pitched tirades. He'd be begging Dad to recognize what I was doing, to admit I was a devious little shit, but Dad maintained his look of serene obliviousness. "Frank, Frank, calm down, you're making a big scene outta nothin', you need to get more sleep, relax, you're dreaming things up out of nowhere ..."

Now that Dad was gone, it was naturally uncomfortable for me to talk to the homicidal uncle I had tortured since birth. The nerves showed. Stalling for time, I asked that mean old fucker anything that came to mind. Whatever ended up coming out of my mouth was *definitely* whacked out in Uncle Frank's estimation.

By the time Gill and Joey came back into the room, Uncle Frank had concluded that I was on "dope"—which drug he meant, I doubt either of us knew. He held to the belief that I was a "druggie" until the day he died. From then on, I was Uncle Frank's druggie nephew. He was a real snap judgment sort of guy.

Back at Joey T's house, Gill was having a ball mimicking Uncle Frank's tirade against me. "You puckin' guys better get this puckin' kid off the puckin' dope before he pucks up the pamily's repu-puckin'-tation!"

After they finished laughing, Gill and Joey revealed why they were in kitchen for so long. "We were looking for a pencil and paper because we got Uncle Franks' credit card number. It was just sitting on that little table, so now all we have to do is figure out what to do with it! We're going to teach him a lesson for what he did to Aunt Carm!"

All of a sudden, God appeared on Joey's television in the form of an infomercial advertising little banana trees you could plant right in your backyard. Joey looked at Gill, and Gill looked at me, and I gave Gill the phone. The revenge on Uncle Frank had begun; we ordered six banana trees that night. This would continue for *months* whenever the mood struck Gill, Joey, or me.

A few days later, Aunt Geri woke us to show Uncle Frank on the news. He had just been indicted with a number of other Outfit suspects.

As I heard this, panic swept through my body, but that was showing my lack of seasoning. Nobody else was too concerned—just another day in the life of a Mafia family. Unlike Iowa, these things happened all the time in Chicago, and they were no big deal. You just called the connected lawyer, and he'd pay off whoever needed to be paid. If you got stressed over it, you were doing it wrong.

In fact, Uncle Frank seemed downright thrilled. It was his chance to be a prick in the cops' own house and get some of the bonus pussy that went along with the press spotlight. He was so excited that he called up Gill and told us to come along as he surrendered himself to be booked and arraigned. I was finally going to get to observe how a real, unambiguous gangster acted in the wild.

The insanity started off bright and early with Frank nearly murdering a gas station attendant for failing to clean the front window of the Lincoln to his satisfaction. Gill hopped out of the car and dragged the attendant back inside the station before Uncle Frank added another felony charge to his arraignment day.

The scene at the Dirksen Federal Building in downtown Chicago was a feeding frenzy of reporters, photographers, cameramen, police, attorneys, gangsters, and groupies. Before getting out of the Lincoln, Uncle Frank took his time primping his hair, checking his teeth, and getting his cuffs *just right* to showcase his huge diamond cluster cufflinks in the shape of his initials FF. "Hey Jimi Hendrix," he barked at me, "my hair okay? Do I look *go-od*?"

Before I could answer, Gill jumped in over me, "Unc, you look like George Raft, only better looking."

"Damn right!" Frank said, hopping out of the car. We walked the long hallway lined with reporters and photographers, and, I gotta tell ya, Uncle Frank looked so cool I remember it in slow motion with a Tarantino-style soundtrack.

I didn't even *like* Uncle Frank, but for those few minutes, the man was *the* stone-cold coolest motherfucker. He was a celebrity, only better; he was a celebrity you had no choice but to fear and respect. If you ever wonder why Italian kids like me make the mistake of following in their father and uncle's footsteps, it all boils down to wanting to be rebellious and glamorous like *that*.

The fingerprinting was a fiasco. Uncle Frank decided to showboat by planting his palm flat down on the paper but refusing to put his fingers down to make the print. This huge meathead cop was pressing down on Frank's hand with all of his might, but he couldn't get Uncle Frank's fingers to move. Frank just laughed, yawned, and checked his watch on the other hand.

This was typical Uncle Frank. Everywhere he went, he'd have a hard rubber handball in one hand he'd be squeezing constantly, building up strength and expending excess anger. Frank's fingers were Superman strong, and he could poke a hole through your chest to your heart. And he was *always* looking for an excuse to display this strength.

This went on for what seemed like a generation before Frank's attorney called him off. "Come on Frank, stop playing games!" The fingers abruptly fell to the paper.

Next was the mug shot, and that was another big joke to my uncle. Frank was goofing off with silly faces, making Gill and I and even the cops bust up with laughter. But, when that camera flashed, Frank's face instantaneously adopted the coldest, meanest, deadest stare you'd ever seen. It was the mug shot of a real fuckin' GANGSTER.

After that, Frank was released—and he was feeling so good that he decided to fuck with me. "Hey John Lennon, you drive?" Frank said as he tossed me the keys to his Lincoln. This was a recurring theme in our relationship. Since there were few wiseguys in Iowa, on his visits he was always trying to recruit me to get behind the wheel since he felt a man of his stature should never drive himself.

"Uncle Frank, I don't have a driver's license, I'm a kid!" I pled with a cracking voice.

Frank gave me this look like I was the biggest pussy ever to be born with the last name Fratto. With a scowl, Frank said, "So?!" in a way that packed more disgust and sarcasm into a single syllable than I thought was even possible.

I was already a drug addict in Uncle Frank's mind for the rest of my life, and if I fucked up here, I'd be a sissy for life as well. Gill gave me an insistent look and whispered, "Don't worry, I'll sit in the front with you. Chill, cuz, it's gonna be fine. Just chill."

A moment later, I was driving a Lincoln the size of an aircraft carrier as Uncle Frank made screwdriver cocktails for himself in the backseat, slamming them back one after another. Gill was sitting real close, ready to take control of the car if I fucked up.

Gill patiently fed me directions that avoided the freeway, and I managed to get along, stopping and starting and barely avoiding accident after accident. The entire time, Uncle Frank's busy replacing his blood with orange juice and vodka.

"STOP HERE!" Uncle Frank suddenly screamed as we passed by the Hyatt House Hotel. I was so relieved! I pulled the car up to the valet, who was shocked to see a child get out of the front seat and a gigantic shitfaced gangster get out of the backseat.

I was a real cherubic kid; I didn't look a day over 11 or 12. The valet looked at me like he had just stumbled upon a scene of child abuse. Gill noticed the valet, so he yelled out, "It's okay! He's really a 40-year-old midget!"

"Don't porget a puckin' junkie!" screamed Uncle Frank, who was starting to lose his ability to say the letter F now that the drinks were kicking in. Why Uncle Frank thought it reflected well on him to be driven around by a drug-addicted midget is unknowable.

Before I even had a chance to let the relief of surviving my crazy cross-town drive with Uncle Frank settle in, I was escorted right into another crisis: the bar. I made the mistake of trying to explain to Uncle Frank that he'd got the wrong impression of me and that I really wasn't a junkie.

Frank sized me up and said, "Alright, I've piggered out a way to prove you're not a doper. Prove to me you can *drink*."

Ok, I know what you're thinking, that this would prove nothing... and you would be right. But remember, we are in Uncle Frank's world in this story, and this is all about what *he* thinks. I know that may not make much sense to the *average* person, but in 1969, Uncle Frank's best intelligence sources had told him drug addicts could not *also* be alcoholics. Obviously, Frank was not a Rolling Stones fan.

Ironically, the only "drug" I had used at that point was bananas...the same drug I was buying in Escobar-scale bulk shipments with Uncle Frank's credit card whenever I got the chance!

As I struggled to hop onto a tall barstool, the bartender looked me up and down with this "Are you fuckin' kiddin' me?" look. I was relieved; surely this fuckin' guy was not going to risk his job and the Hyatt Hotel's liquor license, right?

Wrong!

This bartender was one of Uncle Frank's cronies, which meant that he would have served me rat poison if Frank ordered it for me. Put on the spot, I had no idea what to order—I knew *nothing* about alcohol. Taking a blind step off the plank, I ordered a beer, which was what I normally saw my older brothers drinking.

"Puck, a beer still qualifies you as a junkie!" Frank slurred. The bartender, to his credit, didn't even bat his eyes at this completely inexplicable statement. He had been around Frank long enough to hear and expect worse.

Thinking hard, I remembered that Dad used to drink a scotch and water, so I ordered one. Frank got a wicked grin on his face and laughed. Raising his finger, he shook it from side to side: "Puck that! *No water!*"

"No ice?" I squeak at my uncle, terrified.

"No ice!"

Now this fucking child-abusing lunatic of a bartender pours straight scotch into a glass...with a smile. Gill is screaming that this is going to kill me, which definitely did not help my nerves. With Uncle Frank watching, I sipped one *hard* blast of scotch and, knowing it wasn't going to get any better, I dumped another mouthful down the hatch. I felt like I had been stabbed right between the eyes. There was no way I could finish this glass without taking my mom's second favorite child away from her.

Then I caught a lucky break: Gill walked over, blocked Frank's vision, and subtly dumped most of the scotch into the well on the side of the bar. When Frank got another look at me, all he saw was his thirteen-year-old nephew polishing off the rest of the scotch.

Shit, that wasn't so bad! I had proven to Frank I was not a dirty fucking hippie, and all it cost me was a case of nausea and dizziness that was increasing by the second. I was finally in the clear.

"Hey Ringo, time to get in the puckin' barber's chair!"

Oh fuck! Around the corner from the bar was a barbershop where Uncle Frank got his haircuts, and, now that I had proven not to be a dirty fucking hippie, it was time to get a haircut befitting someone who wasn't a dirty fucking hippie. I had moderately long hair, *Rubber Soul* hair instead of *Abbey Road* hair, so for a cool kid of my generation I was already pretty conservative.

As *Saturday Night Fever* taught the world, it's very important not to mess with an Italian's hair, especially an Italian teenager whose entire reputation is based on his fashion-forward sensibility. A crewcut would *kill* me with the girls.

"A t-t-t-rim?" I asked in terror. The black barber sat me down in the chair, whipped out the clippers, and gave me the look of an executioner—y'know, *sorry it has to be you, but this is just my job.* I had just enough scotch in my system to be drunk, and I saw the executioner approaching through watery, clouded eyes.

"Please . . . please mister . . . j-j-jus' a little trim . . . a trim!" Looking at the fear in my eyes, you would have thought I was about get circumcised with a battle axe!

"Look," the barber said as the clippers approached my hair. "Let's be real. If the man want it cut short, you better believe I'm cuttin' it *short!*"

"No, no, no! Cuz it's *my* hair!"

"I gots a news flash fo' ya, partnah," the barber said with a laugh. "If that man wants me to cut off your head, then you might just want to change your name to Icky-bod Crane. You betta get yo'self a horse! You get it, you little junkie?"

The barber laughed at the confusion in my eyes.

"Yeah, that's *right*, your Uncle Frank told me all about you!" The barber shook his head in disgust at my drug abuse. I can only imagine what he thought of my scotch breath.

Lucky for me, Uncle Frank had sniffed a piece of ass and ran back to the bar to hit on a beautiful woman named Rosie. Gill took the opportunity to run to the barbershop, call up his girlfriend, and tell her to talk to the barber as my mother and tell him to go easy on the haircut. After a little trim, Gill took a handful of grease and flattened my hair down to my skull to make it looked I had been sheared down to almost nothing.

I was moaning and gurgling like a wino who had just been tossed onto the street. Gill was eager to shut me up before I exposed the hair gel ruse to my uncle, so he handed me the piece of paper with the credit card number and 1-800-BANANA number. "Here cuzzie, knock yourself out!"

I grabbed the barber's phone and ordered up another six banana trees. That made me feel better immediately.

When we sat back down at the bar, Uncle Frank was so enthralled with Rosie that he hardly noticed my new haircut. Standing next to Rosie, I noticed one reason Uncle Frank was enamored: she was not hiding the fact that she was buck-ass naked under a long mink coat with a plunging neckline.

I noticed something else strange: there was a line of *thirty-five* screwdriver cocktails on the bar in front Frank and Rosie.

"Hey Unc, what's up with all the screwdrivers?" I asked.

"Look at this nosy prick 'ere," Frank muttered to Rosie before leaning down to my level, "if you must know, I ordered 35 puckin' screwdrivers to make sure Rosie 'ere got drunk enough to *screw*, get it? No reason to leave it up to *chance*."

To her credit, Rosie laughed at this, even though it was clear it was no joke. She was a real sport, that Rosie. She shotgunned a screwdriver and tugged on the collar of her mink coat to expose a little bit more bare chest. She was *exactly* Uncle Frank's type.

Uncle Frank asked Rosie where her lady friends were, and she said they would be there in five minutes. *Friends* ... wow, Rosie was Uncle Frank's dream girl.

We were all sitting there in the bar, and I was feeling pretty okay for the first time since we left the arraignment proceedings. My nausea seemed under control, and my buzz from the banana tree order was still intact.

Then Rosie went and ruined it. The pretty woman turned to me and said, "I know how hard it can be, my brother is an addict." Apparently, Uncle Frank had a new conversation starter he was trying out on all of Chicago.

"I'm no addict!"

"That's okay, honey. My brother is in denial, too."

We were joined at the bar a moment later by two of Rosie's friends, a stunning brunette and a blond that looked identical to Goldie Hawn at her peak. I was just about to give myself the go ahead to get happy again, but I didn't get the chance.

"What time's the concert, Elvis?" the Goldie Hawn lookalike asked with a snicker as she checked out my sculpted hairdo. Man, *that* hurt. Elvis may have been cool to my big brothers' generation, but he was as hokey as Howdy-Doody to a flower child like me.

"That's my cousin from Des Moines," Gill interjected, trying to help and failing.

"*That* explains it," said Goldie, displaying the usual Chicago contempt for the great city of Des Moines and its supposedly backward residents. Even back then, nothing got me indignant like someone who dared to talk shit about the great state of Iowa and Des Moines, so I was ready for a fight.

"*No!*" I slurred with all the force my pubescent drunk voice could muster, which wasn't much. "No, it has nothing to do with Des Moines. See, Uncle Frank thinks I'm a doper, so he made me get a haircut, but I tricked him and didn't get one, and now he still doesn't believe me even after I drank a scotch!"

"What's he on?" Goldie said to Gill, almost admiring how fucking high out of my gourd I was.

Just then, Uncle Frank slid up to the two new girls and threw his big bone-breaking arms around their shoulders. "Who are these beautiful girls? Did they meet my nephew Charlie Parker?"

Rosie cut in and introduced her friends. "Well, that's Frederica, but you can call her Stormy, and this little lady is Joy, but you can call her Windy…"

With the ladies' introductions taken care of, I debonairly introduced the contents of my stomach all over the bar table, the floor, and myself. Uncle Frank's long legs almost hopped clear out of the hotel he was so worried about getting his silk suit stained with vomit. Stormy was not bothered, of course; she had seen *all* of this before.

"It's okay, Charlie," she said in a sweet voice as she lifted my head off the table very gently. "It's very common, you guys, it's called withdrawal." Looking into my eyes, she seemed to be searching for the future in a crystal ball. "Are you okay, Charlie? Poor little guy has a monkey on his back!"

I was eventually cleaned up and dried off, and Gill decided I had been torture enough for one day. He was slowly walking me out of the hotel when I overheard my Uncle Frank sneer, "I'll bet that little hippie pucker didn't throw up at Woodstock!"

Forget a man—even a scotch-drunk *boy* has his limits. I swung around on Uncle Frank like an Old Testament prophet. "I didn't go to Woodstock, *and* my name's not Charlie! I'm just a kid for Christ's sake!"

"C'mon, time to go," Gill said through hysterical laughter. "I think you have a phone call you need to make."

I felt like shit, physically and spiritually, but a couple calls to 1-800-BANANAS on the hotel payphone and I was already starting to feel better.

LET ME TELL YOU A QUICK STORY...

ABOUT UNCLE ROCKY MARCIANO

Rocky had been hanging around my house for as long as I could remember. Since Dad owned a huge piece of America's boxing rackets, just about every major fighter of the 1950s and 1960s visited our home. I got to see everyone from Sugar Ray Robinson to Sonny Liston mincing about our house as cautious and polite as Mormon missionaries. These motherfuckers were terrified!

Though just about every boxer visited, only Rocky stayed. At first, he might stay for a couple days, and then for a few weeks, and then for a few months. My mom finally let me in on the secret that Rocky had a very stormy relationship with his wife. Whenever Rocky's marriage hit the rocks, which happened on a monthly basis, the former heavyweight champion would nonchalantly show up at our door with some luggage and move right in.

Though Dad never showed annoyance with the visits from the most beloved Italian sports star in the world, he would sometimes make a joke about how he now understood why his friend from Providence, godfather Raymond Patriarca, had signed over his stake in Rocky. Marciano made Patriarca millions, but it wasn't worth the price of putting up with him. The champ was like a needy, hyperactive, annoying kid brother.

Since Frankie didn't really have much of a Des Moines Family to inherit besides a few old bookmakers and con artists, he had to lean on Uncle Frank and Rocky Marciano to create the right aura of power around himself as he rebuilt the syndicate from scratch. Frankie figured out that, if Rocky followed him around like a cringing servant all the time, it would imply such terrifying things about Frankie that no one would ever guess he had no other manpower backing him up.

The drawback to this otherwise brilliant scheme was that he was foisting Rocky on the rest of our family—and our house—at all times.

You might think that Rocky's world-class athletic accomplishments must have required world-class motor skills and coordination. I lived with the motherfucker, and he must have destroyed those guys in the ring by stumbling into them and accidentally knocking them out. We had to have new glassware and china shipped to our house every few months.

My poor mom had just lost the love of her life, and now she had to clean up after, cook for, and humor a clumsy, ill-mannered, motormouth boxer with an annoying high-pitched Lou Costello voice. Though she could not hide that she found Rocky's presence irritating, she never said so. She was the sort of sweetheart who wouldn't hear a cross word about Charlie Manson if he were our guest. "Oh, let's give Charlie the benefit of the doubt, he's just *artistic*, you know how *they* are."

It was cool to have a boxing legend living in the bedroom down the hall . . . at first. Rocky was a real athlete—the sort of pain in the ass who deludes himself into thinking that 14-year-old boys need to spend their free time jumping rope and jogging. I didn't go for that shit.

Once I made the mistake of letting Rocky convince me to jump on Carmie's pink tandem bike with him, and that crazy fuck started peddling so fast my legs almost flew out of joint. The whole time, Rocky was yammering at me to speed up. When we got home, I bitched to my mom about Rocky being irresponsible on our romantic tandem bike ride, and Iowa's newest wiseguy took that offense against omerta personally.

That cost me big time at dinner. My suck-up younger brother Willie got the seat of honor to the right of Rocky, while I was stuck on Rocky's left. This was *bad* positioning, like sitting directly behind the horse's ass in a carriage.

When Rocky sat down at a table, he had two plates in front of him—one plate with his food on the right and an empty plate on the left. Usually, the plate on the right was a steak, a *big* steak, a fucking he-man Paul Bunyan porterhouse. You'd look at that piece of meat and want to start *clapping* it was such a fine goddamn piece of red meat. Red was definitely the operative word here, too; Rocky liked his steaks super rare and super fucking bloody.

Why? Because just about the only thing he swallowed was the blood. Rocky would slowly, clumsily slice off the tiniest morsel of steak and stuff it his mouth. At that point, the chewing would *begin*, and fucking world empires would rise and fall before that piece of steak got a reprieve and the chewing ended.

About two or three minutes later, after that piece of steak had every droplet of blood chomped free, Rocky would pause mid-sentence, pool all the blood and phlegm and meat in his mouth, and hock out the gross mess across the table onto his spare plate like he was Wild Bill Cody spitting chew into a spittoon.

Whatever was left of the steak would land on the plate a couple inches from my dinner. The little mound of flesh on the plate looked more like a glistening glob of white mashed potatoes than anything that once belonged inside of a fucking bull.

A couple minutes later, that first steak loogie would be joined by another, and then another, and then another. By the end of the meal, there would be Mount Marciano, a stinking mound of meat mush creeping ever closer to the edge of my plate.

I'd try to eat, but it was impossible. I'd look over to my mom in desperation, and you could *see* the pain on her face. She would never say a word to our honored guest, but she was dropping a dress size a month whenever Rocky was staying with us.

Every once in a while, I'd come into the kitchen after dinner and see my mom body-blocking our dog from getting to Rocky's spittoon plate like Dennis Rodman boxing out a center from grabbing a rebound. *That's* how gross this shit was: my mom wouldn't have respected our *dog* if she saw him eating it.

I eventually served notice that I'd be eating my meals early for the foreseeable future. Now my poor widowed mom had to cook and serve separate meals to two clumsy, finicky, insane Italians a night, indefinitely.

13

WHAT BECOMES OF THE BROKEN HEARTED?

"Frank Farrell can't be real. He's got to be a myth, a dream, something imaginary. He must be a character out of a make-believe story....Frank Farrell is no tall story. A story he is, tall he isn't. Frank is a 5-foot 6½-inch junior...[who has scored] 142 points...in the last seven [basketball] games — a 20.2 average....Despite all his basketball heroics, Farrell insists baseball is his favorite sport. 'I'm a second baseman,' he says, 'and I hit .438 last spring for the high school team [as a sophomore]."

DES MOINES REGISTER

To me, a single song encapsulates my brother Frankie: "What Becomes of the Broken Hearted" by Jimmy Ruffin. That song is the soundtrack of my fondest memory of Frankie. He was sitting in his silver 1965 Impala convertible in our driveway, top down, getting ready to go out for the night. Frankie was carefree, bragging that he was "the coolest guy in town" and that he'd kick the ass of anyone who disagreed. He was tan, muscular, and handsome, Sal Mineo wrapped in 30 pounds of extra muscle—looking every bit the part of the constantly flattered college baseball star and future Yankees second-baseman.

No matter how much he pretended to like Dean Martin and Tony Bennett and all that old-fashioned tuxedo music, Frankie's real passion was for soul, blues, and R&B. He was a Motown Records fan, a Stax Records collector. He could tell you the best deep cuts on every Lou Rawls or Sam Cooke album, and, if he *really* trusted you, he'd show you he could sing every word to every Motown single.

In our driveway that afternoon, Frankie was saying goodbye to me and Willie when "What Becomes of the Broken Hearted" came on the radio. It was his favorite song.

With a spokesmodel smile, he cranked up his radio huge, blasting the song out across the plains of Iowa. It was funny because the song had an instrumental preamble like a lot of soul records, and Frankie took advantage of the chance to break into his shoulder-rolling, white boy groove waiting for the verse to start. When Jimmy started to sing ("As I walk this land of broken dreams..."), Frankie sang duet, hitting every single note on the bull's eye, swinging out his arms and hamming it up like he was performing on *Ed Sullivan*, making his little brothers who idolized him laugh.

Just like the rest of his brothers—all cut-ups and goofballs—Frankie had a lighthearted, humorous side to his personality. The difference was he worked to suppress the light side of his personality in order to look tough and mature from a very young age. He systematically eliminated any trait that might make him look weak, immature, or frivolous.

That's why that rare moment of Frankie singing Jimmy Ruffin and being a carefree kid stayed with me. When I think back to my brother, I remember him as that tan teenager having fun with his two kid brothers.

But that's not how Frankie let the world see him. Once Des Moines saw how the notorious gangster Frank Fratto and the Italian-American hero Rocky Marciano deferred to my brother, Frankie began to attract a crowd. Within months of Dad's death, Frankie was followed everywhere by a posse of tough, young Iowa-bred Italians, real shitkickers in blue jeans who knew nothing about Chicago and traditional organized crime but knew everything about fighting, drinking, gambling, and getting laid.

Those Iowa kids all idolized Frankie, the local sports legend and chosen heir of Lew Farrell, as the best Iowa could ever dream of producing. Frankie was their ticket to credibility. By themselves, these Midwest hoods were crazy, self-destructive rednecks. With Frankie lending his credibility and golden Chicago connections, however, they could reach any height their talent merited.

For a quiet, no-bullshit guy, Frankie had an overpowering charisma. It's not that he was all that charming—he just *looked* powerful. He had the ability to project importance way beyond his young age and inexperience. Eyes were drawn to him wherever he went. You knew instantly, "Here is someone who matters, somehow or somewhere."

Frankie made sure his name rang out. In Dad's last year, Frankie had taken down the name of every bookmaker, loan shark, pimp, sheriff, politician, and union head in Iowa who owed their position to Dad. After Dad's death, Frankie went down that list and showed his face to every single name, reestablishing relationships and cashing in favors and collecting debts. From there, Frankie sat down with every civilian in the Midwest to whom the name Lew Farrell meant anything—making a friend of every priest, barkeep, farmer, and businessman who had ever loved Dad.

Frankie was making the network Dad built over forty years his own.

And he had every intention to expand. When Frankie discovered a place where Lew Farrell's name could not get him access, he used Rocky Marciano's name.

The most incredible thing Rocky did for Frankie was allow him to meet with Vito Genovese, New York's most dangerous godfather, in Leavenworth Prison. Don Vitone and our dad had made an agreement to cut up the proceeds from some racket in Genovese's territory, but the Fratto family share had stopped coming once Lou got too ill to pursue it. Frankie intended to get the money coming to Dad—with interest—and carry over the agreement so that it applied to him, as well. He intended to get *all of this* from Vito Genovese.

Just about everyone in Chicago counseled Frankie not to approach Don Vitone. Genovese was a viper, a heroin kingpin with a long track record of whacking out longtime associates over a single envelope that he felt was a couple bills short. The idea that a 22-year-old kid from Iowa would visit this gangland legend in prison and demand two or three years of proceeds from a racket in *New York City* was preposterous, insulting. Frankie was getting too big for his britches.

Frankie refused to listen. Since the feds would deny Frankie a direct meeting with Don Vitone due to his Mafia ties, Frankie had Rocky contact the prison staff with an offer they couldn't dare refuse. Rocky offered to visit the prison with some reels of his most famous fights and show them to the general population as a way to promote physical fitness and sports as an alternative to the criminal lifestyle. The warden accepted so that he could take a photo with The Champ.

Accompanying The Champ, of course, was Frankie. As the prison film projector played Rocky's fights on a cafeteria wall, Frankie huddled close with Don Vitone. The numerous wiseguys in Leavenworth were staring in confusion, wondering who the fuck this ballsy, olive-skinned kid was and why Don Vitone was talking to him so freely and with such respect.

Frankie must have bullshat that old bastard good, because he left Leavenworth that day with a promise that one of Genovese's men would deliver the entirety of the money owed to the Fratto family within a week. For the rest of Frankie's life, the regular payments from New York allowed our family to live in material comfort.

And it was all thanks to Rocky, really. I know it's hard to believe that a worldwide icon like Rocky Marciano would agree to be the lackey of a 22-year-old in Iowa, but it made sense to us. Rocky was just part of the Fratto family, albeit a member that everyone treated with unending deference and respect, sparing him the normal Italian ball-busting.

Besides Uncle Frank, of course. When Uncle Frank was drunk, he was always trying to bait Rocky Marciano into a fight. Rocky knew better. "Maybe in a ring, Frank, when I was young and healthy," he'd say, humble as a butler.

No matter what my brother Frankie did to mediate, Rocky figured that there was no way he would survive a fight with Frank Fratto. Either he would lose and be beaten to death, or he would win and get shot the next day. Rocky never was at ease with Uncle Frank; he used to tell me he was terrified Frank would just sucker punch him at random.

"That's a man that wants to tell the world he beat up Rocky Marciano," he'd say.

The funny thing is Rocky's mom, Pasqualena Marchegiano, loved Uncle Frank and thought of him as "her little boy's protector." Like her son, Momma Marchegiano was a little goofy. It was the funniest thing watching this sweet old-school Italian mama talk to Uncle Frank like he was a polite young man, blindly ignoring what a gigantic boor he was.

"Now, Frankie, you mussa watch out for my little boy!" Mama Marchegiano would hector Uncle Frank.

"Whaddya mean?" he'd ask, impatient to get back to his drink.

"Now, you gotta make sure nobody messa wit' and hurta my boy!'

"*WHO THE FUCK IS GOING TO MESS WITH HIM?*" Uncle Frank would start yelling, incredulous. "He's the fucking heavyweight champion of the world! Who's going to fuck with *him*?!"

"Now, now, Frankie, you mussa keep my boy outta trouble!"

"Mama Marchegiano, give me a fuckin' break here! You sayin' that somebody gonna look and say, 'Hey, there's fuckin' Rocky Marciano over there, unbeaten heavyweight champ, how 'bout I fuckin' give him a pop in the face just to see what happens?' Get your head checked, woman!"

"Oh, Frankie, you knowa how these young people are nowadays! No respect! They do anything! You gotta keep Rocky safe!"

"Okay, Mama, I promise I'll punch anyone that looks at Rocky," muttered Uncle Frank.

And you could never be sure he didn't mean it. He punched plenty of innocent people for no apparent reason. It happened all the time.

That's what made Uncle Frank so valuable to Dad, and later, Frankie.

The scarier and crazier Uncle Frank was, the nicer and saner the other Frattos got to be—and the easier all of our business partners were to handle. It was in every Fratto's best interest to keep everyone convinced Uncle Frank was a completely out-of-control psychopath so we would receive political capital from granting the *favor* of calling Uncle Frank off.

Only Lou and Frankie wielded that invisible power to control Frank Fratto. He was like a fighting pitbull who unquestioningly trusts his owners and no one else. They had Uncle Frank on a leash—but neither kept a very tight grip.

That would defeat the purpose of Uncle Frank! They didn't want anyone *else* to get comfortable because that decreased their power.

Uncle Frank is the reason just about my entire family believes that Dad and Frankie were saints. He was the Renfield doing all the dirty work that allowed Dracula to maintain his aristocratic bearing and gentlemen's reputation.

14

THE CAR-JACKING VAMPIRE

We come out when the sun goes down. In the dark, we obtain powers of seduction and mind control that seem positively supernatural. We use the power of glamour to attract the helpless victims we mercilessly feed upon to prolong our inhuman, decadent lifestyle. If we focus our predatory attention on you, your only chance of surviving is to hold on until dawn, when we will rush powerless to our black cars with the Secret Service tinted windows and speed away to sleep through the day.

I've always fantasized about becoming a vampire. As a kid, I watched every vampire movie that ever came on TV—usually strange, low-budget films from Europe—and never missed a showing of the classic *Dracula* or its cheesier sequels at the Holiday Theater in town. I learned to cope with my fears about my Mafia bloodline through all of those vampire movies and thousands of hours vampire play.

After Dad's death, I fled to that fantasy.

The result was that I became a criminal at the age of 14.

At night, I'd lay in bed, wide awake and sweating with excitement, waiting for everyone else to fall asleep. When the silence was total, I'd slip out of the house with a throbbing heart and coast my bike down our driveway out onto the moonlit streets.

I'd peddle frantically to put distance between me and my family. Once I felt safe, I'd swing into the middle of the empty road, accelerate my speed until I felt the bike wobble, and then stretch out my arms. I closed my eyes and imagined I was a vampire soaring on bat wings in the moonlight. I felt as free and unaccountable as Uncle Frank.

I felt like a vampire. I felt like a gangster.

Some nights, I'd take my bike out to the very edge of town, where owls silently coasted over empty fields and roaming dogs chased my bike while I imagined they were werewolves. If the moon was full, the countryside could become eerily bright and otherworldy, and I would convince myself I was being followed or chased by some malignant night spirit. I'd swing around and peddle back to town in an exhilarated panic.

Back in town, I would seek entirely different thrills. I'd peddle over to the seedy open-all-night motels that once paid tribute to Dad, circling the block a couple times on the lookout for open or broken blinds. Every once in a while, I'd catch a couple fucking and hide behind the bushes to watch. I'd pass by the bars and lounges that ignored curfew but whose owners were learning not to ignore my brother Frankie. Sometimes I'd catch some of Dad's acquaintances who I knew from our living room laying a solid beating on drunks who had failed to pay their tab.

The idea that I was getting away with flouting all the rules of local society was intoxicating to me. I felt like I was penetrating an enemy camp, trespassing into the dark world of adults that vampires like Uncle Frank and Frankie secretly ruled. Though I was not prepared to be a part of the underworld, I got a junkie's rush from skirting along the edges and swerving back and forth over the boundaries. It was the first step into my destiny.

I let some of my degenerate friends in on my nighttime pastime. While prowling around the neighborhood, they realized that there was nothing stopping us, in those days before car alarms, from just jimmying open the doors of parked cars and stealing their stereos.

The first time one of my friends did this, I was scared enough to piss myself. The second time, I was the first one in the stranger's car and the last one out.

Though I didn't really have much I could personally do with a car stereo, there were other things I could find in a car that were much more useful: cash, clothes, porn, knives, guns, just about anything you could imagine. At fourteen, stealing anything remotely worth keeping—a nice flashlight, a broken watch, a football—felt like a pretty badass thing to do.

The problem with this racket was volume. Bicycle baskets don't make for huge takes. I came up with a solution: I stole my brother's '65 Impala. My day as Uncle Frank's midget chauffeur had given me the confidence to back an Impala out of our garage, fill it full of my friends, and swerve it around town in total darkness for a burglary spree. Whenever we saw a car that looked like a rich target, I let my friends hop out while I waited in the getaway car with my foot shadow-pumping the gas.

The amount of criminal hijinks we were able to get away with in that Impala that night made me feel giddy with freedom and power, much like Dad must have felt the first time he got behind the wheel of a Studebaker as a poor slum kid during Prohibition. We could hit any neighborhood in Des Moines with ample time to get home by morning, and we did our best to do so. We got too cocky. By the time I dropped off my friends and returned home, the sun was rising.

You know what happens to vampires when the sun rises.

I pulled into the garage. I very quietly opened the driver's door and slipped off my shoes so I could sneak in with maximum stealth. As soon as I lifted my two tennis shoes in one hand, a phantom shot out from a dark corner of the garage and slapped me so hard across the face that I felt like my tongue had launched out of my mouth. I was stunned, and before I could open my eyes, an iron grip was squeezing my chin just like I had seen Dad do to Michael Landon.

It was Frankie, and his eyes were lit with hellfire. I now saw in Frankie the anger I had seen in Dad when Alan Rosenberg's fate was sealed. My brother's stout, broad-shouldered, muscular body was identical in shape to Dad's as a young boxer, and he stood with the same self-assured power that allowed both father and son to stand like men in the presence of Tony Accardo, who reduced the best of men to children.

"So you think I'm fucking stupid, do you, Johnny?" Frankie whispered, his voice strained and growling with rage. I felt my chin splintering in his hand.

"You think, just because Dad's gone, that I'm a fucking idiot you can disrespect and get over on? What have I done to you to deserve this? I've got all of Iowa, all of our family looking to me to put the pieces back together and keep food on everyone's table, and I have my own brother betraying me behind my own back in my own household?"

No one gives a better "You betrayed your family!" speech than an Italian—and no one is quicker to pull that card, either.

My eyes were submerged within pools of tears; my face was suffocation red. I had always been careful not to push Frankie too far because I always knew he had within him the ability to become something truly terrifying. I had always doubted that Dad could be a gangster, a killer, but Frankie never hid that he was just waiting for an excuse to lay waste to someone. I had finally given him the opportunity, and I could feel my chin shaking from his arm vibrating like a tuning fork with rage.

"You know what your fucking problem is, Johnny? Dad spoiled you. He made you selfish; he made you a fucking narcissist. He gave you everything you wanted, so you thought that was the point of life: to get what you wanted. That's why you're so fucking stupid. You don't pay attention to what's going on around you."

Frankie let go of my chin and wiped the sweat from his forehead. He stood tall and squared his shoulders at me, pulling his head back like a cobra waiting to spit venom.

"Look around yourself, you selfish bastard! What am I doing? I drop out of college, I give up the major leagues, and I come home. I didn't need to. I could have made my money and left Tommy to watch over all of you. But no! I came home, and I've done my best to keep Uncle Frank under control and to keep Mom from dying of grief. Look at me: I'm there for mom every breakfast, lunch, and dinner that I can spare, there to tell her Dad is in Heaven and she's got something to live for.

"And where the fuck are you, asshole? You're in your room, waiting to eat alone, insisting the poor fucking woman make a second meal! She's lost the love of her life, and you don't even fucking talk to her, you're so busy with your fag records and little whore girlfriends and fucking clothes! Have you noticed how Mom's doing?"

"I..." I tried to speak, flicking my tongue around my mouth to regain my sense of taste, rubbing my sore chin, ducking my eyes away from Frankie. I thought about Mom, how she appeared to pad around the house doing her chores just like before, always keeping herself busy. She seemed to be about the same, but now I realized she had seemed empty, always distracted. "I thought Mom was holding up..."

"No thanks to you, motherfucker!" Frankie hissed, using all of his power not to scream. I had never seen him this enraged and felt ashamed that I was the cause.

"Did you even think about what you would do to her if she woke up this morning and saw you had disappeared with the car? You would have killed her! Don't you think she's gone through enough? She watched Dad die, slowly, for two years, and then she had to have Uncle Frank put the image of Dad roasting in Hell in her fucking mind, and where were you the whole while?!

"You were nowhere, motherfucker! You haven't given her a second thought. You think Dad's death was a fucking license to get away with murder, you little shit!"

I wanted to speak, but I couldn't. Frankie's stare was making me overheated and faint, like a great werewolf was standing over me with dripping fangs.

"It's time for you to grow up, motherfucker. You can't hang with me, Johnny. Look at Willie: he was already good, but he's done *nothing* but stay by mom's side like a lapdog since Dad died. He hasn't dared to be bad because he's *selfless*, his only concern is Mom and, after her, poor Carmie Lou, who is fucking devastated, and helping me where he can. Willie's a good kid, but you're a conceited, selfish little shit who Dad spoiled."

Frankie paused, licked his lips, and furrowed his brow. He was thinking of something. "Johnny..." he said, drawing out my name. "What exactly *were* you doing out all night?"

"I...I..." I couldn't talk. Instead, I opened the door of the car and popped the trunk. Frankie stomped off to the trunk, looked down, and immediately shot back towards me.

"Listen," Frankie said, his voice suddenly cold and flat. "Listen to me like you've never listened before. You need to behave. You shape up immediately. You are not a criminal. You are a little punk, a spoiled kid. Give this shit up. Don't try to outsmart me.

"Don't find out what will happen to you if I catch you, again," Frankie looked down and to the side, as if the sight of me made him want to puke. "Get the fuck upstairs to your room before Mom wakes up. I'll clean this mess up and cover for you, as always."

I felt my voice trying to crawl up out of my mouth to say "I'm sorry, Frankie," but my pride forced it back down. I slunk upstairs without saying a word and lay in bed. I fell asleep almost immediately, willing myself to rest so I did not have to think.

The next night, I went to bed without any expectation of sneaking out. I was imprisoned; all I needed was a harmonica and a stone wall to scratch off each day of hard time I had done. My internal sleep cock was so haywire that I had no chance of actually falling asleep, so I just laid flat with the radio on low, sulking and listening to great music—"Revolution," "Voodoo Child (Slight Return)," "Cloud Nine," and "White Room."

Around midnight, I heard my door open.

"You can't sleep?" whispered Frankie.

"No..." I said, initially intending to continue but deciding not to try my luck with him.

"Come with me," he said flatly. I got up sheepishly and followed Frankie to his bedroom.

In his doorway, he turned to me with a very mellow look. Bags looped his eyes and his skin was sallow. He was exhausted. He was 22 years old, but at that moment he was an old man. "You're gonna sleep with me from now on. I know it's hard without Dad, so I want you to know you're not alone until everything calms down."

This was not what I was expecting. My cynicism took over for a moment, thinking this was Frankie's way to keep an eye on me . . . but the look on Frankie's weary, drained face was not sneaky. Frankie was not a sneaky guy when it came to me; he would have no problem telling me, "Listen, you little shit, you're sleeping in my room until I'm sure you're not going to do nuttin' stupid!"

But that wasn't what he said.

"Johnny," he said with an exhausted voice, "I know you're just acting up because you miss Dad. It's okay. It's going to be okay. Just lean on me."

With all of the incredible stress and pressure he was under, flying back and forth from Iowa to Chicago all the time, fighting for every inch of his legacy and for our family's financial survival, singlehandedly keeping Mom and Carmie from emotional meltdowns—he had taken the time to think about me as a caring big brother. He analyzed me and saw that, beneath my bluff, I was lonely, aimless, and scared.

In the previous 24 hours, I hadn't spent a single second thinking about Frankie besides resenting him for catching me. At the same time, he had been thinking about his ungrateful, petty thief of a little brother who had disrespected him . . . and still somehow found it in himself to have compassion for me. At the end of his very long day, in which he got up first thing to be with Mom and stayed out late to see all the crooks and wiseguys, Frankie had added one more task: to try to be a father to me.

He had shown me he was a good man, and a good brother, and a worthy successor to Lou.

Looking back, I have no doubt that my Dad asked Frankie on his deathbed to be a father to me. I'm so proud of Frankie that he tried to fulfill my dad's wishes.

I lay in bed next to Frankie, and he immediately passed out from fatigue. I couldn't sleep. For the first time in my life, I thought about what I owed him, and Dad, and my mom—and how my behavior should be a form of repayment for the life they had given me.

I looked over my brother's snoring face, the face that resembled my own more than any other in my entire family. His hair was still perfectly combed like an altar boy, but his face was rapidly aging. I promised myself that, for the first time, I would make him proud of me. I would be a good brother, be a good student, and be a good son to Mom.

The next day I actually paid attention in class, and I came home right after school. Frankie found me sitting at the kitchen table with Mom, going over her favorite memories of Dad, how romantic and debonair he had been when she was swept off her feet as a teenager. Frankie did a double-take when he saw that I was giving Mom attention, but then he nodded as if he had expected it to happen. He sat down at the kitchen table with us, and soon Rocky and Willie joined us as well. We all sat down, told stories about Dad, and laughed.

That night, I slept soundly next to my brother. I felt good about myself.

The day after that, I managed to keep it up. After my second straight day as a good student, I came home and spent more time with Mom. I could see that my presence had put a little electricity back into her system, made her feel a little alive again. I once again went to bed next to my brother and slept easily, deeply.

The next night, Frankie came home with a brand new black sports car. Apparently, the effort he spent reconstructing Dad's criminal empire was paying off. Once the rest of the family finished admiring Frankie's car and went back inside, Frankie pulled me aside.

"You know what you were doing with those stereos, Johnny?"

"Don't worry, Frankie, I haven't ever even thought of doing it again."

"That's the thing. Just this once..." Frankie cracked a smile, "how about you steal me a brand new stereo for my car?"

That was the end of my reformation. Frankie got a new car stereo, and I got a license to steal. I wouldn't have another crisis of conscience for decades: Frankie was the only contemporary whom I ever admired, and he had given me his blessing to victimize the innocent.

This permit to do evil would go into mortal sin territory within weeks.

LET ME TELL YOU A QUICK STORY...

ABOUT KICKING A PRIEST'S ASS

I decided that if Frankie deserved a new car, then I deserved his old car. I asked my mom about getting a driver's license, but she reminded me I was only 14, too young to get a license. So I called up the DMV and told them—since I was just a poor country boy whose father was too busy on the farm to drive him to school—was there any way I could be granted a special dispensation to drive?

They fell for it. I was given a special permit that allowed me to drive back and forth to school from my home and nowhere else. Of course, I took this pinhole of freedom and ripped it wide open; once my mom gave me keys to the car, I drove it *everywhere* and fast.

Despite my high-speed chase driving style, we were still late to school. My carload was always full: my little brother Willie, my cousin and schoolyard protector Frankie Renda, my good buddy Don Freeman, and sometimes another cousin, who I won't name. Don Freeman was just about my best friend in the world, but even I didn't know why everyone called this little kid by his full name—Don Freeman, which sounded like the name of an old CPA.

My buddy would come over to play, and my mom would ask him, "Don Freeman, are you hungry? Don Freeman, would you like some orange juice?" People around our house, used to hearing Mafia godfathers go by names like Don Luigi or Don Vitone, would pull my dad inside and ask who this mysterious, imposing "Don Freeman" they were always hearing about was.

Due to my narcissism, I'd always deliver Don Freeman and my family to school late in the morning. This resulted in us spending just about every Saturday in detention.

Early one Saturday, when was I driving my friends and my unnamed cousin to detention, I complained that I wished someone would beat the fuck out of the grumpy old priest who handed out all of our detention slips. After spending a lifetime watching our family blindly obey anything Dad said, my juvenile delinquent cousin took my offhand comment too seriously and decided to act when we got to detention.

"Hey there, Father," my cousin shouted in the dead silence of the classroom, loud and sarcastic. "Why don't you got any niggers in detention? What are you, a nigger lover or something?"

I was scared Jesus Himself would rappel through the classroom window and start kicking the shit out of all of us once He heard that comment. Never did I think it was even *possible* for someone to talk to a priest that way, especially since priests in those days were never above beating up a minor. They couldn't wait to slap a kid.

The priest hopped out from behind the desk with his fists balled, too angry to even say a word. He came over to my cousin with bunched shoulders and a tight-assed waddle like he was holding in a case of the craps. The father cocked his hand back and slowly—so slowly—took a limp-wristed swing at my cousin.

Something happened before the priest's fist landed . . . something that convinced me that Rod Serling was standing outside of the classroom door, that I was having a horrible nightmare. My cousin simply stood up and beat the priest to the punch. My cousin punched that motherfucker so hard his little white collar popped off his neck. That punch was followed by a couple dozen more, and a couple dozen kicks to boot.

Willie, Don Freeman, and Frankie Renda all turned to me, looking for guidance on what to do. I hesitated. I thought back to my poor Mom and what she would think if she found out her little boys had been party to such an unthinkably sacrilegious, horrible crime. I knew what she would want me to do: pull my cousin off and immediately turn him in. My soul depended on it.

Then I thought about my brother Frankie. I thought about that stereo I stole for him. I thought about Uncle Frank and how he got away with brutalizing everyone he met. I thought about what Uncle Frank had told me about the formula that made so much organized crime go unreported: the victim's fear of his abuser and, more importantly, the victim's fear of public humiliation.

"Hey, everyone," I said. "Let's get the fuck out of here. No one says nuttin'. *He* ain't going to say nuttin' either."

That was the last time that priest gave us detention.

15

FEAR OF FLYING

What I'm about to talk about, I've never talked about before. I've never spoken about it with my siblings, with my kids, with my mom, with my women, or with my close friends. I never talked about it with my parole officers, or with my psychiatrist, or with my bosses in the underworld. I've never wanted to hear a word said about it.

I've never shared these secrets with anyone.

Okay, not *anyone*. I talked about it with Oprah. But Oprah doesn't really count because *everyone* would talk about *anything* with Oprah if she asked.

And she asked.

So I talked.

The CIA should hire that woman to interview terrorists.

About fifteen years after the event I'm about to discuss, I was living in Chicago, doing a lot of the things Frattos do in Chicago and some things *no* Frattos prior to me had done. Since I was the sort of person who made it my business to know everyone, I became friendly with the producers of the first talk show Oprah Winfrey ever hosted, *AM Chicago.*

Oprah's producers saw in me a valuable resource: a man who knew every TV-ready weirdo, freakshow, and novelty act in the Midwest. I told every guest I booked on Oprah's show to drop my name during the interview, and, by the time Oprah got her nationally syndicated program in 1986, she had heard my name so often that she asked to meet me. We became quick friends, and, even after she became a global icon, she'd have her limo driver pull up beside me to offer me a ride if she happened to catch me walking through downtown Chicago.

As everyone knows, Oprah is renowned for getting people to choke up and agree to discuss their most painful memories on national television. It's not hype; Oprah did it to me. I shared my most personal recollections with her, and within weeks, I was called in as an emergency replacement for a guest on *Oprah*.

In retrospect, I'm glad I went on the show if only to leave a lasting historical document of my 1980s hair. My hair was so big and magnificent in those days that it looked like my head was a fountain spewing molten silver. It was this lush, all-natural, spaceman silver pompadour I could have chopped off and sold as a concert wig to Mozart or Elton John ...

Sorry, I'm trying to change the subject. The point I was making was I went on *Oprah* and confronted my darkest fear. What was the theme of the episode?

"Fear of Flying."

My fear of flying began on August 31, 1969 ... no, no, it began two years earlier than that, on December 10, 1967. That was the day when one of my brother Frankie's heroes, soul legend Otis Redding, died when his Beechcraft 18 airplane crashed into a lake. Frankie was depressed over the tragedy and creeped out that it occurred on the third anniversary of the murder of his all-time favorite singer, Sam Cooke.

My brother's visible sadness on the day of Otis Redding's plane crash made an impact on me since it was the last time I saw Frankie show weakness after Dad's death. From then on, I was wary of airplanes. Like hospitals, they were places where people came closer to death.

On the night of August 31, 1969, I had just turned fifteen. I was sitting at a bus stop all by myself at sundown, eating a shitty slice of pizza from a five-and-dime store. My father was dead, and my little brother Willie now went to a different school.

I was at this bus stop because of Frankie. Despite giving me extra attention and affection, Frankie noticed he hadn't stopped my transformation into a petty teenage delinquent. Since the carrot had failed, Frankie whipped out the stick. One morning, he bluntly told me I would spend my freshman year of high school at a new, ultra-strict Catholic school in the bad part of town, far away from all of my old friends and partners in crime. Frankie also shut down my illegal car permit and compelled me to take the bus to my new school

I remember sitting at this lonely, desolate bus stop all by myself, chewing on a soggy slice of shit disguised as pizza they sold to rubes who didn't know better. I missed Willie. I missed my old friends. I missed the feeling I used to get around this time of year, in the weeks before Christmas. Instead of looking forward to presents, I was dreading the holidays. I knew the holidays at our home now consisted of my Mom weeping constantly while we all mourned Dad.

Over the bus stop speaker came "The Sound of Silence" by Simon & Garfunkel. This was like a joke played on me by God. My mood could not have been more dreary and depressed and lonely at that shitty ghetto bus stop, and here comes "The Sound of Silence", *the* most dreary, depressing, lonely song on the planet to act as my soundtrack. I was so sad I could cry, so I instead I got mad. I redirected that energy someplace more acceptable for a Fratto.

I know today that being in my face was Frankie's way of expressing love. That was how he showed he cared and that I was important to him. At that moment, however, I thought of Frankie as nothing more than an obnoxious bully who was ruining my life. I remember thinking to myself, over and over, "How can I get this asshole to stop meddling in my life? How can I get rid of him? Please, God, make this fucking asshole go away!"

I regret that thought to this day. I feel responsible for what happened later that evening. That's the superstitious Italian Catholic in me. If only I had been a good brother like Willie . . . if only I had been a good Catholic like Carmella . . . if only I had been something besides myself, Frankie's life would have worked out differently.

I was hanging with my friends at the empty lot in Des Moines where all the kids parked their freshly polished cars, cranked up their radios, and chilled on the hoods of their rides. With all of my old schoolyard friends surrounding me, I was bitching about my big brother and how he was tearing me away from my social circle to go to a shitty school on the shitty side of town. Since Frankie was thought of as the God of Des Moines by the younger generation, I always felt like I was scoring serious badass points by daring to talk shit about him.

A car screeched into the parking lot. At first, I thought it was yet another drunk teenager, but out from the passenger's side staggered my sister Carmie—not the sort of person who would drive drunk. I immediately thought about Frankie; he was sending Carmie to come pick me up and drag me to the party he was throwing for Rocky Marciano across the town. *Why wouldn't he just leave me alone? I didn't need a Dad no more, anyway.*

In my rush to look cool and defiant for my friends, I didn't notice Carmie looked pale, beaten, ghostly like Isabella Rosellini showing up on the lawn in *Blue Velvet*. When I did notice, all I felt was embarrassment, self-conscious teenage embarrassment, because everyone was staring at her. Something was very wrong.

"Johnny," she called, her voice weak and shredded. "Come to the car."

"Why?" I said, nervously looking around at my friends. As a teenage girl, Carmie could be overly melodramatic, especially after Dad's death. I could be hard on her. I should have followed her immediately, but in the back of my head I still was wary of giving in too easily if she had been sent by Frankie to harsh my high.

"*Johnny*, come to the car *now*, it's important."

This was weird. I remember not feeling scared or even worried. I was just confused, a little disembodied. From that moment, my life seemed to end and slip into a dream. I can't say I've *ever* regained what little sense of reality I once had, that sense of knowing my place in the world. Everything since that moment has been twisted, hallucinatory, displaced. I'm sure I could be diagnosed with Post-Traumatic Stress Disorder or something like that, and I would have tried to have been if I had thought good drugs came with the diagnosis.

If people think I act strangely, I agree. I feel like I've lived in a bizarre nightmare ever since... maybe not a nightmare, but an acid dream, an alternate universe. My reality was gone; that's the only way I can say it.

I was sitting in the back of the car. The moment is so nuked with emotion that I don't even recall who was driving the car, or if there was a third person inside. I don't remember the words that were said, or how they were said, or anything. All I know is...

I was told that Frankie and Rocky Marciano had just died in a plane crash. It was too horrible to believe. It did not sink in. Frankie was far too young and far too strong to die. There was no way I was living in a world where the indestructible Frankie Fratto could die while I still lived.

The details of the story seemed off, like some bullshit cooked up to hide a conspiracy. Frankie and Rocky had been in Chicago attending a dinner with Andy Granatelli, the CEO who paid Rocky big money to sponsor STP motor oil. After dinner, Frankie rushed Rocky to O'Hare Airport—allegedly so they could make it back to Des Moines for a business function where Rocky was supposed to speak.

The truth was that Frankie had planned a surprise birthday party for Rocky at my Uncle Bill's restaurant, The Charcoal Room. Since Rocky was planning to spend his 46th birthday with his wife in Florida for once, Frankie decided to throw a surprise party for his most important associate a day early. It was for this reason that, when Frankie and Rocky missed their scheduled commercial flight at O'Hare, Frankie insisted they find an emergency flight back to Des Moines at any cost and by any means.

Frankie called Tommy at his new home, where he had just moved in with the first of many wives and the first of many children, and told him to call local businessman Sam Paterno, who had run The High Flyer Lounge by the Des Moines Airport. Since the High Flyer was frequented by pilots, Frankie told Tommy to get Sam to find some pilot who would fly up to O'Hare, pick them up, and fly back.

On a barstool, Sam Paterno found Glenn Belz, a 37-year-old pilot with very little experience with nighttime air travel and no certification for flying using only in-flight instruments. He was the best Sam Paterno could do on short notice, and since Frankie did not want to disappoint the countless people at the Charcoal Room who had traveled from across the Midwest to honor Rocky, Glenn Belz would have to do.

As Rocky and Frankie boarded the tiny four-seat, single-engine, propeller-powered Cessna 172 plane, the party at the Charcoal Room was already starting. The trip from Chicago to Des Moines was so short that the attendees should have barely been buzzed by the time Frankie dragged an unsuspecting Rocky through the door.

As Glenn Belz crossed into Iowa, he received a radio warning of a storm system obstructing his path to Des Moines. Fearful of losing his license by flying into a storm at night without being instrument rated, Belz instead decided to divert the Cessna to an airfield in Newton, Iowa—about a thirty minute drive from the Charcoal.

Shortly before 9 p.m., Glenn Belz radioed into Des Moines Airport and asked for radar assistance since he was running low on fuel and a row of clouds was blocking his view of the landing strip at Newton Airport. After spending only a moment waiting for the requested assistance, Belz inexplicably radioed again to say that he had supposedly found a clear approach to the airfield and was going to land immediately.

Instead, Belz flew right into the thick patch of clouds, panicked, then blindly swerved the plane. One of the Cessna's wings clipped a great big oak tree that was all by itself in the middle of an empty cornfield. The one-winged plane spun off and crashed into a nearby ravine.

Rocky was crushed beneath the Cessna, and Belz and Frankie were launched more than thirty fleet into an untilled field. The plane's steel engine landed directly on Glenn Belz's chest.

All three passengers were instantly killed. Nothing in the world hurts me like the idea that my brother, who lived his entire life in preparation for some glorious future, may have had enough time to realize what was happening to him and think back to the horrible fate of his hero Otis Redding.

My sister drove my cold, blank, unfeeling body to our home, where the party from the Charcoal had transformed into a chaotic funeral procession. Apparently, the news had been broken at the Charcoal with a series of sudden, bloodcurdling screams. By the time I walked through the door, *everyone* was in absolute hysterics, including the wiseguys. I am talking about grown men just weeping, grown women tearing their hair out, little kids running and puking.

This was an unthinkable tragedy. The young leader of our family was dead. The greatest hero of the Italian-American people was dead. It's impossible for people today to conceive what a Hercules, a larger-than-life superhero, Rocky was at that time. Everyone who cared about Rocky Marciano in the Midwest had congregated together in a room to wait for his arrival and instead got news of his sudden, unexpected death. Instead of a joyous and blushing Rocky ushered through the room, pure horror swept through the party instead.

Rocky was dead. Frankie was dead. It was such a robbery. I heard the phrase over and over again: *A sin! It's a sin!* God Himself had sinned against us with this cruel, stupid, arbitrary act of destruction.

I didn't feel anything. I was just observing, as detached as a ghost visiting my family. I had never seen such pain displayed by human beings as in that room. It was like listening to the excruciating torment of a cat being eaten alive by a coyote.

I felt no pain. I felt no pain until I saw my mom. My pain . . . I didn't feel. The pain I felt was in my mother's eyes. Her eyes were anguished, burning red, unrecognizable. She was broken down past her humanity into something horribly primal. She was just shattered.

My mom's pain was everyone's pain. *Everyone* loved Carmella. Everyone knew how sweet, gentle, and vulnerable she was, and how Frankie was the only thing that kept her from collapse after Lou's death. Everyone would have cried for Frankie and Rocky, but they were hysterical for Carmella.

They knew our family had been destroyed. In Dad's absence, Frankie *was* our family. Frankie was our family's stability, security, and sanity. We had lost the past, but he offered us a future. When Frankie died, our family died. We were still family, but somehow we were not *our* family. We were broken pieces shoved together in the same box, in it together, but never put back together.

Our world had ended. How did I know?

When Uncle Frank arrived at our home, he was weeping. Uncle Frank had been able to displace his grief over Dad's death thanks to Frankie, so now a crushing grief over the loss of his only two friends in the universe landed on him all at once. The toughest man in the world was just wimpering in a pile on the ground.

Uncle Frank was not good at coping. This was the same maniac who was notorious for enslaving the top bookmaker in Chicago and forcing him to follow him around constantly as his personal punching bag. Whenever Uncle Frank got hurt or frustrated with something abstract that he couldn't physically hurt, he would turn to the innocent multimillionaire bookmaker and just beat the shit out of him to work off his anger. To him, Frankie's death was a pain that merely *hurting* an innocent person would not cauterize.

If anything, the idea that Uncle Frank was crying was just as big a loss as Frankie's death, as it represented the loss of any hope for sanity in our family. Uncle Frank's tears increased the terror and panic of everyone in that house, because now the pet tiger my dad and brother had kept in our house was let out of its cage after being horribly wounded. The last person who could have ever restrained the most destructive force in our world was dead, and now that force was going to be free to run wild like no one had ever seen before.

Uncle Frank was unleashed. No scarier four words existed in the English language in 1969. I did not have to wait more than a few minutes after my arrival at Frankie's wake to see the result.

I stood far away from the coffin and brooded. I couldn't stop obsessing over the injustice that Frankie, the best of us, had been taken so young. He was only 22 years old! The strongest person I had ever met was dead at 22. The one person I've ever met who I could identify with certainty as a Man of Destiny, a Napoleon, was dead before he had achieved one millionth of what he had planned. This seemed like an error, a glitch, like the world had gone *wrong*. How the fuck could a weak, fragile, silly shit like me outlive a real man like Frankie?

This could not have been God's plan.

I knew my Catholicism. This *had* to be a punishment. This was a sudden act of wrath by a vengeful God. Frankie had been struck down. I had ignored the nuns for over a decade as they told me, day after day, that horrible things happened to bad boys, to the families of bad boys. If only I had been like Willie, had been good and obedient like Willie, Frankie would not be a smashed-up stain in a closed coffin.

That thought was hacking at my heart. I felt as if my brain had grown huge and throbbing and was pressing up against my skull, on the verge of busting through my forehead. Crying, I ran away from the wake. On my way out to the parking lot, I heard a horrible commotion from an adjacent room. Without thinking, I peeked through the doors where the sound was coming from.

Inside were Uncle Frank and one of his thugs. They were shoving a living man into a coffin already occupied by a dead man, trying to force the door shut. They were beating him, taunting him, calling him a rat, assuring him he was already dead and now he was going to get a sneak peak into his future.

Suddenly, Uncle Frank looked up, his eyes fiery with evil, his face flushed with sweat, a monster. The only sign of humanity was the tears that kept pouring from his inconsolable red eyes. When he saw me standing there, Uncle Frank . . . *smiled*. He *laughed*.

"Hey motherfucker!" he yelled out to me, crying, still pressing down on the coffin lid. "Either *help*, or *get the fuck out!*"

I backed away, but slowly. I felt my grief igniting into rage, into violence, into evil. I hated the world for what it had done to Frankie. I was furious. I felt far too damned to ever be saved; I resented the universe that *owed* me for the crime of stealing my brother. I wanted to hop atop the coffin lid and jump up and down until that rat motherfucker was trapped inside.

At that moment, I started to become a gangster. Uncle Frank was unleashed, and in retrospect, so was I.

Frankie was gone. It was time for me to step up.

I was going to be a gangster. I was going to resolve Dad's identity crisis one crime at a time.

16

JAIL BREAK

The difference that Frankie's death had on my life all comes down to paper. If Frankie had lived, I probably would be the same person I am today—only I'd have the paper. I'd have diplomas and the law degree I would need to be the sleazy, bullshit-spouting attorney Frankie told me was my calling.

The Ds and Fs were always going to be the only letters on my report card, but Frankie would have muscled and cheated me through to graduation day. Frankie would have come to school every day and performed spot checks in my classes to make sure I attended often enough for him to arrange for me to get "my papers."

My papers would be my parole.

And then, on September 1, 1969, my brother was gone. The warden was gone. So I escaped from prison and stopped attending school. Drugs, music, and free love became my only concern. I could spend all day on the phone, stay out all night, and never work.

After a very long time away from school, I dropped by high school shortly before the day ended to meet some friends. However, I was stopped at the front entrance by my old nemesis, the principal.

"Johnny, what are you doing here?" the principal asked, looking at me like I was a notorious pimp coming to pick up his daughter for a date.

"Oh, just a friendly visit," I taunted.

"Well, we appreciate it, but you're not allowed on the premises since you were expelled for truancy."

"No, buddy," I smirked, "I'm afraid you're mistaken. I was *not* expelled, I dropped out."

"Actually, you stayed enrolled at this school until *I* expelled you, so you were *expelled*."

"Wait a second, here!" I said, suddenly very irritated. For some reason, I found the idea that this guy thought he could kick me out of a club I didn't want to be a part of absolutely infuriating. It was like dumping a girlfriend who smugly responds that she had already dumped *me* in her mind. "You can't kick me out for *quitting!* I stopped coming, so I *dropped out.*"

"No, you never informed anyone you were dropping out, so I'm informing you that you were expelled!"

"Are you telling me I have to file paperwork to drop out of school? I informed you by not coming to school!"

"*Okay*, Johnny," the principal said skeptically, "if you quit, why are you here today?"

"To meet with my friends!"

"*Su-u-ure . . .*"

"*What?!* You think I came here to *attend class?* Are you mental!?" I was now yelling and flailing my hands about in classic irate Italian style. I never could stand this fucking guy. "This is not a chicken or egg fuckin' scenario! I stopped coming, therefore I quit."

"Well, Johnny, the record shows that you were expelled."

"Okay, *fine*, readmit me so I can file the papers to drop out!"

"I'm afraid you're going to stay expelled!"

I would have spent all afternoon arguing with the principal for my reentrance if not for a long-legged, large-breasted Scandinavian blond who just happened to walk past the front of school on her way home. *Fuck this*, I thought, as I stomped back down the front steps of the school and started stalking my prey. Her name was Barbara, and she would become the mother of my first three children.

We had known each other since kindergarten without ever liking each other. Barb was an uptight, stuck-up goody-goody, and I was an annoying brat pretty boy. Puberty took care of our mutually incompatible personalities. The couple years I spent away from school did us both good. Her body became a woman's, and I got what I like to call my Good Bad Reputation.

A Good Bad Reputation is when you are well-known as the sort of scoundrel women want to fuck and men want to be. I was the guy who your parents warned you about. I was the boy your girlfriends warned you about. Now that it was the early 1970s, my Anglophilia had me dressing like Marc Bolan: long hair with long bell-bottoms jeans and bright, flashy tops. I was an evil pretty boy with bad intentions.

You would think that sort of reputation would scare the good girls away, but in reality I found the opposite to be true. The smarter, the kinder, the more incredible a girl was, the more she was attracted to a shameless degenerate like me. They wanted to redeem me, tame me. Good girls like Barbara threw themselves at me like they were jumping off a cliff.

I was a sucker for Barbara, too. She was my type exactly: a standoffish, tan, California-style blonde with huge cans and a superior high-class attitude. The condescension in her bearing, that sense that she thought she was just *so* much better than me, made her irresistible to the son of a guy who stole a NASA space capsule just because someone told him he couldn't. I ran after her, flirted with her, seduced her. Soon, she was pregnant and we were married. My first child, the beautiful and brilliant Angela Fratto, was born.

I was eighteen when she was born. I was far too young, far too attractive, and *far* too immature to be a husband. I definitely was going to be a helpless zero as a father.

I knew this was true and made no effort to fight against reality. The party never stopped. I rarely spent time at the small home I moved into with Barbara and Angela besides to sleep off my hangovers. I had no intention of being a family man.

I also had no legitimate means of supporting a family. I was an unemployed teenager with no diploma, no resume, no job skills, and no work ethic. All I had going for me was a wiseguy last name and a host of wiseguy connections. It wasn't hard to see where my life was going: to Tommy's The Extra Point Lounge, a rock 'n' roll club where all the half-ass wiseguys from Frankie's young crew gravitated if they had nothing else going on.

The smart gangsters in Iowa spun off and did their own thing since there was no Family left in Iowa to support them or compel them to pay tribute. There were others, however, who were so enthralled by Lou and Frankie's personality cults that it just felt more secure being crooks with a Fratto around as a lucky charm, and, in Frankie's absence, Tommy was their guy.

My poor brother Tommy may have had it worst of all Frattos. Frankie and Tommy had been like twins. Celebrating birthdays was ruined forever for Tommy when he had to spend his 23rd birthday at Frankie's funeral. With Frankie dead, 23-year-old Tommy was now responsible—not only for his own new wife and newborn child—but also for babysitting his siblings, Uncle Frank, and Mom, now a zombie perpetually puttering from the bedroom to the kitchen in slippers and then back again.

We all knew that Tommy was different from Frankie and would never be the same type of family leader. Tommy was a laidback, fun-loving ladies' man who had become a very young club owner—he was all about "Seize the day!"

or whatever caught his eye at the bar. He wasn't as bold as Frankie, nor was he interested in being the authority figure or my surrogate father.

Technically, of course, the real boss was Uncle Frank, who continued to split his time between Chicago and Des Moines to fill the power vacuum in Iowa and keep other families from thinking it was open country. The "Iowa Family" was now just a minor crew in a backwater outpost of the Outfit's empire, a couple old bookmakers and too many half-ass young wannabes who paid off Uncle Frank whenever he swept into town.

When I began hanging around The Extra Point, I was consciously beginning my career as a gangster. Though it could not have been a sorrier and more small-time scene, I didn't know any better. I felt like Lucky Luciano hanging around with all the teenage delinquents, petty con men, and degenerate gamblers as we listened to Mott the Hoople, Led Zeppelin, and The Who. I wanted nothing more than to get in on their sleazebag cons, their petty scores.

But Tommy had no more faith in me than Frankie. He really wanted to kick me out of the club altogether, but he couldn't since it was the only business in the Midwest that would conceivably employ me. He asked me if I could handle the responsibility of sweeping the floor twice a night.

I said yes, but I was lying. I had no intention of doing anything but becoming a criminal and picking up girls. After a week, a cocktail table tipped over, revealing the gigantic mound of dust bunnies and pretzels I had swept under it. This would have earned me a beating from Tommy, but unfortunately Tommy wasn't the one who witnessed the table topple over. Nope, the man who caught me red-handed was Frankie's most terrifying friend Petey Marasco, an Iowan who looked exactly like an Italian Muhammad Ali.

Petey dragged me by my hair around the bar, kicking over cocktail tables so that I could sweep out the secret stash of dust under each. From that night, Petey began to watch me as I worked, like a CO supervising a chain gang on the side of the road.

I couldn't live with a new, Muhammad Ali-looking Frankie. I begged Tommy to let me quit working altogether. Tommy was too focused on his own business to spend his life striving to make something out of me. It was more cost-effective to just slip me money to supplement the money Barbara was making as a nurse, so he never asked me to work anymore.

"If you want to be a gangster, knock yourself the fuck out," he said, laughing at the idea of Johnny Fratto making something of himself in the Mafia in 1970s Iowa of all places.

ABOVE The three Fratto brothers of Chicago in their fighting prime: my Dad, Lou, is standing on the far right; Uncle Rudolph is seated on the right, Uncle Frank seated on the left. They're accompanied (left to right) by my Dad's brother-in-law Tony Cordaro and family friends Babe Bisignano and Johnny Crittelli. (*Photo courtesy of Johnny Fratto Jr.*)

LEFT My Dad and I. (*Photo courtesy of Johnny Fratto Jr.*)

ABOVE Uncle Frank sitting across from Frank
Sinatra at his 21ˢᵗ birthday party, allegedly right
before he intentionally pissed on Sinatra's shoe
in the men's room. (*Photo courtesy of Johnny
Fratto Jr.*)

OPPOSITE My Uncle Frank with his very good
buddy Sammy Davis Jr. These two were thick
as thieves, especially since Uncle Frank loved to
bully Sinatra and even up the score on Sammy's
behalf. (*Photos courtesy of Johnny Fratto Jr.*)

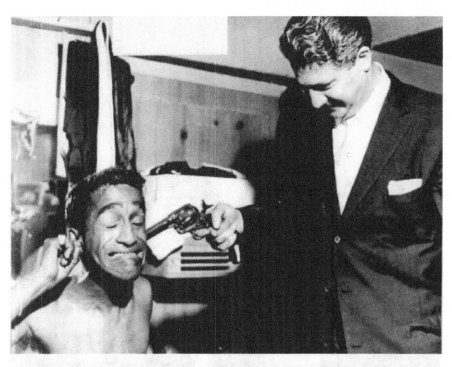

ABOVE My dearly missed brother Frankie and
my honorary uncle Rocky Marciano.
(*Photo courtesy of Johnny Fratto Jr.*)

OPPOSITE Frankie and Rocky enjoying some
good times with family friends Sam Ancona
on the left and Chuckie Morgan on the right—
both serious heavyweights (of a different sort).
(*Photo courtesy of Johnny Fratto Jr.*)

ABOVE Uncle Frank with his own pretty blond heiress, his onetime mistress Zsa Zsa Gabor. (*Photo courtesy of Johnny Fratto Jr.*)

RIGHT Fatherhood, Round 2:
my sons Willie and Joey with
their mom Jowanka. (*Photos
courtesy of Johnny Fratto Jr.*)

ABOVE AND OPPOSITE The great comedy team of Eric Lynch and I, both posing next to my elevator at my Beverly Hills penthouse. (*Photos courtesy of Johnny Fratto Jr.*)

ABOVE AND OPPOSITE A couple glamorous
photos from iconic fashion photographer Tyler
Shields, inspired by a certain family secret about
what happened in Skokie, Illinois . . . (*Photos
courtesy of Tyler Shields*)

ABOVE Here you see the artist presiding over
a photo shoot during my 1980s fashion period.
(*Photo courtesy of Johnny Fratto Jr.*)

17

THE CAFFEINE CARTEL

Confidence man was just about the only job I was qualified for: I had confidence, and I was a man. Throw in my good looks and last name, and that was it when it came to my skill set.

It was all I needed.

A lifetime of watching Frattos get away with everything had taught me to be confident that I could get away with anything. This confidence rubbed off on my marks and made them feel comfortable with giving me their money for any conceivable cockamamie scheme. The biggest obstacle to becoming a professional criminal is the daring to just grab whatever money comes your way without hesitation, without remorse, and without a second thought.

I had *that* confidence all day long. Every dollar that touched my hand felt like something I was richly owed by the world after Lou and Frankie's death. I never felt guilty about taking people's money.

I had grown up in a family where that's all we did to each other: beg, scam, and bully each other out of money we had scammed or bullied from someone else. As far as I knew, that's how people treated each other. If I stole from you, then my Uncle Frank stole from me, that made us even.

That's not to say crime came easy to me. Old timers have a saying: a real crook can walk through the rain without getting wet. That description had nothing to do with me—at least not at the start. I'd walk into a drizzle and just about drown. Dad's generation acted like they could tool around clipping Presidents and purchasing Caribbean dictators and never get caught. Meanwhile, I nearly blew myself up trying to bootleg barley.

My accomplice in this ridiculous plot was my friend Antonio. I can tell you everything you need to know about Antonio with three facts: he was 40 years old; his nickname "Timmy" still fit; and he lived with his mom in the house where he grew up. Willie loved to call hangaround guys like Timmy "porch kids." Timmy was the prototypical porch kid: a tubby, middle-aged petty crook in a slick suit who drove his brand new Cadillac home every night to get tucked into bed by mama in the home where he grew up. The poor sonofabitch had to rent out dumpy apartments around town so he could have a place to lay his sleazy girlfriends without upsetting his mom and fucking up his comfortable situation.

You might call it pathetic, but Timmy thought he was being strategic. Timmy had the money to live a life of leisure because his father, a self-made Italian businessman with the right connections, had built a wildly profitable food brokerage business. Timmy's dad and uncles ran a grocery warehouse that employed half the Italians in Iowa and wholesaled to grocery stores across the Midwest. Timmy figured his dad's multimillion-dollar business would be his by generational gravity so long as he was patient and stayed tight with his folks, which he did by never leaving.

Timmy was wrong. Since Timmy had never proven himself competent at anything besides eating, sleeping, and talking shit, his uncles cut him out of the family business when his dad died. This cataclysm caused Timmy to call me, angry and in desperate need of money.

"The motherfuckers stole everything, Johnny!" the forty year old yelled at me on his front porch, loud enough to get his point across but not so loud that his hard-of-hearing mom might hear as she washed the dishes.

Timmy gestured for me to lean in so he could whisper his plan for revenge. "It's my turn, Johnny, it's my time to make my move, make my name, make something of myself."

Timmy's big idea? Well, if alcohol bootlegging built the Mob in Al Capone's days, and heroin had made the Syndicate untold billions, then Timmy would construct his empire by bootlegging an even more addictive substance: coffee.

That's right—at the perfect time to catch the coming cocaine boom, Timmy asked me to join a Caffeine Cartel instead—and I said yes.

In the summer of 1976, when I was at the age when most kids are grad-uating from college, I was naïve enough to be convinced that Timmy's plot to get even with his uncles might be the beginning of my own criminal empire. In retrospect, it's not hard to understand why Frankie and Tommy didn't rate me too highly as an organized crime prospect.

Thanks to his knowledge of the family business, Timmy sounded pretty damn informed when he broke down the fundamentals of the coffee importation business. "The price of coffee is always fuckin' rising," he'd say, leaning over from his rocking chair on the porch to whisper into my ear. "It's got so fuckin' high out 'ere that the average working class motherfucker can't even afford a cuppa joe no more, know whatta I mean? So, I get the idea that the way to make money is to give the blue collars a cheap cup of coffee."

My eyes focused on the histrionic gestures his chubby-fingered hands were making between his legs.

"I got my inspiration, see," Timmy continued in his best conspiratorial Ralph Kramden voice, "from dis article about Colombian cocaine smugglers who 'cut' their product with shit like baby powder or laxatives to increase their profit. So that's it! All we gotta do is find something cheap to mix in with ground coffee beans to increase our profit margin, and that way we can price war the other coffee makers and corner the market. We'll be millionaires!"

Sounds good, I thought, which shows you that at that point I was every bit the dumb motherfucker as Timmy. I knew about as much about coffee, "cutting," and grocery distribution as Timmy knew about independent living. At least I wasn't the guy that read an article about cocaine smuggling in 1976 and left with every takeaway *besides* how easy it was to make a 10,000% profit from a single plane trip smuggling cocaine.

Timmy was an ass-backwards crook: the Colombians were inspired by Juan Valdez to take their coca distribution business international; Timmy was inspired by coke smugglers to become Juan Valdez!

At least the first part of Timmy's plan proved solid: obtaining eight to nine hundred cases of free coffee really was as easy as renting a Ryder truck and paying a couple of grunts at Timmy's uncles' warehouse a C-note apiece. A real crook would have driven the coffee across the state line to Illinois and took 35 cents on the dollar from Uncle Frank's stolen goods fence and come home with a few Gs.

But I wasn't a real crook...yet.

Apparently, I was an experimental agricultural scientist. As if we didn't have enough trouble filling our dad's shoes, Timmy and I were now trying to become the goombah versions of Louis Pasteur and George Washington Carver. In our many planning sessions, it had never occurred to us how hard it would be to concoct a cheap cutting agent that could be packaged and roasted with real coffee without leaving a trace of taste. After we filled the shithole apartment Timmy used for his dates to the ceiling with stolen Folger's and Maxwell House coffee cans, we looked at each other and realized we had no idea what step to take next.

As the days rolled by, Timmy became paranoid that his uncles were catching onto him and insisted we move the coffee out from his apartment and into the basement of my duplex. At first, I didn't mind storing the coffee since I got a real manly guido feeling with all that stolen loot around, but I quickly learned that keeping a couple tons of coffee in one building creates a smell so intense that it qualifies as chemical warfare.

Even while still in the packaging, the coffee's smell was so potent that it gave Barbara's dog a permanent caffeine contact high. This poor fucking mutt started to chase his tail for nine hours at a time like a tweaker Lassie. My newborn daughter Angela began to smell like a burnt out roaster, and my hot blond wife's hair was somehow turning black.

I had to get this shit out of my house.

"Johnny, we can't move dat coffee, man, be real," Timmy whispered to me on his porch, "I'm too worried my uncles will catch wind of our racket to risk moving that coffee."

"Jesus Christ, it won't be too hard for them to 'catch wind' of our fuckin' scheme here, Timmy," I whispered back, "because any draft that passes by my house must spread the stench of coffee fuckin' beans across the entire sovereign state of Iowa!"

Eventually, I convinced Timmy to let me move the coffee to a warehouse in Mitchellville, Iowa, where we planned to do our experiments with cutting agents. Since Timmy was paranoid about the possibility that his multimillionaire uncles had launched a statewide investigation into some missing coffee cans, we couldn't simply rent a moving truck to take the coffee across town.

Instead, to avoid "being conspicuous", he told me to empty each of the 900 cans of coffee into garbage bags for transportation—since sweaty, nervous Italians loading heavy, nondescript black bags into the back of a truck would never arouse anyone's suspicions. Once this stealthy operation was completed, Timmy wanted me to make a separate trip to transport the cans in the middle of the night to the garbage dump.

This sounded like way too much work, so I simply tossed 900 empty coffee cans in a giant heap for the garbage man to pick up. If anyone was investigating the coffee theft, they could have solved the mystery by driving within ten miles of the Great Pyramid of Folgers on my doorstep.

In Mitchellville, Timmy unveiled the coffee brand that would make us millionaires: Antonio's Morning Brew. If nothing else, Timmy had talent as a product packager. The brand name was attractively displayed on a colorful label, which was wrapped around an ahead-of-its-time plastic coffee jar that looked nicer than any of the tin cans on my lawn.

For the first time, I was impressed with Timmy, but that thought instantly made me skeptical of my judgment. So I checked the can again...

"Timmy, I gotta say, you did a nice job in a lot of ways," I said with an edge of sarcasm in my voice. "The jar looks *great*. Nice and lightweight, unbreakable even."

I paused for dramatic effect.

"The name! The name is great too—'Antonio's Morning Brew!' I can see it in stores. I can see myself buying it!"

I paused again, looking at Timmy with a scowl that must have made my eyes look like they were about to burst.

"Timmy, there's only one problem. Though I can see Antonio's Morning Brew taking off, I *cannot* picture 'ANGIANO'S' Morning Brew' in stores!

"You dumb motherfucker, you misspelled your own name!" I screamed, raising my hands in exasperation and doing my best impression of Frankie during his many lectures of me. "Now I know why they called you Timmy—at least you could spell *that!* I can't believe I'm in business with a guy who steals from his own family and can't spell his own fucking name!"

This was pretty rich, now that I think about it, given my Uncle Frank stole from his own family and couldn't *say* his own name...

Unfortunately, at this point, I was pretty much "pot committed" to Antonio's Morning Brew. Combining the cost of a couple thousand jars and new labels with the moving truck and bribery expenses, we were officially deep in the red. And it's not like either of us had cash to spare. We had to turn a profit somehow, with our only asset being a grimy warehouse full of garbage bags of stinking, migraine-inducing coffee in Mitchellville, Iowa.

All that was standing in our way was *science*. We needed a cutting agent.

Timmy and I started our experiments in the kitchen at my house. We tested everything from soybeans to sawdust in our quest to find a cheap, widely available ingredient that could be invisibly, tastelessly, and scentlessly roasted and ground with coffee.

Finally, the two street corner alchemists discovered their philosopher's stone: barley. Barley burnt to tasteless ash in experiment after experiment; the coffee tasted like shit, but no more than any other shitty cheap coffee. We were made; we had our secret recipe. Timmy was positive he was going to become the Pablo Escobar of coffee.

After an attempt to partner with some old friends in the Kansas City Mob fell apart when neither side agreed to let the other motherfuck it on the deal, I called up on old friend who I *knew* would be easier to exploit.

Ok, time for some fake names to protect the innocent: meet "Duffy", a dweeby lifelong acquaintance of mine who married the heiress to "The Laval-lee Coffee Company" of Des Moines. Duffy was a pushover with badly parted hair who carried himself like a down-on-his-luck door-to-door salesman from the Eisenhower era, so I had no trouble muscling him into letting us roast our barley at his wife's factory.

Duffy looked like he was going puke on his lap when I told him what we were going to do. "Johnny, my wife is going to kill me!" he squealed, his jowls instantly glistening with sweat.

"Duffy, it'll be great," I said with all the insincere calm of a customer service representative.

"Johnny, the police are going to find out!" cried Duffy as if the G-men were already camped outside, just waiting to hang a case on an infamous menace to society like him.

"Duffy, our parents are friends how long? I've known you forever! You *have* to do it!" I cooed to him with a reassuring hand on his shoulder.

"Johnny, I'm going to get divorced!" he bawled.

"Duffy, you deserve a little cash in your own pocket," I reasoned with him. "Do you always want to be begging your mother-in-law for an allowance?"

"Johnny, I really don't want to do this!" he screamed, reduced almost to madness.

"Sure you do!" I retorted unflappably.

"*Johnny!* Do you even *hear* what I'm saying?" the wild-eyed maniac asked.

"No, Duffy, I honestly don't," I said with the same sunnily indifferent tone. Every "no" was just another "yes" to me. "I don't hear what you're saying because you're going to roast this fucking barley no matter what you say... *and* take care of yourself, too." I always tried to remind him that, *deep down*, this was really *me* doing *him* a favor—an involuntary favor, yes, but a favor nonetheless. A rape favor, if you will.

What Duffy didn't know is that I had already lined up a supermarket buyer for 100 cases of Antonio's Morning Brew, and after hassling with the Kansas City Family, a square like Duffy couldn't possibly stop me.

Late one night, I drove up to the Lavallee Coffee factory in a cattle feed truck as Duffy waited in the shadows, chewing on his lips and pacing around the perimeter of a small invisible circle. The truck went *BEEP BEEP BEEP* as I backed it up in front of the little nebbish, and, to give him a little shock, I pulled a lever so that a ton of barley came rushing out of a chute right at his feet.

Duffy nearly stroked out. "Johnny! You can't put this coffee on the fucking ground! This is unsanitary! People are going to get poisoned! That isn't fit to feed to humans!"

"Duffy, what the fuck are you talking about?" I said in the most soothing tone I could muster as I hopped out of the truck, impersonating the way Dad would gracefully disembark from one of his garbage company trucks.

"We are burning this shit, see?" I continued, acting as the lawyer Frankie always wanted me to be. "Think about it, Duffy. If you cook food, you can *eat* food. Why should this be any different? We are going to roast some barley, mix it with ground coffee beans, and then people will soak the ashes in hot water, and drink it. Nothing is going to happen; just calm down and let your friend Johnny handle this."

I needed to roast about 800 pounds of barley to make enough cut for the supermarket owner's bulk purchase of Antonio's Morning Brew, but there was a problem. Normally, that much volume would have to be split up into multiple batches, each taking 2-3 hours to roast in Lavallee Coffee's industrial roasters. Unfortunately, it was clear Duffy's psyche would not withstand an all-night job. After a cop car innocently drove by, Duffy snapped and began maniacally ranting.

"It's over, Johnny! The cops are coming! I'm going down! This is what I get for letting fuckers push me around! No one's pushing Duffy around any more! Ya hear me, world? Duffy's fucking *done*! If my wife finds out, I'm a DEAD MAN!"

I tuned out Duffy's babbling freakout and started dumping as much of the load as possible into a single roaster batch. I drastically exceeded the machine's suggested limit on the first load, but that's how an impatient prick like me does his laundry and dishes at home. What's the worst that could happen? It was just barley for fuck's sake.

Not looking forward to spending more time than necessary with Duffy, I ran to the truck and drove to the nearest phone booth to call Timmy. I tried to suggest to him that one big batch would be enough, but Timmy was having none of it. "Listen, we got 800 pounds of coffee in your basement for this batch. That means you need to roast *all 800 pounds* of barley for the cut. You're going to be burning barley all fucking night."

I drove back to the factory and parked across the street. I was immediately joined by Duffy running over to me, his face the color of a flaming red pimple. This dumpy little toad had pressure-cooked to the point of insanity in my absence. I was no longer dealing with Duffy the pussy-whipped nerd. Now I was dealing with Duffy the Gangster.

"Where the fuck did you think you were going? Who the fuck are you to leave me here, motherfucker? You're going to get me killed!" he barked at me like a real tough guy.

I leaned out of my window and started waving a roll of cash in his face like I was fanning a fainting woman. I had seen this trick used on angry, disrespected accomplices all my life. It was how it worked: squeeze civilians of everything they're worth until you can't get away with it anymore, and then you buy them off with a little sugar right before they blow.

Just as I got ready to sweet-talk Duffy into complacence, the temperature spiked twenty degrees in an instant. I'm talking twenty degrees *centigrade*. It was like being suddenly bitchslapped by the *sun*.

BOOM! The Lavallee Coffee building detonated. This wasn't a case for the Fire Department; this blast made geologists double-check that there were no active volcanoes in Des Moines. The building was just a crater in the middle of downtown Des Moines.

Duffy was already very white. When he staggered off the pavement, I saw he had turned practically albino. His livelihood and marriage was demolished in a moment. I had ruined his life . . . all because I was too impatient to obey the directions and loaded too much barley into a coffee roaster.

When Duffy turned his teary eyes to me, you'd think I'd have a moment of remorse over what I had done to him. You would think that, but you'd be wrong.

This was where that unflappable, demonic confidence that *defines* a confidence man comes into play. Once I came to terms with the fact that I was not dead, my easy smile and sense of humor returned.

"Aren't you going to thank me?" I asked Duffy gently.

"Wha . . . wha . . . wha . . ." the shellshocked little man sputtered, his face pancaked in dust from the explosion.

"I mean, if I hadn't gone to make a phone call and returned at right that moment, you'd have still been inside. You be *dead* right now. I saved your life!" I paused to knuckle some dirt or asbestos or something out of my eye sockets. "I mean, shouldn't *you* be thanking *me* right now? If it wasn't for me, farmers would be finding your limbs across the Midwest!"

This was something of a social experiment for me. I figured this was like one of them free plays in football where the referees have already called a penalty against the defense and you can pretty much do anything you want, since you'll have the option of calling back the play when it's done. Since I already had done the worst thing I could ever do to Duffy, what was the point in sucking up to him?

After a few moments of incredulous blinking in front of the flaming ruins of his family business, Duffy threw his hands to the air, screamed like Janet Leigh in the shower in *Psycho*, and ran away into the night.

The next time I saw Duffy, a lightning bolt of grey had been singed across his scalp. To me, it looked like my signature etched onto his head.

A month later, Duffy called me on the telephone. "Hello, Johnny," he said in a very loud, stilted voice. "I know it has been a long time since we last saw each other and broke into the Lavallee Coffee factory together. How have you been?"

Well, this wasn't the most subtle sting operation I would ever encounter. Despite what you may think, I held no hard feelings against Duffy for cooperating with the police. If anything, I thought I deserved it since I hadn't even bothered to give him the few hundred bucks I had promised him in exchange for roasting the barley in the first place. I didn't feel guilty about blowing up his family business—that was an unforeseen act of God that I couldn't help—just about the cash I promised him.

Anyway, it all worked out for Duffy. His wife's family received a healthy insurance settlement for their business, and Duffy today is a well-respected executive at a Fortune 500 company. Like I said, I did him a favor: now *he* is the breadwinner and shotcaller in his family.

You might think that, in the aftermath of the detonation of Lavallee Coffee, I would have immediately abandoned the cursed Antonio's Morning Brew brand. Nope; I was a born confidence man. Nothing, including reality, could deter me from believing in my own predestined success.

A new batch of barley was roasted in a brickyard industrial kiln, and the ashes were sent in garbage bags to Mitchellville to be mixed with the stolen coffee and packaged in our attractive plastic jars.

A few weeks later, I walked into my meeting with the sales management of the Safeway supermarket chain in a dazzling silk business suit. If nothing else, I have always looked the part of the important, put-together businessman.

I pitched Safeway on Antonio's Morning Brew, complete with a full brochure displaying our planned national ad campaign: "Antonio's Morning Brew: Same Great Taste, Half the Caffeine!" By filling our coffee jars halfway with barley ashes, we had legitimately reduced the caffeine level of our coffee by 50%. Granted, we had also reduced the coffee level by 50%, but "Antonio's Morning Brew: Same Great Taste, Half the Coffee!" didn't have the same hook.

I had three pots of coffee on the table—one Folger's, one Maxwell House, and one Antonio's. I passed the pots around to the dozen finely dressed, smiling businesspeople sitting around the boardroom table. They looked like easy marks for a handsome spokesperson like me.

"These are three cups of coffee: one from Folger's, one from Maxwell House, and one from Antonio's Morning Brew. Take a sip of each one . . . and concentrate," I said in a slow, dramatic delivery that I thought raised the suspense level in the room. The Safeway representatives began to sip from my samples.

"Even though Antonio's has *fifty percent* less caffeine than the other two brands, I *DEFY* anyone . . ." I bellowed like a carnival barker with a great sweep of my arm . . . "in this room to tell me which cup contains Antonio's."

Fuck, what an amateur I was! Today, I would just fill all of the cups with Folger's.

Every single hand in the room pointed without hesitation to the pot that only *I* was supposed to know contained Antonio's. I scanned from the shaking fingers up to faces contorted and distorted in reeling expressions of disgust. In a panic, I grabbed the pot in question, poured a shot, and slurped it down with the confidence I was about to enjoy something that at least resembled coffee.

It was like I had just licked a dirty ashtray. Never in the history of college dorms has a freshman girl performed a walk of shame half as humiliating as my stumbling, apologetic exit from that Safeway boardroom. I was defeated.

But only for a minute. So what if Antonio's tasted like it was poured from a Clydesdale's ass? There are places where substandard products thrive: mental hospitals, prisons, halfway houses, homeless shelters. Championing the rock bottom price and the reduced caffeine ratio, I called on some of Dad's old contacts and convinced the Iowa state government to purchase our entire stock of Antonio's Morning Brew and distribute it to the jailhouses and mental wards.

Whenever there was an ax murderer in need of a pick-me-up, Antonio's Morning Brew was there; whenever a macho nurse tipped a cup into a straitjacketed maniac's drooling mouth, Antonio's Morning Brew was there.

My cut was $100,000 on the deal—a decent payday for a 22-year-old without any clue what the fuck he's doing. And with his share, Timmy finally left home . . . nope, actually the motherfucker blew it on cars and clothes. He really was a porch kid.

But me? I was pretty damn sure I was a gangster.

PUMPING OFF!

Grifting isn't like masturbation; you can't teach yourself.

After a couple near-death experiences like Antonio's Morning Brew, I was sane enough to seek tutelage. In my early years in the rackets, I studied under many masters, whom it would be insulting or endangering to name. Still, there's one in particular who deserves credit: The Master of All Cons, Joey.

Joey knows who he is, and that's everyone who needs to know.

More than anyone, Joey was my guru. He showed me how to swagger and smile my way through any obstacle. He put the finish on the gangster.

The most educational trip I ever made to Chicago began with Joey picking me up in a brand new limousine. "Did you rent this for me?" I asked Joey.

"Fuck no... I *own* this motherfucker!" Joey said. That was Joey all the way: always carry yourself like someone so rich and powerful they can get away with anything.

In keeping with his fraudulent high-roller status, Joey had his driver take us to The Pump Room in the Ambassador Hotel, the elegant restaurant immortalized in Frank Sinatra's song "My Kind of Town (Chicago Is)" and countless movies. Since I was still nothing more than a sleazy kid, I was very wary of drinking in a snooty, ultra-expensive place like the Pump Room, where I figured I could only get in trouble.

"Fuggeddaboutit, cuz," Joey told me. "Just chill. Just watch me operate."

First, Joey used the Pump Room's phone to call every friend in his address book and tell them to come over for free booze. Once a good crowd got going, Joey started ordering bottle after bottle of the most expensive champagne, bourbon, scotch, and wine you could find in Chicago. At first I was worried, but then I was drunk and wasn't worried anymore.

At the end of the night, our host at the Pump Room came over with an $8000 bill. This guy was an old, uptight Chinese immigrant who spoke in broken English, but he seemed very relaxed as he handed Joey the bill. By design, Joey looked like the sort of elegantly wasted rich kid who could buy a yacht a day without worrying about his bank balance. My cousin barely even glanced at the bill; without hesitation, Joey gave the waiter a credit card.

"Joey, what the fuck are you doing . . . ?" I asked.

"Teaching *you* something, you little prick. Just watch!"

Of course, that first credit card was declined. So was the second, third, fourth, fifth, and twelfth that Joey gave the host. At no point in this charade did Joey acknowledge the increasingly exasperated and worried old man as he returned to our table, not even bothering to pause his conversations or make eye contact as he casually handed the old man yet another credit card.

Finally, the host lost his temper and interrupted a funny story Joey was telling to the table. "Hey!" he barked as our table of drunken, giggling, red-faced Italian socialites slowly turned to pay attention. "I don't get you, mister! Listen! Why you come here and drink and don't got no money to pay! I call the cops!"

With his same easygoing, friendly demeanor, Joey responded, "Listen, we both know you ain't callin' the cops. *You* know we'll just kick your ass if you did that."

The old man blinked. This was apparently not the response he was expecting.

"Besides, do I *look* like the sort of guy who can't pay a bar tab?" Joey asked with a yawn as he leaned back in his chair. "See that limo out there?" Joey asked as he pointed out the window to his limo, which was parked intentionally so that it would be in view of our table. "That limo's *mine*. I *own* it, brother. I don't know if you don't know how to use a credit card machine in your country or somethin', but since you can't get my cards to work, I'll go to the bank first thing tomorrow morning and get you $8000 cash and a $1000 tip for you and bring it right over here. That work for you?"

The little man looked back and forth for help. The Pump Room had been around since Dad's days in Chicago, so it had ample experience with spoiled young Italian kids with enough juice to get away with torturing waiters and managers. That was one difference about Chicago and Des Moines: the Windy City was so accustomed to wiseguy behavior that you were granted *way* more latitude to be a lout since every business owner was always wondering if you were related to the wrong guy.

And Joey and I were related to *all* the wrong guys. Of course, the host didn't know that, but he nonetheless let us go with a promise to return the next day.

Of course, Joey and I never went back to The Pump Room, which was way too stuffy for us anyway.

By chance, I was at Joey's modest bachelor pad six months later when the Chinese host from The Pump Room called. Who knows how he got Joey's number? You might think Joey would be worried, but instead he was positively giddy, bouncing on the couch and giggling.

"Sorry...I didn't quite hear what you're were saying," he said into the phone while lifting his finger to his lips.

"I say, I looking for Mister Joe..."

"Listen 'ere, you sadistic fuck!" my cousin screamed, his voice haggard with rage. "What type of sick motherfucker would call me up and ask if Joe is here? Huh?"

"Ahh, sorry? I just ask for Mister Joe..."

"Listen 'ere, you cumstain, everyone knows that Joe and his buddy Johnny died after they spent all night drinking at some bar and then crashed their limo into a school bus full of fucking kids. The cops are still searching for the bar that irresponsibly kept serving them liquor so they can press charges for being accessories to the murder of all those poor kids.... *You* wouldn't know where they were at?"

"OH SHIT!" yelped the host from the Pump Room. "N-n-n-n-n-n-nooo, I just old friend of Mr. Joe..."

"You *were* with them that night, weren't you! Who the fuck are you, you lyin' cocksucker?"

Dial tone.

"And *that's* how you get out of paying a bill, Johnny," Joey said with a raised eyebrow.

With teachers like this, how could I ever go wrong?

18

JOHNNY VS. THE GYPSIES

By the late 1970s, I had swaggered through my initial rough patch as a con-man and became recognized as one of the elite confidence men in the Midwest. In the circles that mattered, I was widely acknowledged as one of very best up-and-coming "Openers"—the cocky, glamorous, good-looking first-impression-merchant who attracts the money marks through envy and sexual attraction. Once I charmed the discretion and skepticism out of the mark, I'd hand them pocketbook-first to the "closer"—the conman who would actually do the motherfucking, who credibly looked the part of someone you'd trust on a serious business transaction.

I had one advantage over the other openers: my longstanding ties with the London fashion community. The same SoHo designers who had imported cutting edge threads for me back when I was a prepubescent Beatlemaniac and pubescent hippie continued right on designing the stage costumes for every major rock band of the 1970s. I was the only person in the Midwest who could get Mick Jagger's designer on the phone and order a custom-tailored version of anything in his wardrobe.

When actual rock stars played The Extra Point or one of my cousins' clubs in Chicago, I was invariably better dressed. Since this was the era before music videos, when I'd show up before the show, the groupies would often figure I *must be part of the band* and drag me into the ladies' room for a quick fuck.

As an Anglophile, I was into Bowie-style glam rock to a way more flamboyant degree than most Americans. I would be walking around Iowa in skintight silver leather pants, alligator skin boots, a completely unbuttoned metallic blue silk shirt, floor-length fur coat, and immaculately feathered black-and-silver hair. I started going grey while still very young, but I *owned* that shit to the point that most people thought I had intentionally dyed my hair to attain that Pepe Le Pew look.

Soon, all of my shirts were doused in glitter, and I constantly wore a pair of snakeskin pants so tight that they looked like two anacondas were digesting my legs, and so shiny that my crotch reflected light like a disco ball. Then came the long silver leather trench coat designed for Robert Plant that he sent back for being too small, which made me look like a kid playing superhero in a cape made of tin foil.

Finally, there came my ultimate accessory: a pair of space alien blue contact lenses. This was back in like 1978, before strangely colored contacts became widely available; I had to special order these motherfuckers from some mad scientist in Bulgaria.

These contacts, I was sure, would be the accessory that would put me over the top in my pussy-chasing contest with my brothers Tommy (the Babe Ruth of ladies men) and Willie. Though nowhere near as flashy as me, Tommy had this classic Fabian look to him that women loved, and Willie had the unfair advantage of looking and dressing like a more muscular John Travolta at the peak of his *Saturday Night Fever* stardom.

Tommy could have Fabian and Willie could have John Travolta; *I* had my space alien blue contact lenses. I was convinced my blue eyes were going to fuck their shit up.

I showed up at The Extra Point in my Robert Plant trenchcoat, snakeskin pants, and my new blue contacts, unveiling my masterpiece to Tommy and Willie. "Whaddya think?" I asked, throwing out my arms as if showcasing the most perfect example of American manhood yet fashioned.

Willie studied my long silver-and-black bouffant hair, the glittery shirt, my over-tanned skin, my skintight pants, my heeled boots, and my blue eyes. "Jesus Christ! I got it! Now I know exactly who you look like . . ." he said, getting my hopes *way* up.

Which rock star could it be? Jimmy Page? Marc Bolan? Joe Perry?

"Yeah, you *really* look great. With the blue eyes, now it's unmistakable. Johnny, now you look like the fucking *spitting image* of Elizabeth Taylor!"

Though my non-threatening appearance made marks feel comfortable, the other benefit of looking like Elizabeth Taylor was that the other conmen and crooks would still look at me as someone who could be fucked with. Part of being an opener was making yourself an available, approachable, and attractive target for other con artists of varying skill—kinda like Great White sharks who eat smaller sharks. I had to have the confidence to let them run their game and play their tricks on me in order to draw them close enough to defraud and rob.

A great example of this sort of conman battle came in 1979, shortly before the birth of my son Lil' Johnny. I was 25 years old, rapidly becoming such an accomplished grifter that my uncles and cousins in Chicago were frequently flying me north to play a part in their schemes. Though I was not yet at the peak of my talents, I was definitely at the peak of my arrogance; I was positive no one could out-swindle me.

This explains my behavior in the story I'm about to tell you.

I was sitting at a stoplight when the most beautiful lipstick-red 1975 Cadillac custom convertible purred up next to me. I knew my luxury cars, and this vehicle was a true work of art, probably the best looking car I had ever laid eyes on. I was envious to see that I knew the prick in the driver's seat: a local character named Mike the Gypsy.

Mike the Gypsy was actually a real Gypsy, a young Romani tramp on the make. I'm not saying all Gypsies pursue the stereotypical Gypsy trade of scamming the honkies, but the large extended clan in Des Moines certainly did. The Gypsy men were all fixtures in the Iowa underworld, conmen and pickpockets and cat burglars who drove beautiful cars, wore immaculate jewelry, and lived in abject terror of their bloodthirsty Gypsy fortuneteller wives.

I'm not judging them—my life was almost identical! We both inherited a family tradition of parasiting off white people; only I called it Mafia and they called it Gypsy. The Italians and Gypsies were very similar, the only obvious difference being that most Italians aren't so uptight about marrying virgins as the Gypsies are.

Though the Des Moines Gypsies had far too much respect to ever fuck with my dad or Frankie or even Tommy, my reputation as a superficial club kid made me an attractive target for an inexperienced young hood like Mike the Gypsy. He decided to try one of the Gypsy's most reliable scams on me.

"Hey, Johnny, I got a business proposition for you," he called out over the roar of the Cadillac's engine, which he revved for effect.

"I'm always listening!" I called out as I revved *my* Cadillac's engine.

We pulled our cars over to the side of road and greeted each other with the wiseguy hug. I was fully aware I was about to be conned, but I had a feeling there would be a way to turn this play to my advantage.

"Listen, Johnny, so I got this problem..." Mike said with a Hollywood-ready smile and relaxed demeanor. He was good, but not as good as me.

"Well, there's a reason they call me 'The Problem Solver,'" I responded. In case you're wondering, no one has called me "The Problem Solver."

"Here's the thing. I need $3500 quick. I got a sure thing, and I can flip that $3500 within thirty days and give you back $7000. That's double your investment in a month."

"The juice sounds good," I said, feigning interest, knowing it sounded *way* too good to be true. "But whaddya got for collateral?"

"How 'bout this Cadillac?" the Gypsy volunteered after a moment of pretend-thought. "I have the title, and I'll sign it right over to you to hold until I pay you back."

This was a transparent ploy—obviously the title was fraudulent. I wasn't going to give a Gypsy $3500 for a piece of paper and a handshake. "Fuck the title," I said with my finger pointing to his chest, "I need the *physical* car *and* the title, too. Give me both, and I'll get you $3500 by tomorrow."

At that moment, both of us thought we had our mark just where we wanted him. Raised within families that repeatedly got away with scamming the rest of the world, both Mike and I were positive our opponent had no idea what he was getting himself into. The only difference between us was Mike was under the impression that I was any old idiot mark—and *I* knew that I was engaged in a battle of conman chess.

"Fine, no problem!" Mike said with a slap on my shoulder, "I'll come over to your house tomorrow and drop off the Cadillac and title in exchange for $3500 cash. In thirty days, I'll come back, give you $7000, and pick up the Cadillac. Deal?"

"Oh yes," I said as I shook his hand with mine tilted upright so he could see the diamond rings, "We got ourselves a fucking deal."

Things went down according to the agreement the next day, just as I knew they would. You never pull confidence tricks in a rush . . . because that would betray a lack of confidence. You have to let the mark "get pregnant" with the deal.

Once Mike left with his loan, I took stock of the situation and figured I was definitely way ahead. I had in my possession a priceless custom Cadillac convertible, and all I had given up was $3500 in local restaurateur Pete Riccelli's cash. A lifelong friend, old Pete was so eager to see how I was going to out-scam the Gypsies that he advanced me the cash just so he could reserve a front row seat for the show.

He wouldn't have been thrilled to learn that I wasn't exactly sure how I was going to scam the Gypsies yet since I didn't know what their play was going to be. Surely, they would come in a couple days to reclaim the Cadillac, whether by con or by burglary, so I took precautions. I buried the Caddy deep in my garage, surrounded it by heavy, borderline-immovable objects, and fortified my garage door to the extent that it would take dynamite to open it. I went next door to talk to my cousin and future state senator Tony Bisagnano, who I informed of the situation in the hope that he would keep an eye out for me in case there was trouble.

And then I waited.

Two days later, a few tough Gypsies rang my doorbell in their finest suits. I thought back to how Joey had taught me to neutralize an angry mark through an incredibly aggressive counterattack.

I knew what I had to do.

I wildly disheveled my hair, pulled my boxer shorts askew so as to expose a testicle, and lifted up my undershirt up over my belly. If I was going to win this battle of wits, I would need to have the power of *crazy* on my side.

"What you want?" I gruffly asked like Mr. T as I opened the door.

"Well, I hate to say it, but there's a problem," the lead Gypsy said with a pained expression on his face, as if he *really* hated to trouble me. "I've been informed that a member of our family named Michael gave you a certain Cadillac as collateral for a personal loan. That car was unfortunately not his to give; it belongs to his uncle."

"Why should I give a shit?" I asked before lifting a finger to press against one nostril so I could shoot a jet of snot out of the other nostril.

There's no finer sight in the world than a flustered Gypsy. It took the speaker a moment to collect himself and continued. "Well, you should care because it's a stolen car. His uncle is very upset, and he intends to call the police and report that you have stolen the car and refuse to return it."

I blinked rapidly, as if I were having trouble comprehending the situation. "Well, what you goin' to do about it?"

"Well, it's very easy," the Gypsy continued, speaking with the reassuring tone of an infomercial host offering a miracle product that would solve all of my household needs. "We don't want anyone to get in trouble, and we want to make sure this entire situation is settled amicably since Mike acted so immaturely. What we suggest is that you give us the car, and we'll bring you the full amount Mike owes you in a couple days, and then everything will be square."

"Hmmmm..." I said with one hand rubbing my chin and the other scratching an exposed nut. "That sounds pretty good, but I got me a better idea. How 'bout *you* motherfuckers give me the money *first*, and *then* I'll give you the fuckin' car?"

Now here was a moment to cherish: the head Gypsy conman cocking an eyebrow, biting his lip, and finally turning his head in either direction to check with his accomplices to see if *they* had any idea on how to proceed. I'm sure that, in all their time operating in innocent, eager-to-please Iowa, never had these guys encountered a white guy who sincerely didn't give a shit about the threat—*oooh, scary!*—of a stolen vehicle report.

"B-b-b-b-ut," the Gypsy continued, "see, that, *that* won't work. The uncle is already *very* pissed. The uncle ain't gonna wait. He's just gonna report the Cadillac stolen and get both you and Mike in trouble. You don't want to see your name and mug shot in the newspaper..."

"Ha, that's where you got me *completely* wrong," I said, cackling. "You motherfuckers got *no* idea what I want to see in the newspaper. Listen, there are two options: either I keep the Cadillac and the old uncle can do whatever the fuck he wants, or...you motherfuckers are going to give me the $7000 you owe me."

Now the Gypsies were all rapidly swinging their heads back and forth to each other, trying to find someone who had an idea what to do next. I could read their minds: *white people don't act this way.* I'm sure they had run this scam hundreds of times across the world without ever encountering someone who was willing to face a gang of angry Gypsies *and* felony carjacking *and* loansharking charges—all over $3500.

My reaction was unthinkable.

You could tell the entire con itself was extremely well-designed by the sum of the loan: just big enough to be a good payday, but not so large that it would break the mark and make him desperate enough to do something stupid. An amateur will shoot too high and indebt his mark so deeply that he'll never write the cash off as lost, leading to years of bad blood and pursuit. These Gypsies were professionals: they milked me for pretty much the exact amount of cash that a normal person could lose and move on with their lives.

Their problem was that they weren't dealing with a normal person.

They were dealing with a professional asshole.

As I slammed the door in the Gypsies' faces, I knew that my victory was only temporary. Round 2 definitely went to me—probably a 10-8 round on any fair judge's scorecard—but they were guaranteed to come back for many rounds to come. Gypsies don't give up on Cadillacs easily.

The Gypsies next move was to approach their local Italian contacts and beseech them to intercede on their behalf with me for *my* sake, since I obviously didn't know what I was getting into. The old Italians laughed in the Gyspies' faces, informing them that *they* didn't know what they had gotten themselves into by picking on the crazy dopehead nephew that Chicago Outfit killer Frank Fratto couldn't stop warning everyone about.

"That kid's a *maniac*, everyone knows he doesn't give a shit about nuthin'," one veteran bookmaker told the Gypsies. "Besides...it's not like you can muscle a Fratto in Iowa, anyway. That's just against the rules."

Well, the Gypsies didn't play by the rules of any society besides their own. Since diplomacy didn't work, they showed up at my doorstep with a full contingent of their toughest street fighters. Luckily for me, my cousin Tony had been keeping an eye on my home and took precautions the moment he saw the Gypsy cars pull up. Tony grabbed the collar of his enormous Great Dane, Fonzee—which stood 6½ feet tall on its hind legs and weighed over 150 pounds—and led him through my backyard and into my house.

When I opened the door for the Gypsies, they were surprised to meet *at eye level* the vicious, snapping fangs of a Great Dane. Those Gypsies disappeared so fast you would think they had knocked up one of my daughters.

I had an entire clan of outlaw Gypsies on the ropes, and I knew the knockout blow was coming when I started to receive desperate, pleading phone calls at all hours.

"Listen, Mr. Fratto, we're trying to *help* you!"

"*Help* me, cocksucker?" I'd scream into the phone, doing my best unhinged Joey impression. "How would you go about helpin' a motherfucker like me that doesn't need your help? Eat shit and die, fuckface, and stop calling here, too!"

Finally, the Gypsies took the extraordinary step of approaching my lawyer, John Robert Sandre. You know you're a real motherfucker when you can drive a secretive band of outlaw nomads who have been on the run since medieval times to seek solace in the American judicial system.

John Sandre had a reputation in Iowa as the one man who could talk sense to me, the good angel on my shoulder—otherwise known as my Good Cop. It was said that I trusted him with my life due to his magical ability to keep me out of jail. The Gypsies counted on Sandre's ability to act as a good influence and arrange a settlement to our standoff.

What the Gypsies didn't count on was that John Robert Sandre really *was* that close to me...and, back then, I definitely didn't let *good* influences get that close to me. Do you think I was tight with the motherfucker because he persuaded me *not* to get my way? The whole point of a lawyer is to let you get your way without paying the consequences.

The Gypsies arrived in Sandre's office at 3 p.m. on a Tuesday and were escorted to a conference room where my attorney and I waited in matching black suits. We were the very picture of relaxed friendliness. By the looks on our faces, they should have immediately known they had walked into a setup.

In the center of the huge circus troupe of Gypsies that sat down all around us in the conference room was a short, thickset, tough-looking older gentleman whom I had never seen before. This rough character introduces himself as the uncle, the *real* owner of the Cadillac in question. He explained to Robert that his nephew Mike had gotten a fraudulent second title to the car and signed it over to me as collateral for a $3500 loan.

John Sandre nodded, smiled, and turned to me on cue. "So, Johnny, is that the way *you* recall it happening?"

"John," I said, adopting a grave tone and a frowning, reluctant face, "I really hate to be put in this position, but I must tell the truth. It is my duty to inform you... *that* is *not* the way it happened at all. The person who signed over the title of the car is *that* man, the one talking, the so-called 'uncle!'" I threw my accusatory index finger into the face of the old man, jabbing it all about his personal space.

To say the Gypsies were disquieted would be an understatement.

"What the fuck?!" the uncle screamed, bewildered and angry. "Motherfucker, I don't even *know* you! This is the first time in my life I've ever seen you!"

"Sorry, sir," I said, my face breaking into a real motherfucker of a giggly smile, "I don't know what's gotten into you, but I have to tell the truth. I gave you the money, and then *you* and *only you* signed over the title to the Cadillac. I'm sorry you're having remorse over you actions..."

"THE MOTHERFUCKER'S LYING!" one of the Gypsies started raving, "THE MOTHERFUCKER IS A MOTHERFUCKER WHO LIES!"

"NO!" I yelled right back while laughing hysterically like the Joker. "*That* motherfucker's lying! That motherfucker can't *help* but lie!"

As rehearsed, John Sandre threw up his hands in exasperation. "I think you're both lying! There's nothing I can do about this. It's he said/he said, and in those instances, you know what they say?"

The room fell silent. The Gypsies leaned in. The uncle wiped the spittle from his salt-and-pepper beard and blinked his bulging eyes. I could barely contain myself.

"In those instances where ownership is disputed," John Sandre, Esq., continued. "...*possession* is 9/10ths of the law... and my client has *possession* of the Cadillac!"

"And, guess what else, motherfuckers?" I yelled out, as defiant and wild-eyed as Jack Nicholson at his best, my voice coursing with vindictive evil. "For putting me through this bullshit, I ain't giving you the car back *ever*, no matter how much money you give me! How do you like *them* apples, fuckos?"

The meeting started at 3 p.m. It took *nine hours* for the screaming, threats, taunts, teases, recriminations, small talk, and finally friendly tall-tale-swapping to come to an end. With each hour, the two sides begrudgingly came more and more admire to the chutzpah, toughness, and persistence of the guys on the other side of the table.

At the stroke of midnight, the Gypsy uncle asked to use the conference room telephone to make a phone call to the "king" of his tribe, who resided among a related clan in Kansas City. The uncle explained the situation and asked the Gypsy king what he should do in the face of such an obstinate, insane enemy. The answer that came over Sandre's speaker phone system was greeted in the room like the announcement that we had won World War II: "Fuck it, just give the motherfucker the fucking car!"

Three days later, the Gypsy uncle threw a party in honor of John and me. It's one of that clan's unique cultural traditions: if an outsider out-scams a Gypsy, the defeated Gypsy is duty-bound to honor the white guy with a party at his home and induct him as an honorary member of the clan. We drank heavily, ate heartily, and danced with dark-eyed, dark-haired, dark-skinned Gypsy broads with shapely bodies they definitely knew how to move.

At the end of the night, the uncle told me that the clan had *nineteen* fake titles out on my Cadillac that they had been using to defraud civilians across the Midwest. Each young Gypsy would get a day with the Cadillac in rotation, driving it around for eighteen hours in the hope of snagging as many loans and handing out as many titles as possible. This scam had operated without a single failure for *years* . . . until they met Johnny Fratto.

I had unwittingly broken up one of the most durable and successful fraud rings in America. More importantly, I was the owner of the most criminalized vehicle on Earth, which made the act of driving it feel *very* cool.

Weeks after he helped defeat the Gypsies, Sandre managed to get me out of jail on my first ever arrest, a conspiracy to deliver cocaine charge handed down on Christmas Day, a couple days after I impregnated Barbara for the second time.

Needless to say, my official position is that I was completely innocent, as were my associates from those days who are still alive. I won't bore you with the details.

By the time Barbara went into labor with our second child, I had been temporarily put in state custody and was being held until trial. Even though the police called me a dangerous "organized crime figure," Sandre managed to play on the sympathy of a kindly old judge to spring me so that I could see the birth of my firstborn son.

People think I named my son John Robert Fratto after me, but I was *never* that dago. I named Lil' Johnny after the attorney that defeated the Gypsies, sprung me from jail, negotiated a plea deal for me of a suspended five-year sentence and at least four months in a half-way house, and *somehow* got the judge to discharge me completely after only eleven days of my sentence.

Once sprung, Sandre and my accomplices in the underworld told me to "lay low" from now on since I had a felony on my record. That offended me for some reason, so I decided to do the opposite to prove a point.

What exactly that point was, I don't know, but I sure as fucked proved it. I pimped out my Gypsy Cadillac. Using exclusively stolen merchandise, I installed around $25,000 worth of elaborate embellishments to the Caddy: pure golden side pipes, huge silver grille, gangsta white wall tires. Best of all, I took $10,000 worth of diamonds, crushed them, and blew them into the new Candy Brandywine paint job. My Caddy sparkled with a fine pixie dusting of diamonds.

That car became its own racket. I made major scratch loaning it out to parades, car shows, and even movies such as *Car Wash* and *Dr. Detroit*. Today, it lives in some Cadillac museum.

19

SHITTING DIAMONDS

"Confidential Informant Omaha T-7 advised on December 11, 1959 that he had heard rumors to the effect that FARRELL was bringing in out-of-town hoods to Des Moines for big safe jobs which FARRELL would finger and case and in which FARRELL would receive the largest share of the loot."

SPECIAL AGENT ROSSITER C. MULLANEY
Federal Bureau of Investigation
File OM 92-74

There are very few gentlemen gangsters left. A lot of people are sold on the idea that the Mafia's cash flow generally comes from classy suit-and-tie crimes like skimming casino profits, manipulating dirty labor unions, cutting under-the-table deals with corrupt politicians—the "Make him an offer he can't refuse" school of backroom power politics.

That's all bullshit.

Yeah, those tuxedo crimes exist at the highest levels of the Mob, but it makes up a tiny percentage of the real cash flow. In reality, for most of history, the Mafia's profits came from two things: street level gambling (and the loan-sharking that comes with it) and burglary.

Yes, I said burglary.

Besides gambling, the real bread and butter of the Mob is stealing: burglary, home invasion, armed robbery, container hijacking, stolen goods fencing. The Mob is all about what can be stolen and resold. It may not sound glamorous, but it can be incredibly profitable. There have been years when a guy *like* me (like *identical* to me) might make a few *million* dollars just by stealing.

Even my Dad was arrested for hijacking an armored car.

And like him, in my twenties and thirties, I too became known as an old hand at the art of stealing. I know it sounds like some petty hood shit, but I was living like a rock star during my burglary years. You'll soon find out why.

My first burglary was a surprise, even to myself. The inspiration came so quickly that I did not even have time to second-guess myself. I would have plenty of time to second-guess myself afterward while I wallowed in my own shit for days at a time.

I was in a jewelry store in Omaha, Nebraska. A pretty female jeweler was pouring out loads of loose diamonds onto a black velvet handkerchief, convinced that classy gentlemen such as us were likely bulk buyers. An associate pointed to a piece in a case behind the counter, and the jeweler turned away for a moment to identify it for him.

There was no premeditation. We really were there to *buy* jewelry. Then I got a flash of inspiration: while her attention was diverted, I slid my right hand along the surface of the glass case and tapped my index finger into the pile of diamonds. The moisture on my sweating hands causing a two-karat diamond to stick to the fingertip. I lifted the hand from the counter and scratched the corner of my lip, depositing the diamond in my mouth. I breathed deep . . . and I swallowed.

We walked out twenty minutes later undisturbed. I believe my family is still friendly with the family that owns the store.

When I returned to my hotel room that night, I was positive I had performed the easiest score of my career.

You know how they say diamonds are the hardest thing in all of nature? Well, they are right, at least when it comes to digestion.

The next morning—okay, afternoon—I rolled out of bed, poured my normal piping, pipe-cleansing mug of coffee, and headed to the bathroom with the morning paper. The newspaper wasn't for reading. It was for kennel lining.

I laid out the newspaper across the bathtub, hopped in, dropped my boxers, and popped a squat right over a front-page picture of a local police chief. A squint and a grunt later, a hefty helping of reincarnated pasta and sausage splatted onto the newsprint. I stood up, turned around, and bent over, expecting to see my special little jewel shining like a cherry atop a chocolate sundae.

There was no diamond visible. But how did I know what lay *inside*? I looked around the bathroom for a utensil to dismember my sample and found only a toothbrush, hair dryer, plunger, and cotton swabs. So I pulled up my boxers, slammed the bathroom door, and ran to the kitchen for a pair of dish gloves, praying that no one opened the door and discovered that Daddy had shit in the bathtub.

I returned to my brown treasure trove with a pair of thick dish gloves and, taking a deep breath, got down on my knees and started playing with my fecal matter like a kid looking for a penny hidden within a mound of Play-Doh. No diamond—and no self-respect left either. I thought of Dad having dinner with Harry Truman and Pope Pius and what he would think of his adult son rifling through his own shit like a kid looking for a prize in a box of Cocoa Pebbles cereal.

Finally, it was clear that my diamond wasn't in *this* load, so I needed to clean up. Unfortunately, I was no expert at the dissection of shit, and there was crap all over the tub, the newspaper, and the gloves.

Have you ever wondered if you can take off a pair of shit-covered gloves without drenching your free hand in shit when you remove the second glove? Well, let me tell you it's impossible.

With the second glove snapped off, a piece of Iowa corn flicked onto my stubble like they were both made of Velcro. I very carefully balled up the entire mess in a towel, but *that* towel got so shitty that I needed a second towel...and *that* towel got so shitty that it required a third. By the time I was finished, my family saw me go to the bathroom and emerge an hour later carrying a globe of balled-up towels the size of a planet outside to the garbage can. I gave them no explanation, and no explanation for why I had to throw away the garbage can, too.

The next day, I had a new plan. I noticed Lil' Johnny had a sandbox playset that included a small plastic sifter perfectly sized to fit under my asshole like a pail under a milking cow. I therefore went to the local toy store and bought ten sandbox sets, and then took a detour to the grocery to get some more kitchen gloves. Once again, my family received no explanation for why Lil' Johnny now had eleven sandbox sets, or why I kept ten pairs of kitchen gloves and ten plastic sand sifters in the bathroom.

I was a gangster, after all; I was allowed my secrets.

Over the next three days, I shit myself sore, but there was no diamond. By the time I was even running low on sifters and gloves, I figured something must have been desperately wrong with my digestive system. I called Mom and asked her how solve constipation. "Oh, Johnny, that's no problem. Just go to the store and get that laxative that comes in chocolate bars and then drink a lot of water."

No problem, the woman said! Ha. So, somehow the laxatives turned me from regular to actually constipated within minutes. After twenty-four hours bereft of bowel movements, I ignored the recommended serving size on the laxative chocolate bar and, instead of eating one tiny square, I ate all 25 remaining squares at once.

This had to work. I cancelled all my *many* appointments for the next two days and took up a position on the couch closest to the shitter.

Nothing—not even a little ketchup bottle squirt. Nothing.

I gave up on ever seeing that diamond again. On the third shitless day, I gave in to Barbara's nagging and took her out to the movies just to convince her that my increasingly eccentric, hermetic behavior was not a sign of drug abuse. After all, I couldn't tell her it *was* a side effect of drug abuse, namely laxative chocolates.

I ordered up a soda, a big bucket of butter-drenched popcorn, and took a seat on my tightly puckered asshole next to my wife in the theater. Finally, I could relax and be distracted from my diamond digestion dilemma.

Fifteen minutes into the movie, a hole was opened up in the wall of my anal dam. This was no time for niceties; my wife did not get so much as a "Be right back!" before I hopped out of my seat, jumped over the chair in front of me, and hobbled out of the theater with my hands squeezing shut my clenched asscheeks.

The maintenance man standing beside the theater's Men's Room was amused to see me stagger through the swinging door . . . and stagger right back out. I realized immediately upon entering the Men's Room that, if I shit there, I could have no hope of finding my diamond. Instead, I would have to drive *all the way home*, abandoning Barbara at the theater, to get to my specialized shit-sifting lab and equipment.

No car chase I had ever participated in during my time in the underworld was more suspenseful than my drive home from the movie theater, mumbling "*Please God, please God, please God, please God, no! No! NO!*" the entire way. I was the cartoon character plugging up the hole in the dam with a single finger as the cracks spread through the concrete. At any moment, I was going to flood my car.

Pulling up to my driveway, I was pantless and shoe-less by the time I reached the front door. I could waste no time. I felt like Moses weakening as he suspended the Red Sea in the air. At the very last possible second, I snatched the second-to-last plastic sifter from under the sink, covered my asshole, and leaned over the edge of the tub.

The cleanup crew at the Exxon Valdez spill had an easier time than me that night. What was left was an unholy toxic mess that contained everything produced by my body, naturally or unnaturally, everything *besides* the diamond. I was positive it was lost, lodged in an artery somewhere. I had no diamond, no dignity, and, by the time Barb figured out I left her at the movie theater, possibly no wife.

The next morning, I dejectedly drank my coffee and stumbled into the bathroom where so many horrors had occurred. I contemplated seating myself on my porcelain throne—though I felt like no king—but I decided I might as well use my last plastic sifter just to see this debacle through to the shitty end.

One easy squeeze later, and there was my diamond, perched on the tip of a long turd like Leonardo DiCaprio standing atop the bow of the *Titanic*. It was dazzling, sparkling, beautiful, visibly unstained and undamaged. No sifting was necessary, only a pair of tweezers.

Talk about a diamond in the rough!

This was the poo that dreams were made of.

It was like *The Maltese Falcon* if that movie were about a priceless bejeweled turd.

After all I had gone through to reach this moment, you may think I was happy to see that diamond. You'd be wrong. Never had I felt so ashamed and disgusted with myself as I did looking down at that little hunk of rock . . . and realizing what I had reduced myself to in the process of chasing it.

I felt like Lady Macbeth after I extracted my diamond. No matter what I did, nothing could get my hands and the diamond clean. I scrubbed the diamond furiously in the sink, soaked it in a glass of Windex for a day, even had it professionally cleaned and polished by a jeweler. You may think I would be quick to dispose of a diamond that had spent a considerable amount of time being incorporated into a shit sausage, but I was too ashamed to fence it. When I had it beautifully mounted on a ring, I could rarely bring myself to wear it.

After a few years, a restaurateur friend of mine asked if he could buy "that beautiful diamond ring I only see you wear every once in a while" for $5000. Morals were morals, but five Gs was five Gs. I sold it.

But, once again, my greed was its own punishment. It never occurred to me that my restaurateur friend would forever after *wear the turd-stone while cooking and serving my table's food.* That ruined one of my favorite restaurants for me.

Still, I wouldn't be who I am if my conscience and self-respect were things that could get in the way of me and a buck. I did the math and realized, if stealing *one* diamond gave me $5000, then my charitable organizations of choice would be in *great* shape if I could steal in bulk.

Besides, though I love diamonds, what I really loved was *watches* covered in diamonds.

I put out word through the Network that I was looking for anyone who moved high-quality, diamond-studded watches in bulk. I got a tip that there was a traveling Rolex salesman who picked up large parcels of watches from a store in Des Moines and drove them cross-country in a moderately priced sedan, making deliveries and sales along the way to a regular clientele of jewelry shops and big spenders.

This tubby, middle-aged Rolex salesman was practically the mascot for why stealing is the bread and butter of the American Mafia. Could you imagine an easier way to make a couple hundred thousand dollars? All I had to do was intercept an unarmed, unsuspecting, unprepared white civilian as he transported enormously valuable watches in an unlocked briefcase across hundreds of miles of empty highway.

On the day I knew the salesman was supposed to make his pickup in Des Moines, I rented a car at the airport and hired out two West Coast muscle guys, one of whom was dating a smoking hot stripper who would make a perfect decoy. I shadowed the Rolex salesman in my rental car as he left the jewelry shop and had the meatheads with the stripper shadow me in a big white van. After a few hours, he turned off at a Denny's for dinner; we kept going, took the next exit, and swung back around.

The stripper and I went into the Denny's to have a bite to eat and, naturally, she happened to bump into our mark as he got up to take a leak and started flirting. Before they were finished discussing each other's astrological signs, the salesman's car was already well on its way back to Des Moines.

Inside this salesman's trunk was a briefcase containing *thirty* Rolex Presidents, the watch of choice for cocaine dealers the world over. My cut was half, *fifteen* Rolex Presidents. What did I do with them?

Well, I sent them in unmarked boxes to the heroic firefighters of Des Moines, of course. I *definitely* didn't take them to Chicago, fence them with a reliable old friend who would modify them beyond recognition, and take home $100,000 for one's day's work.

But if I *had*, I would have been *really* encouraged to make heists my main sideline in the Midwest. I'd have been encouraged to think big, *real* big.

And if you're annoyed at me for not naming names, times, and places—get over it. Regardless of whether I'm alive or dead, plenty of my accomplices are still around, and Johnny Fratto isn't going down as a rat.

For example, let's say that I had an in at a major department store in the Midwest. For argument's sake, let's say I had a *number* of ins at department stores across America. Hypothetically, let me break down how I would have gone about breaking into a lovely department store in the Midwest back in those days.

I would have a relative, or a friend, or friend of a relative, or a relative of a friend who worked there. I would have that person precisely locate the most valuable jewelry display case and identify an easily accessible, lightly trafficked spot in the store where no security camera and motion sensors were present. I would then send a couple local teenage hoods to seek out that obscure corner of the department store and hide in the clothes racks ten minutes before closing time.

In this fictional scenario, I would be waiting in the parking lot in a rented Ford pickup truck, a Walkie Talkie on my lap and a police scanner on the passenger's seat. I would wait a couple hours until the surrounding streets were free of traffic and a major disturbance was distracting the police elsewhere in town. Then I'd yell "GO! NOW!" into my Walkie Talkie.

Though the motion sensor alarms would immediately start blaring, my two teenage hoods would run directly to the most valuable display case, crack it open, sweep the contents into a bag with one easy motion, and run out to the truck in less than 120 seconds. We'd be on the other side of town before the cops ever got around to arriving.

How much in unreported, untaxed illicit income would that night of work conceivably bring? Oh, I don't know... maybe around $200,000!

You could see why someone with an addictive personality like me would shy away from something like that. If I did it once, I'd probably do it over... and over... and over... and over again throughout the 1980s, across the United States. I would have probably been thought of *pretty highly* in Chicago if I managed to get away with such a profitable racket for so long.

As I entered my thirties, my identity crisis was a distant memory like my virginity and my Elizabeth Taylor blue contacts. With my swagger and my jewels and my easily won reputation, I couldn't conceive of *who* was a gangster if I wasn't one. Sure, I wasn't violent, but committing crimes seemed to be my calling, my destiny. Just like a panda can only eat bamboo, Johnny Fratto could only be a criminal. Unlike Dad, there was no conflict—nothing holding me back. There was nothing else in the world for me besides crime.

I was a vampire that was about to walk into the sunlight and realize that, all things being equal, I preferred a tan.

20

THE TURD MAN OF ALCATRAZ

In 1984, I turned thirty. My hair was now a well-burnished silver, sculpted into this monolithic 1980s pompadour the size of a Buick. Whatever I was doing, I was no longer an amateur at it, yet my surroundings seemed very smalltime. Though I was by now a real player in the Iowa underworld, that was a pretty tiny and uneventful fishbowl. I had gone about as far as I could. I was bored.

My home life sure as fuck didn't help the situation. The problem was simple: I was a selfish asshole married to a good woman who wouldn't give up on me. I loved Barb, but I also loved staying out late, answering to no one, and fucking every pretty girl I met. For whatever reason, it took Barb decades to realize I wasn't just immature; I was an incurable prick.

Being an asshole wasn't a phase I was going to grow out of—it was my calling.

Nonetheless, Barb argued with me, pled with me, nagged me, did all the things desperate, lonely wives do to try to reach their husbands. This made spending time at home incredibly unpleasant for a partied-out narcissist who just wanted to relax, not face his own faults.

Besides my catastrophic failures as a husband, I was also a pretty half-ass father. After the birth of my youngest daughter Alexis in 1982, I now had *three* kids who I saw exclusively way after their supposed bedtimes or way after mine the next morning. You can ask Lil' Johnny, and he'd tell you that most of his childhood memories of me involve sunrise sessions counting, banding, and stacking piles of cash. If Barbara couldn't take the kids to school in the morning, I'd groggily tell them "Good news! Sick day!" and go back to sleep.

I didn't make any excuses to myself. I knew I didn't have it in me to be anything but a disgrace as a family man. So I did what I generously termed "taking responsibility": I blamed myself for everything. I sought to canonize Barbara in the eyes of our kids and demonize myself in the hope that Angela, Johnny, and Alexis would seek to comfort their mom and, in turn, go to her when they needed comfort.

The family tree was sick, so I amputated and cauterized the doomed limb. In 1984, I left for Chicago. Technically, I never "moved"—I just spent the majority of my life away from home on "business trips."

The excuse my friends in Chicago used to relocate me was an editorial job at a new "high fashion" magazine named *Exeter* and later renamed *Metro*. Basically, a certain somebody dumped a comical amount of money in the lap of a local *Playboy* and *Penthouse* photographer in the hope that he would create Chicago's own *Harper's Bazaar*.

The shadowy figure in question gradually realized that betting an enormous amount of money on a photographer's ability to launch an upstart publishing venture was not a particularly safe investment. So, to increase his chances of recouping his money, he decided to implant a Fratto in the editorial offices to watch over expenses and ensure we exploited any available opportunity for a quick buck.

As the only person in the Midwest underworld with even a passing familiarity with modern fashion, I was the obvious candidate for the job. I could easily fit in at the offices of a couture magazine without looking out of place or drawing police attention. And, by bringing me into the fold full-time in Chicago, I could also bring all sorts of new income into the local crews through my nightly output of schemes, cons, and heists.

The editor job at *Exeter* was theoretically a no-show job. I was supposed to occasionally stop by the offices, but I wasn't actually supposed to *work* full-time. After all, I was a 30-year-old high school dropout with absolutely zero work experience anywhere and no discernible work ethic. It was inconceivable that a thrill-seeking party animal like me would ever dream of rolling up his sleeves and putting in long, high-pressure hours at the cramped offices of a magazine.

What neither my friends nor I counted on was the *women*. Though I realized I would be working at a fashion magazine, I didn't realize until my arrival that the magazines offices would be overflowing with—get this—models!

In my first week at *Exeter*, I saw everyone from Gia Garangi to Carol Alt to Joan Severance to a bubbly local teenager named Cindy Crawford. When these helpless creatures stepped into my office with their little portfolios clutched to their perky little chests, I thought of the travel-weary maidens who approached the castle of Dracula seeking respite and safe sleeping quarters.

I *never* left the offices during business hours. There was just about nowhere else on Earth I wanted to be! It was an almost magical place, an alternate dimension where famous designers gave you free clothes and the most beautiful women come from thousands of miles in every direction to grovel for your approval.

Since I found myself hanging around the offices all day long waiting for chicks and schwag, I began to amuse myself by doing busy work on the magazine. To my everlasting shock, I found myself not only enjoying, but *loving* the work. Here I was, a 30-year-old who had never held a job, suddenly discovering that fruitful employment could be fulfilling and fun! Imagine my surprise!

Before I arrived in Chicago, my only creative outlet had been my clothes, hair, and jewelry, and it makes sense that I spent an inordinate amount of time and money tweaking how I expressed myself through my appearance. I was an artist, and my canvas was me. All the while, I figured I was just a narcissist, never suspecting that I was also a creative guy in search of an artistic outlet.

I arrived at *Exeter* with the expectation that I would do absolutely no editorial work. Within a couple weeks, I was doing *all* the editorial work: concocting the premises for the bizarre couture editorial shoots, casting the models, touching up and captioning the photos, writing ad copy, drawing the cartoons, and interviewing the celebrities that passed through town. I was actually great at all of these jobs—besides celebrity interviewer, because shutting up didn't come easily to me.

Still, I managed to discover a couple future celebrities that, until my interviews with them were published, had toiled in unmitigated obscurity. Granted, the celebrities in question were Jeff Foxworthy and Tom Arnold, but whom have *you* discovered?

Exactly.

As the magazine's secret owner had expected, my job at *Exeter* did allow me to spot unforeseen opportunities for illicit profit. In the process of hunting a rich girl, I accidentally ended up following her to an art gallery. The price tags on the paintings were *most* intriguing. Who knew avant garde fingerpainted bullshit could fetch $10,000 or $20,000?

In other words, in addition to Fashion Magazine Editor, I now added Art Dealer to my growing resume. It wasn't too hard to find an obscure painter in Iowa who was positively ecstatic to get paid $500 to exactly replicate any painting I gave him. Today, if you visit the wealthiest and most powerful families in Chicago, you just might find the same one-of-a-kind masterpiece hanging in multiple homes.

The funny thing is that *this* sort of crime did not feel all that criminal. After all, I was no more a thief than the art dealers selling identical paintings for $20,000.

At the magazine, I experienced a sort of life—glamorous, sexy, creative, professionally fulfilling, and risk-free—that in every way trumped any potential life I could live in the Mob. Even if I became every bit the gangster Dad was in his heyday, I could read the newspapers in 1986 and see that *all five* of New York's godfathers were being prosecuted together in one case. It was hard to overlook the grisly reality that, without Dad to intercede on their behalf, family friends Sam Giancana, Jimmy Hoffa, Paul Castellano, Johnny Roselli, and Anthony Spilotro had all been slaughtered by our own people. Besides the immortal, untouchable Accardo and my uncannily lucky uncles Frank and Rudy, most of the Old Guard was dead or in jail.

I had spent my life wondering if I were a gangster. Ever since Frankie's death, it had seemed like a settled issue; after all, I made my living committing crimes. However, it only took a few months in the offices of *Exeter* for me to realize that, as good as a criminal as I was, I felt just as natural, comfortable, and entertained as a fashion editor. All things being equal, why would I choose to pursue the profession that came with the work hazard of being imprisoned or murdered if I could be a fashion editor instead?

There was only one good reason: the now-elderly Uncle Frank. Uncle Frank had no intention of letting me embarrass the family by being some sort of artsy fancy pants without a gangster cover. Always watching me far too closely for comfort, it did not take him long to show me what he thought of my newfound gigs as a Fashion Editor and Art Dealer.

I would get phone calls in the middle of the night at my apartment in Chicago. "Hello?" I'd ask, secretly terrified I was receiving "the call" that came only late at night and without warning, the call out to meet someone terrifying somewhere remote to do something unforgivable.

There would be a pause on the line. This pause was not for dramatic effect; Uncle Frank would just be so drunk that it would take a little longer than usual for data to be processed by his good ear and transported to his brain. "So, Mr. Pashion Plate," he'd finally start, the sound of his head bobbing and the liquids inside his skull sloshing around clearly audible over the line.

"Isn't it about time you just admit you like to suck cock? Ain't that right, you mudderpucker you? Puckin' Handsome Johnny, I knew all along you were a pag! Johnny Diamonds, a puckin' asshole if I ever saw one!"

"Well, good night to you, too, Uncle Frank."

Breaking into my family's criminal empire was easy. Escaping would be far harder. I thought I was making a jail break when I dropped out of school and embraced crime; little did I realize I was really checking myself into a Maximum Security Prison with Uncle Frank as warden.

I was now the Turd Man of Alcatraz.

LET ME TELL YOU A QUICK STORY...

ABOUT MORTY

One unavoidable side effect of living in Chicago was that, out of respect, I had to spend more time with Uncle Frank than I had since Frankie was alive. It would be wrong to say the man mellowed or sobered up with age.

Completely wrong.

Uncle Frank knew this bookmaker named Morty whom he did business with, but never completely trusted. Uncle Frank was the sort of guy who saw rats everywhere, all the time, and Morty had a sorta rat-like look to him by nature. Uncle Frank was always very careful about what he said and how much he drank in Morty's presence.

Anyway, one day Morty died, and his family entrusted Uncle Frank with the ashes on the promise that Uncle Frank would fulfill Morty's dying wish to have his remains scattered on Soldier Field, home of the Chicago Bears. The family knew that not just anyone could get away with dumping human remains on a major sports field, but that Uncle Frank had plenty of experience getting away with dumping dead bodies anywhere and everywhere.

The problem was that Uncle Frank was a busy guy—what with his drinking and all—and it took him a long time to get around to visiting Soldier Field. In the meantime, Morty's urn chilled in the front seat of Uncle Frank's car. Whenever you drove with Uncle Frank during this time period, the old man would give you the stink eye if you began to talk about underworld business.

Just like he did in life, he'd point silently to the urn to say *Not in front of Morty! He's not trustworthy!*

Only he wasn't joking. We had to sit in perfect silence. We couldn't even look at the urn. I was relieved when Morty was finally dumped in his chosen resting spot.

Not even when my best friend Mike Tenini hallucinated that we were being tailed by an evil midget have I ever experienced more awkward car rides—and yes, that story is coming later.

I would never tease when it comes to evil midgets.

21

TOM CRUISE

I drop names like my dad's buddy Harry Truman dropped bombs. I'm strictly A-list—and the A stands for atomic. I've left entire blocks of prime Beverly Hills real estate radioactive with envy in my wake.

I don't fuck around.

As I said in the last chapter, I'm not a tease. Let me demonstrate. Get a load of this Hiroshima and Nagasaki 1-2 punch:

Whenever I think of my time with Tom Cruise, I recall what my longtime friend Oprah Winfrey once said: "If you come to fame not understanding who you are, it will define who you are."

You couldn't have summed up the Tom Cruise I met in 1985 any better. The poor kid's identity was *fame*—it was practically the name on his birth certificate. That's how green and impressionable he was. Hot on the heels of *The Outsiders* and *Risky Business*, Tom Cruise came to Chicago as Hollywood's newest fad. Tom was only 23, but, in person, he looked and sounded like a teenager. He was not an imposing presence at all—as a good-looking young guy of modest stature myself, I could tell which one of my people were predators and which were prey.

The poor kid was definitely still *prey*, and unfortunately he had been cast as a world-class predator: director Martin Scorcese had picked Cruise to play a slick pool shark and conman for his next film, *The Color of Money.*

That's the reason a local casting director wanted to introduce him to me. Cruise had let him know he was worried that he couldn't credibly pull off the role of a barroom hustler. He was humble enough to ask for expert advice. The casting director, knowing my reputation, introduced him to me at Faces, a popular dance club on Rush Street, which I made my home away from the office.

Due to my upbringing, I'm not a guy who gets starstruck, so my only response to meeting this small, too young actor was a brotherly pity for how much pressure he was under. I was in my thirties and still found it impossible to handle responsibility, yet this kid had a multimillion-dollar Scorcese film resting on his narrow shoulders!

For whatever reason, Cruise took a liking to me. Perhaps he dug my personality, or maybe he got off on my real-life stories of hustling in the underworld that made his script look dry and uninspired by comparison. Whatever the reason, he invited me to spend the day at the set with him.

The moment I stepped on location the next morning, I could see Martin Scorcese scoping me out. He called over one of his assistants and whispered something in her ear. A minute later, the PA was tapping me on the shoulder. "The director would like to know if you'd like to stand in as one of pool sharks in this scene?"

I guess there was no substitute for the real thing, especially since I had moved on from my snakeskin and leather wardrobe and graduated to a closet full of the immaculate Italian silk suits that would have made my father proud. There was no one on that set who looked more like a hustler and carried himself more believably as a hustler than me. Even a square like Scorcese could see *that*.

You can imagine my excitement when I heard Martin Scorcese wanted me in one of his movies, and you can also imagine my disappointment when I realized Uncle Frank would murder me if he found out I had risked "heating up the family" by accepting a role as a criminal in a major motion picture. I could also picture my Chicago cousins calling me "Johnny Goes To Hollywood" as a pun on that gay '80s band Frankie Goes To Hollywood, and that didn't appeal to me either. I reluctantly declined Scorcese's generous offer.

Once filming had wrapped for the day, Cruise promised to meet me at Faces later that night. While I was waiting for my new buddy on one of the couches, two smoking hot party girls from Des Moines came over to say hello.

"Hey Johnny, what are you up to?"

"Waiting for my buddy Tom Cruise to show up."

"*S-u-u-ure*, Johnny," the one girl said, incredulous. "We believe *that*."

"Do you think we were born yesterday?" squawked the other crow.

"Okay, fine, fine," I said, smiling and laughing to myself since I could already see Tom slowly making his way through the crowd. "Why don't you two ladies take a seat and hang for a moment?"

Right as the two Des Moines chicks settled down onto the couch across from me, Tom Cruise threw his arms around their shoulders and stuck his head between theirs. "What's going on, ladies?" he asked with that mischievous superstar smile that made that fucker *billions* of dollars.

It wasn't hard to see why: in all my years of being gorgeous, I had never seen women actually swoon in real life. Once they realized Tom Cruise had *his* arms around *their* shoulders, these bitches *swooned*.

Which brings me to something I've been meaning to say for a long time: despite whatever rumors you've heard, I can vouch from firsthand experience that Tom Cruise is not a homosexual. No, I didn't hit on him, but I did party with him and watch him go on an unstoppable tear through the female populace of Chicago during the filming of that movie. I saw him go to town in the back of limousines, in club bathrooms, and across hotel hallway carpets. If there was anything gay about Tom Cruise, I sure as fuck didn't see it, and neither did the Doubting Thomas girl from Des Moines whom he picked up from the couch at Faces and took back to his hotel room that night.

The next night at the club, I saw the same girl back at Faces, glowing like a saint. "So, how was it?" I asked her.

"What do you mean?"

"How was . . . *Tom?*"

"What do you mean? Nothing happened!" she insisted, none too believably.

"What? You're trying to tell me that *you*, the girl who fucked *everyone* I know in Des Moines, drew the line at fucking Tom Cruise? Is that *really* what you want me to believe?"

"Okay! Okay! And it was great!"

That night, Tom introduced me to a square cousin of his who was visiting from out of town. Now, the only reason I remember that is because, after introducing his cousin, Tom leaned up close to me and whispered the strangest thing I've ever heard into my ear.

"Listen, Johnny," Tom said, "you gotta help me here. This cousin of mine, he doesn't have any luck with girls. You gotta help me get him *some slickum on his hangdown.*"

Whatever the fuck that means. I took a guess and got the cousin laid. I think that's what Tom wanted, because from that point on, he was obsessed with the idea of taking me back to Hollywood and making me a star.

"Listen to me, Johnny," Tom said with that intense tunnel vision stare he always has in the movies when he's focused on something. Turns out it isn't acting; that's what he really looks like when he's concentrating. "I know movies, and your life would make an incredible movie. The story of your childhood with your Dad, growing up surrounded by gangsters, trying to find your identity amongst all these sociopaths and weirdos . . . I'm tellin' you, man, it's *great!* It's a one-of-a-kind coming-of-age story! You have to let me introduce you to my manager. She'll set it all up."

Tom Cruise wasn't a Jew, but he might as well have been my Moses. For a vain narcissist with delusions of grandeur and a religious devotion to tan California blondes with big titties, Tom Cruise's offers of Hollywood stardom sure sounded like the Land of Milk and Honey. In that way, I was more in the Cherry Nose *90210* state of mind than the Lou Fratto *Green Acres* state of mind.

I had come to Chicago nursing secret dreams of fulfilling Frankie's destiny of rising to the top of the Outfit, but now I had a new dream, an even *more unlikely* dream: adapting my childhood into a major motion picture.

I even had a great title—*Son of a Gun!*

Thinking a meeting couldn't hurt anything, I let Tom put me in a room with his management team. What would be the harm if I gave myself the challenge of making a film pitch to a group of hardened, cynical Hollywood professionals? Despite fifteen years of experience as a street-level conman, certainly there was no way I could win over an entire room of L.A. hardcases without having any experience or knowledge of how the movie industry worked. I would probably be better off having my delusional, preposterous Hollywood fantasies dispelled in one short, brutal meeting.

Call it beginner's luck, but the entire room was sold on *Son of Gun* within fifteen minutes. Tom couldn't wait to play superstar high school athlete Frankie. I had sold my first major motion picture without trying. I was going to be rich, famous, a Hollywood player . . .

That is, if Uncle Frank gave me permission. Hey, if I could pitch a room full of disingenuous Hollywood sharks, how hard could it be to win over my own uncle on a movie glorifying the big brother he idolized? I even went through the trouble of tracking down Uncle Frank just early enough in the morning to catch his thirty minutes or so of sobriety for the day.

All *that* ended up meaning is he said "Fuck you!" instead of "Puck you!"

If the revelation that I was a fashion magazine editor and art dealer convinced him that I was a closeted homosexual, the news that I was aspiring Hollywood producer partnered with Tom Cruise confirmed for him that I was the gayest man in the world.

"Listen up, you fuckin' lunatic," Uncle Frank told me after I got about fifteen seconds into my pitch, "If I ever hear anything about you putting our family name up on a fuckin' movie screen...If I so much as hear one *peep* about you tarnishing Lou's name...If you even so much as *think* about trying to disgrace the Fratto family's reputation by opening your motherfucking mouth about family business..."

"Well guess what, you smiling motherfucker? You'll be going for a little ride in my trunk, and I won't be fucking sneaking you into a drive-in movie..."

"Those don't exist anymore, Uncle Frank..."

"You hear me, Liberace? You better go back to trying on high heels for your fuckin' fashion magazine, you dicksucker, or you'll be one dead motherfucker."

I had to say no to Tom Cruise. Though there were no hard feelings, after *The Color of Money* left Chicago, so did he. He went on to become the biggest star on planet Earth, just like my old *A.M. Chicago* buddy Oprah went on to become the most powerful woman in the Universe. I watched as they got bigger and bigger, and I got smaller and smaller.

After a few years of treading water in Chicago, unable to commit to a life in the creative arts and unwilling to fully pursue a life of crime, I returned to Iowa. In Des Moines, I was only the third biggest star in my own family, far behind local institution Tommy Farrell and my little brother, Willie, who had become a major touring standup comedian.

I tried to tell my brother that his act would go over better under the name Will Fratto, but he disagreed. "Will Farrell" would be the brand name that brought him to stardom, he insisted. Turns out, "Will Ferrell" would be the name a California comedian born John Ferrell would utilize as he achieved *Saturday Night Live* and movie stardom. Willie should've listened to his big brother!

For the time being, however, the joke was on me. I no longer dreamed of Outfit glory, of living up to my Dad's legacy. All I wanted was the one thing I couldn't have.

I wanted to live the life that Dad's predecessor in Iowa, Charles "Cherry Nose" Gioe, had never managed to pull off: moving to Beverly Hills and conquering Hollywood.

The only reason I didn't follow my dream is that I remembered what happened to Cherry Nose when *his* Beverly Hills excursion went wrong: Uncle Frank shot him to death.

22
THE RAT

Dejected and feeling hopeless, I returned home to Iowa like a kid who flunks out of college and moves back in with Mom & Dad. For me, the role of Dad was played by my big brother, Tommy, whose ego and influence had grown greatly since my departure from The Extra Point.

Unlike me, Tommy would rather be a huge Fratto fish in a tiny pond than a little guppy in Chicago, or a microscopic amoeba in Los Angeles. When I returned fulltime to Iowa by the early 1990s, Tommy graciously shared his fishbowl with me and helped me get started in the local club business. Tommy had been the innovator and dominating influence on Des Moines nightlife for nearly twenty years at that point through his various clubs and lounges around town. For the moment, he was willing to share the crown of Des Moines' nightlife king with his moody little brother.

Together, Tommy and I made a great team as nightlife hosts: great looks, great clothes, and great party stamina. We were the lords of darkness, the baddest brothers in the state of Iowa. Des Moines may not have been known for its mean streets, but that didn't stop us from taking pride in being the biggest fuck-off dogs on our suburban block.

The funny thing about Tommy is no one told him you're supposed to be a lover or a fighter. Tommy's an all-purpose threat like Uncle Frank. This fucking guy loves picking fights over bullshit and loves getting married; that's his bread and butter. He was already getting up there in years and was always a small man, but to this day Tommy will fuck anyone up, regardless of size. He doesn't care if he's five foot tall; he walks around in flip flops or flat sneakers, carrying himself like a giant. You'd think getting punched in the face felt good to this guy.

Tommy's other quirk is that he has the magic touch when it comes to women. I could never get away with the shit he pulls. His ex-wives and countless children and grandchildren will get together and throw huge parties in his honor where he's sitting at the head of the table and bathing in love like Jesus at the Last Supper. The sixty-year-old ex-wife will be chatting around the chips and dip with the forty-year-old ex-wife and Tommy's freshly pregnant twenty-year-old girlfriend, all falling over each other to be the first to say what a great guy Tommy is.

So, when we were business partners in nightclubs, we were always looking for cash to replace the money Tommy had just flushed down the divorce toilet.

In this instance, that meant that our 1950s-themed bar Jukebox Saturday Night was going to be open *far* later than the mandatory 2 a.m. closing time legislated by the Iowa state government. The government had *its* business, and we had *ours*. We just locked the front doors and kept the party going.

You should have seen us in '88, looking like the hosts of a retro '80s night party at a 1950s nostalgia bar. The thing was, at the time, we just thought we were *cool*. We would stand around at Jukebox Saturday Night in our gigantic man-poodle hairdos and *Miami Vice* Armani pastel sports coats with the rolled up sleeves thinking, *Shit, all these 1950s styles were corny as hell*!

Man, that club really was off the chain. I think Quentin Tarantino stole the idea for Jack Rabbit Slims in *Pulp Fiction* from Jukebox Saturday Night. Jukebox got its name from the gigantic 30-foot-tall jukebox up front, and we completed the ambience with a 1957 Chevy convertible as a DJ booth and a roster of pretty waitresses in poodle skirts and pony tails.

That night, Tommy and I were making obscene money and thinking obscene thoughts in the illegal after-hours shift. After all, my brother was a bachelor once again—however briefly—and I was married and didn't give a shit! That meant we needed to celebrate. That's what we called a "bachelor party" in the Fratto family: the short breaks between my brother's marriages.

But then the party came to a premature—very premature—end. Our grim, bloody responsibilities intervened. I was no longer in Chicago, but that didn't mean I was a free man.

Marcia, our beautiful Spanish waitress, sashayed over to Tommy with the bar phone. "Hello," Tommy said, sounding very businesslike for a drunk man fielding a call at 3:30 a.m. in a raucous club. Whatever he was hearing sobered Tommy up right quick; the smile on his face evaporated, his head slumped down, and I could see his jaw lock. "He's there now?" Tommy asked solemnly. "Okay...okay. We will be right there."

That "we" in "we will be right there" just about made me want to kick him in the fucking balls. What was Tommy committing me to?

I loved my life and my freedom too much to entrust it to a snap decision made by Tommy after a two minute phone call at 3:30 a.m. There was nothing like sudden phone calls in the middle of the night to make me hate The Life—I've seen many lives ruined by phone calls like the one Tommy had apparently taken. Those rash phone calls that came in the thick of the night were the fuckers that tore apart families and destroyed a man's soul.

"Tom, what the fuck's wrong!?"

"Come on. We gotta go take a ride," said Tommy, avoiding eye contact.

"Oh no no no," I said, panicking. This was not how my wonderful night was supposed to end. "A ride *where*?"

"By my house. We need to take a ride by *my* house. That fucking rat is there again."

"Tom, seriously, don't be hasty," I said in my most persuasive shitting-my-pants tone. "There are professionals who do this, no problem at all. We have friends, *our* friends, who do this. You just pay them!"

"NO!" Tommy barked, his eyes on fire. "Men do their own work. Frattos do their own work." Sometimes, I wonder what fucking family tree this gorilla crawled out of, but I'd never say that to Tommy's face.

As we were driving out to the suburbs in Tommy's bright red XJS Jaguar with the windows down and Steve Winwood's "Higher Love" pumping from the stereo system, my older brother spoke to me out of the corner of his mouth. "Johnny, get the gun out of the money bag. I'm going to fix this fuckin' problem once and for all."

I rolled my eyes, wiped the sweat off my forehead, and checked my watch to see if it was still *19-fucking-88* and I wasn't hallucinating that we were actually going to the mattresses like it was 1929. For a moment, I wished it all away, leaned back in my seat and let the breeze blow on my face.

Des Moines can be such a beautiful city for a moonlit drive . . . the breeze is so nice on late nights like this . . . so nice and relaxing . . .

"IS IT FUCKING LOADED?!" Tommy shouted, yanking me out of the rabbit hole and reminding me how shitty my reality was in comparison at the moment.

"Yes, it's loaded," I said as I clicked the clip on the little 25-automatic pistol back into place.

Tommy parked the car around the corner from his house, but he was in no hurry to get out. He exhaled hard, looked off at nothing for a few seconds, licked his lips—and then turned to me with a hard stare and nodded. It was the sort of stare that was hard, by design, since Tommy's brain sent a message to his eyes that said, "Try to look really hard right now so Johnny can't tell you're nervous!"

We quietly slipped out of the car and crept up to Tommy's porch. Since he was concentrating so intently on being silent, my brother did not pay attention to where he was stepping and loudly tripped over a baseball bat lying in his yard.

Hopping back upright, Tommy handed me the bat like he had meant to pick it up with his feet. "Just in case!"

"Gee, thanks, Tommy," I said as I tested the grip on the bat. "If you needed someone to bat clean-up, don't ya think you should have called Willie?"

Tommy shushed me. He led with the drawn gun, and I took up the rear with the bat. We slowly tiptoed towards the porch.

"Can you see him?" I asked. Tom nodded and gestured to the porch. Tom aimed the 25, and his biceps tensed, ready to fire. At just this moment, Tommy's young son Louie popped up in the window like a jack-in-the-box.

"STOP!" I squeaked to Tom. "Louie's in the fuckin' window!"

Tom flailed his hand and gave Louie his best bug-eyed, flushed cheeks "GET THE FUCK TO YOUR ROOM!" look. Louie ran away like he had seen Freddie Krueger. Once he was gone, Tommy lifted the gun again.

"Okay," Tommy said, his hand shaking, "on the count of three!" With a finger in the hair, he counted up 1-2-3. On three, I brandished that bat over my head and clenched my asscheeks tight. Tommy was buzzing like an epileptic, his knees knocking. He screamed "YOU MOTHERFUCKER!" and I saw his forearms tense.

But there was no gunshot.

"Tommy, just shoot him! Just get it over with!"

"I...I...I can't."

"Why?" I asked in disbelief. Tommy was hardly an "I can't" sort of guy. He was a shoot-now-and-don't-even-bother-thinking-about-it later sort of Fratto. He was Uncle Frank compared to me.

"I can't... cause he looks old. He looks *old.*"

I'd had enough of this shit. I'm no cold-blooded killer, but I'm not going to get caught with my pants down suffering from performance anxiety. I grabbed the gun out of Tommy's hand, aimed, and squeezed the trigger. As the hammer fell, Tommy lunged and yanked the gun up above my head so that it fired into the air.

BOOM!

"TOMMY! You fucking maniac! What the fuck are you doing—trying to get yourself shot?"

"Look at him!" Tommy hissed through gritted teeth, his right index finger outstretched. "I think he had a heart attack!"

Our target was keeled over on his side, lifeless and drooling with his eyes open. "Let's pick him up," Tommy said, sounding cold and resolute, "and put him in the woods."

"I'm not touching that dirty motherfucker!" I said, still getting over the shock of being unexpectedly manhandled as I fired a gun.

The house lights flashed on, and Tommy's newly divorced wife Lori was standing in the doorway looking at us with the bat and the gun.

As usual, I was the only brother with the balls to talk.

"Hi Lori," I said sheepishly. Tommy didn't say a thing; he knew Lori and what she was capable of. He knew that we were beyond saving.

"WHAT ARE YOU TWO STUPID MOTHERFUCKERS DOING OUT HERE MAKING ALL THAT NOISE, AND WHY IS THERE A DEAD OPOSSUM ON MY PORCH?!"

Now, you might be thinking that it is little excessive for me to tell my writer Randazzo to hold down his trusty Caps Lock for so many words, but, trust me, the rage in this woman's voice could never be communicated in mere lowercase letters.

"Well," Tommy said in a tiny, meek, begging voice. "Louie called and said he saw that opossum through the window, and he was scared of it. So...I thought...I would come in and handle it." Tommy gestured at the gigantic rat that was upturned on its back like a turtle. "I mean, c'mon Lori, these opossums carry disease and..."

"LISTEN UP, YOU SHITHEAD!" Lori screamed, "IT'S 4:30 IN THE FUCKING MORNING! THE KIDS ARE SLEEPING, AND YOU ARE SHOOTING A PISTOL LIKE A FUCKING IDIOT IN THE MIDDLE OF A NICE NEIGHBHORHOOD! GET THAT MOTHERFUCKING THING OFF MY PORCH AND GO FUCK YOURSELF!"

I took a deep breath. For once, I had avoided the business end of an angry spouse...

"YOU TOO, JOHNNY!" Lori grabbed a broom that was inside the doorway and launched it at me like God tossing a thunderbolt. The broom handle clunked off the top of my forehead, staggering me backwards until I almost stepped on the dead opossum.

"Now…GET IT OUT OF HERE AND BE QUIET YOU FUCKING IDIOTS!" The door slammed. Tommy and I both exhaled.

As we were slowly sweeping this heavy woodland rat down the driveway, Tommy looked to me and whined, "Boy, you try to do something nice…I mean, Lord knows what diseases this thing has…"

"Tommy," I said, "the reality is she likes that rat better than she likes the two of us! You know it's a sad day when the mother of a Fratto prefers a rat to another Fratto."

Once the carcass was rolled down to the side of the road where we meant to leave him, Tommy cast down his eyes and shook his head. "Poor old guy…just got too old for the game…Fuckin' rat."

The sun was coming up as Tommy's Jaguar did a U-turn in the street and began to drive away. Before we got more than a few feet, that motherfucking opossum hopped up from its death crouch and ran in front of the car. Tommy, who only moments before was trying to shoot this fucking thing, slammed on the brakes to avoid running over it. The opossum frolicked off into the woods, as good as new. Apparently, he wasn't such a poor old guy after all!

I shot Tommy a disgusted look. "What the fuck type of *man* are you supposed to be here, Tommy? We come over here to kill that fucking rat, and you get a chance to run over him, and you hit the brakes? You wasted my whole night, asshole!"

Seeing that Tommy was bummed out, I relented. I had a conscience just like my older brother. I hated seeing the poor old guy so helpless. Tommy was like a bite-size Atlas with that big broken ego to shoulder.

"Don't worry, he'll be back, then we'll get him…" I mumbled, but the poor guy's spirit was broken. Between his ex-wife's ridicule and his shameful inability to pull the trigger when the pressure was on, this was not Tommy's night. Our father hung with Al Capone and Tony Accardo, and here Tommy couldn't kill an elderly opossum!

"You know, Tommy, in all fairness, this isn't a total waste. At least, now I know where the phrase 'playing opossum' comes from. That fucker had it down to a T!"

When we got back to Jukebox Saturday Night, all of our employees were milling about pissed off at the delay in getting their nightly cut from the till. Standing in the front of the line of employees was Eb. Eb was this gigantic football-playing hillbilly we called Eb because, well, his goofball parents actually named him Eb after a character on *Green Acres*. That made sense—everyone on the show besides Zsa Zsa was an incurable hayseed just like him.

"Well, where is it?" Eb asked as we walked in the door.

"Your money's coming..."

"No, no, not my money, the opossum!" Tommy and I both stopped mid-stride, looking at this giant like he had just asked whether we wear boxers or briefs. "What?" the nervous redneck asked. "What's the big deal? They make for some real good eatin'. My mom knows how to boil 'em till the meat falls of the bone."

This at least solved one mystery for us: how did a huge, barrel-chested sasquatch like this fucking moron stay so well-fed on the minimum wage salary we paid him? Well, apparently his family was eating whatever they could find in the woods. These people had no fucking overhead!

"Listen, you freak," I said, completely fed up with life in Iowa after my sojourn in the big city. "Next time we go to breakfast, I'm just goin' to drive you to Interstate 80 and let you get out and pick up a bite to eat, you hillbilly fucker! And, shit, the thought keeps hittin' me that I don't belong anywhere near anyone who fucking eats rats for dinner. Tommy, you close up... I need to get the fuck out of here!"

I went home that night and watched *The Color of Money* on HBO. I pictured myself in the roles of the various pool sharks, imagined how great my hair would look billowing across the upper reaches of my big screen TV.

Instead, I was hanging around Iowa botching hits on opossums and trading witticisms with motherfuckers named Eb.

Whatever patience I had left for the Midwest underworld was disappearing. Most Frattos are depressed because their last name made it harder for them to get away with committing crimes. I think I was the only Fratto in history to ever be outraged at my last name for keeping me from becoming an artist!

THE PIZZA SPEAKEASY

The best pizza in America was made by this Des Moines goofball nicknamed Bammie Jr. When the I.R.S. seized the legendary family pizzeria founded by Bammie Sr., Bammie Jr. appeared to cope by crawling inside a big fuck-off bag of cocaine.

Allegedly, of course.

Since such hypothetical hobbies are not cheap, Bammie needed money. He decided to reopen the family pizza business in his nice home in suburban Des Moines. Bammie's home wasn't zoned for business, so everything had to be done on the down low to save Bammie from further government harassment. The poor guy's home basically became an illegal pizza speakeasy.

When you combined his sudden outlaw status with Bammie's belief that the I.R.S. was going to send black helicopters out to seize his pepperonis, this made for one paranoid, uncomfortable environment for ordering pizzas. It was practically espionage to get a large pie with extra cheese.

You heard of the Soup Nazi from *Seinfeld*? Well, this guy was the Pizza Nazi of Iowa. If you didn't follow his insanely detailed protocol for ordering a pizza, no pizza for you!

To order a pizza from Bammie Jr., first you had to know him well enough to be trusted with his unlisted private number. If you weren't already tight with Bammie? You were fucked.

If you *did* have the special number that went straight to an answering machine, the next step was to slowly place an order for pickup at a precise time *two days in the future*. Let me repeat that: you needed to give this mad pizza scientist *48 fucking hours* to conduct counter-surveillance, perform the necessary background checks, and come to terms with making your pizza.

Even if you gave Bammie a full two days heads-up, he would only accept orders within a narrow dinnertime window. If you wanted a pizza late at night or on less than two days notice, then no pizza for you! The worst part was, you only found out you were out of luck when you showed up and saw your pizza wasn't there.

Picking up the pizza was also an ordeal. If you were two minutes early or two minutes late, or if you shut off your car's ignition when you parked outside of his house, your pizza went right in the trash, and all future orders would be ignored. If I said I would be there at 7:13 p.m., I would be sitting in my idling car outside Bammie's house at 7:00, sweating as my Rolex counted down the seconds and my car's battery and gas tank emptied.

At the appointed time, Bammie's customers had to skulk through the darkness, sneak behind Bammie's house to the backyard, *quietly* open up the sliding glass doors, and enter the home's back entrance. Once there, you'd find yourself in eerily empty room with nothing but a counter covered with boxes of pizza. After scanning the boxes for the order with your name on it, you'd put the *exact* amount of money you owed on the counter and very slowly, very cautiously, very silently extract yourself from the home.

At no point did you see Bammie during this transaction—but you could *feel* his eyes watching you. You felt like a cat burglar. The weirdest experience was when you ran into another customer at the deserted home like two pathetic junkies scoring from their dealer at the same time. You both felt *ashamed* for ordering that damn pie and humoring a fucking dingbat like Bammie.

But we had no choice! We needed that pizza pipeline to stay open!

23

DEATH OR DISHONOR

They say there is only two ways out of the Mafia: death or dishonor. As I entered my forties, I did my best to shoot for both.

For the same reasons that I loved my job at *Exeter/Metro*—easy access to hot young poontang and ample opportunities for creative expression—I embraced the job of being a club owner. You couldn't find a better club owner in the Midwest, but that had little to do with busting heads and *everything* to do with my taste as a musical scout, booker, interior decorator, culinary director, and live event promoter.

For example, my signature creation, The CroBar, was about as far from a stereotypical wiseguy social club or Brooklyn guido disco as can be imagined. The CroBar was like *The Dance Club of Dr. Caligari*—an abandoned railroad station in Des Moines' empty warehouse district that I transformed into a demented underworld nightclub for freaks, gangstas, and vampires.

And I literally mean vampires.

The CroBar was a department store of sin with different evils serviced on each of the building's three stories. On the top floor was a techno and hip-hop club full of ecstasy dealers and wannabe gangbangers. In the middle was a ritzy acid-rock bar and restaurant catering to hipsters, yuppie druggies, and burnt out old hippies. On the bottom floor was a gothic club for vampires, real or imaginary. All those kids playing dress-up with their pancake makeup and fake fangs would look at a tan, smiling, Robin Leach-looking guy like me and never suspect that I was actually the real thing.

The CroBar got special real late at night, when all of the different scene kids got so fucked up that they started to roam around and cross-pollinate. It was a summit of freaks, outcasts, and degenerates of all different stripes. The

CroBar was a special place, an irreplaceable little corner of Hell, and I was its Mephistopheles. You can imagine the look on Uncle Frank's face when he visited and found me surrounded by a flock of goth kids dressed up like Bela Lugosi who were chewing on stuntman blood capsules.

In the early-to-mid 1990s, The CroBar was Iowa's nightlife hotspot, the cutting edge club that allowed Iowa kids to claim a little shred of big city cool. I helped make Iowa hip and revive the dormant warehouse district. I can't tell you how many bands I helped to discover by giving them regular spots at The CroBar, unsigned multi-platinum superstars-to-be like Green Day, Blues Traveler, and Iowa's own Slipknot who I let slip through my fingers.

My sense that I was missing out on my artistic destiny was greatly exacerbated when I would start seeing those familiar faces on MTV...while I was still stewing in Des Moines as Tommy's second banana. While Tom Cruise was flossing with Nicole Kidman's panties, I was fighting with Barbara constantly and looking forward to the few moments of peace I got to spend with my kids during visits with Aunt Carmie or the still brokenhearted Grandma Carmella.

I was depressed, stuck in what appeared to be an unending malaise. Luckily, my fortieth birthday provided an excuse to break this malaise with a desperate psychopathic breakdown. It would normally be called a mid-life crisis, but that sounds like a pretty limp term for something that convinced me to embark on an armed robbery...without being armed.

I had absolutely no good reason to rob that jewelry store. I mean, I had something like 100,000 good reasons to have someone *else* break into that jewelry store and rob it, but it went against everything I was taught to risk my own good name and freedom by personally including myself in the break-in team.

Even though I had been out of the heist game for a while, I did not hesitate to act on a tip given to me that a small, family-owned jewelry store with an abnormally valuable inventory had let their security systems lapse. Within minutes, I had assembled a team of two muscle guys and an experienced getaway driver. Since the people behind the counter were roughly 70 years old, two screaming thugs in ski masks would have been sufficient force.

So why in the name of everything holy did I throw on black pants, black shoes, and a black ski mask? Why did I wait until closing time before kicking open that fingerprint-smudged glass door with the little bell on the handle and pointing my right index finger in my pocket at the old couple behind the counter? Why did a successful 40-year-old businessman risk everything in his world for no good reason?

The answer is simple: I was bored, depressed, and suffering from rapidly declining testosterone levels. I didn't feel like the man that Lou, Frankie, and Uncle Frank raised me to be. Even Tommy and Willie were two guys you never wanted to trade punches with. Meanwhile, I was starting to feel more like the sort of guy who would more likely throw a slap than a haymaker. My self-prescribed remedy was an armed robbery.

In the getaway car, while all of my young accomplices were cracking jokes and laughing and giddily enjoying the adrenaline high, I was a sweating, blanching, panting, googly-eyed mess. I couldn't talk, couldn't even keep my head upright. I sank my head between my knees and tried not to puke.

My heart skipped a beat. Skipped two. Jesus fucking Christ, skipped three... then did a drum-roll of three or four beats in a second. *Holy shit, I'm dying.* I grabbed my chest like Redd Foxx and called for Barbara... only I didn't have the voice to be heard. All the whippersnappers in the car were too high from the robbery to even notice my distress. I was positive I was going to die.

My mind was frantic—not with fear but with ridicule. *You stupid motherfucker, you killed yourself over a fuckin' jewelry store! White hair is the sign you shouldn't be throwing ski masks over your fucking head, you idiot! This is how you end! When you die, Chicago will take out an obituary that will read "Stupid Mudderpucker Proves Uncle Frank Right!"*

More out of anger than desperation, I started punching my chest, trying to bash through my ribcage to my hiccupping heart. A couple punches turned out to do the trick: suddenly my heartbeat was regular and my lungs were working as usual. I guess my heart was like our old TV set: you just needed to hit it a couple times when it started to short out and everything would go back to normal.

When I got home that afternoon, I didn't want to talk to anybody. I retreated to the bedroom, shut off the lights, and laid in bed, alone. I had permanently alienated my wife and daughters—there would always be stress, drama, and bitterness there. Even Lil' Johnny was like *Rain Man* if he had been played by Tom Cruise, this gorgeous kid with the brain of an obsessive-compulsive mad scientist. Lil' Johnny was *way* too smart for me, to the point that he usually made me feel like a goddamn idiot within five minutes of any conversation, so our conversations usually ended with me preemptively calling him stupid to cover up my insecurity.

As far as the underworld, I had proven to myself that I was no longer cut out for that life, if I ever was. The only path to a fulfilling, respectable life for me was to leave the Midwest and pursue my artistic dreams in Hollywood, but that could never happen as long as Uncle Frank was still alive.

I was stuck.

On what seems like the very next day in retrospect, but may in fact have been months later, I got a little bit of karmic retribution.

I got up late one afternoon as usual and shuffled to the kitchen for something to eat. I was perusing our cereal selection when the doorbell rang. I clomped over and opened the door, squinting in the harsh sunlight.

Oh great, I thought to myself. My unannounced visitor was this ignorant redneck drug dealer from Texas who looked and dressed like Eminem.

This goofball had been passed around the Midwest underworld like a bitch at a biker rally; everyone was lifting money off him because he was cash rich and brain cell poor. He was the sort of dumbfuck who might pay $10,000 for some cheap piece of shit ghetto jewelry. In fact, I had just sold this cracker some cheap watches for $10,000.

"Hey buddy, what's up?" I said nonchalantly, hiding my annoyance at his presence. One of the primary rules of a conman is to never show your stress, never give anyone a peek at your hole cards. You're always happy, relaxed, and ready to do business. Even during my existential crisis, I wasn't going to show this dirtbag that I was hurting.

My only thought was getting this fuckface out of the house since Lil' Johnny and Alexis were due home any minute from school. Just like me, my kids had grown up with seriously damaged felons around the house on a daily basis, but, like Dad, I tried to only expose them to *professional* sociopaths who had paid their dues and proven their reliability. This kid was a complete amateur and potential loose cannon, so I wanted him gone as quickly as possible from my family home without causing offense.

I motioned for the kid to follow me and shuffled over to the kitchen to talk with him. When I reached the refrigerator, I turned around and nearly clipped my nose on the barrel of a 45-caliber revolver.

When nostril-to-barrel with a huge fuck-off cowboy gun, any father should only have one thought: *my kids!* If I had been anywhere else, I would bet my life on my ability to talk myself out of this situation, but Johnny and Alexis' lives weren't mine to wager. Without thinking, I threw my potbellied middle-aged body at this young drug dealer in an uncoordinated flounce. We toppled in a heap onto the kitchen's tile floor.

We were wrestling on the linoleum, all four hands on this gigantic *Dirty Harry* revolver, twisting it in every direction, trying to keep it away from our faces. Our torsos were wildly struggling and wiggling against each other; my feet were doing a spazzy, high-angle doggy paddle in search of his nuts.

We looked like two cockroaches getting busy on the kitchen floor. This fucking kid was definitely no Charles Bronson. How could he not overpower a panting forty-year-old chainsmoker who never had to fight his own fights?

After about thirty seconds, the drug dealer yells in my ear. "I ain't leaving here until you give my fucking money back!"

"Wait a second..." I panted, searching for enough breath to chew this asshole out. "Don't tell me you pulled a fuckin' gun over $10,000?!"

"I want my 10 Gs!"

"You fuckin' cocksucker, all you had to do was *ask!*" This wasn't true, but it *felt* true now that I was fighting a life-or-death battle five minutes after rolling out of bed. "Listen, calm fuckin' down, put away the gun, and I'll give you whatever I have in my safe!"

The skinhead stopped struggling. So did I. We looked at each other awkwardly for a moment, neither of us feeling particularly confident in our manhood. Both of us were so depressed by the pathetic Greco-Roman snugglefest we had just engaged in that we decided to trust each other and just move on. I let go of the gun, and we both got up and brushed the crushed Captain Crunch crumbs off our clothes. The kid stuffed the gun down his jeans, and, shaking my head like a scandalized old man, I led him to my office safe.

"Listen," I told Marshall Mathers as I spun the safe's dial, "I'll give you everything I got, but, I gotta warn you. No matter what you do, you're *not* going to get away with this; you're *not* going to get very far at all. But if you want it..." I threw open the safe door, "here's all I got in the world."

Of course, I had money stashed all around the house. The first rule of owning a visible safe is to only use it as a decoy, putting just enough in there to satisfy any robber so that he stops looking and immediately leaves.

Naturally, this inexperienced dope slinger fell for the trick. He shoved me out of the way, snatched a handful of jewels and a couple bricks of banded cash from the mostly empty safe, and ran like a Kenyan out of my house. He didn't even bother to hide the cash or the jewels or the gun sticking out of his waistline.

The police sirens were blaring before I even reached my open doorway. My buddy was plastered face-first on my lawn, four plain-clothes cops planting knees in his spine. Ever since I had returned from my credibility-enhancing tour of duty in Chicago, there had never been a moment's time when my home or club wasn't under blanket police surveillance.

"See?" I taunted the drug dealer as he spit out grit from an ant pile. "I *told* you that you weren't going to get very far. These guys are sitting over there all day long! They got nothing better to do!"

My triumphant mood changed drastically when my kids started to arrive home to the sight of an armed burglary bust. That's when what I had done hit me. It was one thing for me to needlessly endanger my own life in an armed jewelry heist. It was another thing for someone like Dad to bring powerhouse racketeers to our house since he did business the right way with people who followed the rules and showed respect. He was a real gangster *and* a real father.

I was neither. I had been derelict in my duties as a father *and* a gangster by bringing half-ass, lowlife criminals with no sense into my home. I had risked my son's life, my daughter Alexis' life, and my wife's life.

I needed to get away. I did not trust myself around my kids, did not trust my abilities to navigate the dangerous world I had to navigate without hurting them. Uncle Frank *was* right: I *was* a sick fuck.

I needed help.

So did the cops in prosecuting that kid.

The incredible thing is that *I* got some.

The police and prosecutors didn't get shit from me because, you know, fuck them.

Lou Fratto didn't raise a cooperating witness.

24

DR. GREENFELD

A couple years before *The Sopranos* and *Analyze This*, I had my mafioso ways changed through visits to a shrink. At the time, this confession would have marked me as an untrustworthy "half-a-fag" and potential rat in the books of Chicago. If I did it today, everyone in Elmwood Park would just say I'm getting desperate in my search for a TV or movie deal.

Since The CroBar's opening night, the local cops, FBI agents, and IRS investigators had sulked in the futility of trying to nail me for one criminal racket or another at the club. They sniffed around the warehouse district for years, dumping out every garbage can and interrogating every fired bartender—all for nothing. There was nothing to find. I was a good, upstanding businessman who just happened to serve drinks to vampires and play host to alleged Chicago Outfit kingpins.

Still, I could feel the heat. You didn't need to be a genius to see that the empire my family had built was coming to an end. Besides my uncles Rudy and Frank and their longtime partner Marshall Caifano, the rest of the Old Guard of the Outfit was dead. Even Accardo was dead, never having spent a single night in jail in his entire life. With the untouchable "Joe Batters" gone and the investigation-killing influence he had built up since the 1920s lost, I knew the feds were going to make up for lost time very quickly.

I needed to get the fuck out of Dodge if I wanted to stay a free man. I didn't want to be caught under indictment, pleading that I really wasn't a gangster at heart! I didn't think "Innocent By Way of Identity Crisis" would hold up in court.

Temporary Insanity, on the other hand . . .

Tiring of all the bullshit, I sold off a managing stake of The CroBar. Since I was expecting The End to come at any moment, I had taken reasonable precautions. I owned an insurance policy that would cover all of my bills in case I was unemployed and in no state of mind to obtain a new job. All I had to do was visit a therapist once a week and prove to him I was too fucked up to hold down a 9-to-5. *Fuck it*, I thought, *if the Chin could do it, so could I!*

Vincent "The Chin" Gigante was just about the only New York mobster who impressed the FBI or the guys in Chicago with his intelligence. Don't get me wrong, we all respected Gotti's attitude and swagger, but he wasn't exactly a brainiac.

Chin, on the other hand, was a thinking man's gangster. Dad and my uncles in Chicago always talked highly of Chin as "that smart kid with Don Vitone"—Chin's mentor, Vito Genovese. While everyone else in New York was going to jail, Chin stayed free by relying on his wits and laying low. *Real* low. *Ridiculously* low.

For decades, Chin avoided prison by voluntarily booking himself into mental institutions. It was a brilliant strategy: Chin, just about the only smart and sane gangster in New York, spent his free time convincing Greenwich Village that he was a brain-damaged ex-boxer.

Even the feds fell for his performances: since their little Mafia rulebooks told them no "man of honor" could visit a psychiatrist or wear a scraggly beard, the coppers had no choice but to disqualify Chin as a major organized crime suspect. It took the FBI almost a decade to realize that the wheezing, drooling, mumbling old boxer puttering around Greenwich Village in ketchup-stained pajamas was really New York's most powerful godfather.

Chin was my inspiration. If Gigante could sucker the best psychiatrists in New York City into believing he was crazy, then certainly an accomplished conman like me should have been able to trick one mediocre Iowan shrink.

For my first doctor's visit, I dressed up in my best Chin Gigante Halloween costume: disheveled pajamas, fucked up slippers, my sunglasses skewed completely sideways on my face, my hair left unwashed, and a big robe with a boxer's hood thrown over the entire mess. To go the extra mile, I got my smoking hot Polish mistress Jowanka to play the nurse and gently guide me into the office as I shivered and stumbled and whispered to myself.

The doctor seemed pretty wary of me as I gently lowered myself onto the couch as if I were recuperating from an exploded hemorrhoid.

"So, Mr. Fratto, what's wrong with you?" Dr. Greenfeld asked. I looked him up and down and decided he would be a pushover. The doc was nerdy—

a Buddy Holly fucker with badly dyed hair and the frumpiest white boy clothes I had ever seen.

If I made a convincing mental patient, I figured I might even get a prescription for some happy pills in addition to a free insurance paycheck, so I left nothing to chance. I had memorized the symptoms of severe depression on the way to the appointment.

"Oh, it's *horrible*," I mumbled, imagining myself to be Brando at the end of *Apocalypse Now*. I looked like a homeless, senile version of Chicago Cubs announcer Harry Carey, so I did my best to impersonate his demented warble. "Depending on the time of day, I suffer from aggression, alcohol dependency, anger, anxiety, appetite diminishment..."

It never occurred to me to shuffle the textbook symptoms of depression so they didn't come out in alphabetical order. I mechanically reeled those fucking symptoms off like a four-year-old practicing his ABCs. I had blown my cover within one minute of sitting down. Chin I wasn't.

My community theater acting chops were further exposed by my decision to improvise a new life story to discuss. After all, it's not like I could tell this complete stranger *everything* about my life. I was arrogant enough to believe that I could *improvise on the spot* a completely new identity for myself and maintain its believability through multiple sessions with a psychiatric expert who was taking detailed notes.

All I can say is thank God for my stupidity and rapidly atrophying skills as a conman. If the 1984 version of Johnny Fratto had visited Dr. Greenfeld, I never would have received the help I needed.

When I handed the good doctor the slip from my insurance company he needed to sign to authorize the unfit-for-work payments, he looked at it for a moment and then gave me this disappointed TV dad look.

"Mr. Fratto, let me be honest with you," the good doctor said. "I'm going to sign this paper, but I have one reservation. I don't want you to get the wrong idea. The thing that's bothering me is that you apparently believe I'm so stupid that your silly act is fooling me."

I was stunned. Dr. Greenfield sighed and tapped his pen on his note-taking pad like a judge's gavel.

"The scary thing, Mr. Fratto, is that all of this is unnecessary," the doctor said in almost pleading tone. "You don't need to fake it. To use language you will understand, you sincerely are *very* fucked up."

I was told this all the time, but hearing it from a human being besides Uncle Frank and Barb was a revelation. It was like I had gone my entire life thinking I was invisible and suddenly realized that everyone had always been able to see me.

"I mean, Johnny, no kidding—you're pretty much nuts. The fact that you don't realize it just proves how badly you need help. So... I'm signing this paper because you really and truly are a disturbed individual who needs intensive psychiatric care before being trusted in the workplace... and *not* because you're getting one over on me."

Dr. Greenfeld slowly extended his arm to give me my paycheck permission slip back. "Seriously, you really are a fucking mess. No joke. I can't stress how serious I am about that. I advise you to take that seriously and reconsider your approach to therapy."

I thought about the jewelry store robbery. I thought about the murder that almost transpired in the home where my thirteen-year-old daughter Alexis lived. I needed help.

"Can I be fixed?" I heard myself asking in an almost childlike voice.

"Absolutely."

"THEN FIX ME!" I blurted out with way too much enthusiasm. Never in my life have I said any sentence with that much emphasis without using the words "fuck", "suck," or "money."

"Next time. We'll get down to the real, hard questions," Dr. Greenfield threatened. That sentence ended my feelings of excitement and liberation.

Terror. I was just about ready to shit myself. The secrets I kept were my armor, my protection from the insane life I led and, I guess, the insanity I never confronted in myself.

As a so-called gangster, I was just like the vampires I dreamt I was catering to at CroBar, deriving power from the darkness and mystery that surrounded me. To open up about my fears and insecurities about my lifestyle would have been as unthinkable to me as a vampire willingly walking into the sunlight and melting away. My shut mouth was voodoo that made me feel like bullets and indictments would bounce off me harmlessly.

This code of secrecy is a psychological survival mechanism as well as a physical one. There's a strange sense of security that comes from living your entire life according to the rules of *Omerta*. Silence made me untouchable. I gave the world nothing to grab a hold of and hurt. Every fact I kept to myself was a vulnerable part of me hidden away behind armor.

My conman mentors had taught me to only show the world a meticulously fictional persona, a costume designed and tailored to fit the needs of the con at hand. No one ever saw the real me, even my wife. That's why I wear sunglasses always; you never meet my eyes, can never look in the window of my soul.

The next week I made my appointment. I had no choice—I needed the check. There was no Johnny "The Chin" Fratto. Fuck that! This time, Dr. Greenfeld met "Handsome" Johnny Fratto. I arrived in a beautiful steel blue silk suit, brand new Italian leather shoes, diamond-encrusted watch and jewelry, blue sunglasses screwed on straight, and a panty-dampening smile on my face. My whole attitude was "Tell me I'm crazy *now*, motherfucker!"

All Dr. Greenfeld had to do then was make a single innocuous suggestion: "Why don't you tell me about your father, Johnny?"

That was my mortal weakness. I sucked in a deep breath of air and then expelled a gust of pent-up childhood memories so mighty that I must have looked like that grey-bearded guy who blows the ships across the oceans in old maps.

It felt like I was deflating the world's largest and oldest gas bubble in my chest. I just let it rip. Obviously, I didn't tell this yuppie anything incriminating about anyone, but I gave myself the freedom to explore how I felt about Dad, my mom, my Uncle Frank, my brothers, and my position in the world as a Fratto.

"Doc, let me level with you," I said with a devilish laugh. "I know what my problem is. I suffer from an identity crisis. Deep down in my heart, I want to be a good person, but my brain thinks normal people are nerds or pussies. I don't wanna become a square, doc.

"I honestly think I'm somehow *better* than them. If nothing else, I get my way—do what I want to do. Normal people just seem to take orders all day long from their wives, their moms, their bosses, their kids. Me? I do want what I want. That's the good side of being me.

"But, to be honest," I changed my tone, looking a little worried. "I mean, to be completely honest . . . the more I'm around gangsters, the less I want to *be* one. I mean, they need to take some refresher classes and get certified before I'd even call them human. I deal with some fucking world-class subhuman morons on a regular basis. Try explaining anything to these people; you might as well piss up a tree.

"Actually . . . *that's* the problem. I honestly believe I was born better than everyone else, and that's why I don't try. I am a complete failure. I was born on third base and somehow managed to strike out!"

"Why are you here?" Dr. Greenfeld asked like an amnesia patient waking up after a long nap.

"What? You told me to be here! Did I get the wrong appointment time?"

"No, no. Johnny, why are you *here*?"

"What? On *Earth*? Because my parents fucked!"

"*Johnny*, what are you doing in *Iowa*?"

"Well, I was born here..."

"You can leave..."

"Yes, yes I can."

"Have you ever heard the phrase, 'Go West, young man'?"

"Sure," I said, trying to remember where I heard it. It sounded like a Village People lyric, which made me a little unsure of the doctor's intentions.

"That's you, Johnny. It's talking to you. Go West. You're too eccentric and creative and weird to be in Des Moines."

"Des Moines was good enough for my dad!"

"Johnny, did your Dad ever tell you why he came to Des Moines in the first place?"

"No...uh...he was pretty thoroughly silent on that subject."

"I have a feeling there was a pretty good reason, and it wasn't a happy rainbow sort of reason."

That got me ruminating on the mystery of my Dad's life and transformation again, distracting me from interrupting the good doctor.

"Besides, Johnny, even if your Dad was a born-again farmer, you don't fit in here, and the social circle you inherited from your dad is nothing like the social circle you would make based on your creative, colorful, open-minded personality. You need to escape and go somewhere where high-functioning artistic nutballs like you are understood and appreciated. You need to go somewhere where eccentric is the norm. The only place for you to go is to Hollywood."

"Are you fuckin' crazy, doc?"

"Listen, Johnny, you belong at Paramount Pictures. Your only problem is there's no Paramount in Iowa. Go West. That's where you'll find yourself, and find the distance and context you need to find out exactly who your dad was, and who he would have wanted you to be."

It all made sense. There's no way you could look at a postmodern piece of art like The CroBar and say the maniac who transformed an abandoned train station into *that* belonged in the prairie country.

I wanted the opportunity to prove that my suspicions in Chicago were correct: I *was* a sincerely talented artist and legitimate businessman. I wanted to see if I could *really* hang without the Fratto and Outfit safety net...and without the obstacles presented by those same people. I wanted to find out if I was actually as smart as I thought I was, or if I was just smart in comparison to the goombahs around me.

Dr. Greenfeld was right. I needed to go West. A pretentious Mobbed-up club owner in the grip of a nearly fatal mid-life crisis *belonged* in Hollywood. That was where I needed to be to prove myself and find myself. That was where I could achieve my dream of developing *Son of a Gun* into a major motion picture.

There was only one problem, the same problem as always: Uncle Frank.

25

THE GOLDEN TALON

"FRATTO, GRIFFIN TEAM FOR SERIES

Johnny Lew Fratto, son of Iowa mob boss Louis 'Cock-Eyed' Fratto (aka Lew Farrell), has linked up with Merv Griffin Entertainment, which has optioned the right to make both a feature and a television series based on Fratto's family life."

VARIETY

After Frankie's death, I lived my life surrounded by violence and chaos. The only way I stayed sane is by simulating security through routine and protocol, staying within the invisible boundaries of the kingdom Dad created. As long I lived within the rules and geographical boundaries of the Outfit's territory, I believed nothing from the outside world could hurt me. According to Dr. Greenfeld, it was a form of obsessive-compulsive disorder.

When Dr. Greenfeld first told me I needed to go West, I theoretically accepted his course of treatment only because I knew, in practice, it was unworkable. "I agree with you Dr. Greenfeld, I need to go to Hollywood. I would jump on the next plane if I could... *but*, as long as my Uncle Frank is alive, I would be endangering the lives of my brothers and even my *children* to leave. So I can't go until he is gone."

Of course, I figured that motherfucker would never, ever die. Despite the least healthy diet and the most pathologically aggressive personality imaginable, Uncle Frank survived *seven decades* within the toughest crime family in the toughest town in the toughest nation in human history. I had no doubt the crazy fucker was invincible.

The wait lasted about five days. On May 25, 1996, Frank E. Fratto died of cancer. Just like Dad, his death was memorialized in the press in he said/she said fashion; depending on the paragraph you read, he was either a Chicago socialite obsessed with raising money for retarded children or an Outfit assassin and strong-arm guy.

I was sad, though my biggest sense of loss was that the best source for information on my dad, and his secrets, was now gone. I figured I would never know what brought my Dad to Iowa and made him change who he was. I felt like my ties to the past were now severed.

Now I had no excuse. Afraid of losing face, I told Dr. Greenfeld I was making preparations to uproot myself. I actually did nothing at all. A couple years passed. I'm a creative guy; new excuses occurred to me all the time.

I was hoping for an act of God to save me.

My prayers were answered. I didn't get an act of God—I got something *better*. I got an act of Merv.

My normal schedule of patiently collecting my unemployment insurance and fretting over my relationship with Dr. Greenfeld was interrupted by a phone call early one afternoon. It was my cousin Renee—Merv Griffin's assistant. "Merv wants to talk about making a movie about you and your dad's life. You have a meeting in his office in two days, first thing in the morning! Don't be late!"

"Thank Christ!" I yelled in ecstatic joy. At that moment, I wasn't thinking about the stroke of luck that delivered one of Hollywood's most legendary super-producers directly into my lap . . . or, I guess, dropped me into *his* lap. I was thinking about how relieved I was that someone else had intervened and made my decision to go to California *for* me.

Merv Griffin's sudden interest in *Son of a Gun* wasn't as big of a surprise as you might imagine. Merv owed the Fratto family. Dad had been the "friend" that gave Merv the muscle he needed to get the labor unions in line and become a major TV producer in the 1960s. If Merv was anything, he was gracious and loyal, and he repaid his debt to the Frattos by hiring my cousin Renee as his personal assistant and adopting me as his pet project when I became useful to his ends.

Towards the end of the 1990s as HBO's *The Sopranos* took off on TV, Merv decided he wanted to produce an organized crime movie—but not any old wise-guy story. He had seen enough to know that the usual East Coast "dese dem dose" goombah stereotype was going to be run right back into the ground long before he could get a movie released. He needed a gangster movie with a twist.

Luckily, my cousin Renee was there to remind him about his old buddy Lou Fratto, the charming godfather of corn country. She didn't even have to sell Merv; he told her to book me for a meeting in his office in two days.

After months of waffling, I was now officially headed to Hollywood. That also meant that, after 25 years of mostly unhappy marriage, I was finally leaving Barb and my daughters behind. I say "my daughters" since Lil' Johnny had already moved to Los Angeles to pursue his dreams of becoming a Hollywood scriptwriter. Though I knew I most likely wouldn't be back, I told the women that I would be in California only for as long as it took to develop, film, and release *Son of a Gun.*

Technically, so far I haven't been proven a liar.

Over a decade after the dream of *Son of a Gun* was planted in my head by Tom Cruise, I was finally on my way to achieving it. I wish I could tell you some details about my journey from Iowa to California . . . I really do. The flight from Des Moines to Los Angeles was long—and so was my memory of what happened to Frankie and Rocky Marciano. Anesthesia was required.

With my future resting on my ability to get to Beverly Hills immediately, I paid some local muscle to physically kidnap me and get me on that fucking airplane, regardless of what I said or did. I told them to tie me up if necessary. No matter what, they were to put me on that plane and stand guard at the gate to make sure I *stayed* on the plane.

Once I was strapped into my seat, I felt paralyzing existential dread, like I was waiting in a boat that was about to land in Normandy on D-Day. So I popped pills—*lots* of pills, *all* of the pills at my disposal. I aimed for tranquilized, overshot, and landed on *tripping balls* instead.

All I remember clearly from the first long-distance airplane ride in decades are brief splashes of psychedelic hallucinations, pants-shitting horror, and physical discomfort as I writhed like a waterboarded terrorist in my airplane seat. I was a prisoner, and the correctional officers were named Officer Xanax, Officer Vicodin, and Officer Ambien.

I was fucked up like no Fratto has ever been fucked up before. Everyone around me was on a 747, but I was at Woodstock.

By the time we were airborne, I had the stewardesses convinced I was a mental defective. I was reeling in my seat like an infant, slapping my hands against my chest and twisting my fingers in painful contorted knots . . . mumbling and moaning and licking my cake-white lips like Dave Chapelle playing a crackhead.

I had my little CD player with the noise-cancelling headphones cranked up so loud that my ears felt like someone was pouring boiling hot sauce into my brain. I was listening to twisted, trippy songs like "I Am the Walrus", and my player was cranked so loud that people in the bathroom were singing along with the "Goo goo cachoo!"

I was stuck ass-over-head in a Satanic H.R. Pufnstuf cartoon. When the stewardess asked me for my drink order, the words came out of a miniature copy of her head that sprung out of her mouth like in *Alien*; when she poured my drink, she did so out of the skull of Buddy Hackett; when I opened my bag of peanuts, *dreams* came out.

I foggily recall the flight attendants peeling me out of my seat, throwing me into a wheelchair, and kicking me down the concourse like that runaway baby carriage in *The Untouchables*. Somehow, the driver that Merv sent to pick me up at the airport found me and convinced me to get in the back of his limo.

The first clear memory I have of California is of watching myself on TV during a massive high-speed car chase. Contrary to what you might be thinking, this was *not* a hallucination. This actually happened.

I was passed out in a suite at the Beverly Hilton, Merv's prized real estate property. This was the luxurious hotel that traditionally hosted the Oscars. I was woken up from my golden slumbers by an outrageously loud symphony of police sirens, pounding car horns, screeching tires, and helicopter propellers chopping. Looking through fuzzy eyes at the TV, my first thought was *Man, this fucking thing has great Surround Sound!*

Then I realized there were no speakers in the suite. The sound of a car chase was coming from my TV screen, but it was *also* coming from outside my window.

Stumbling like Dudley Moore to my sixth floor balcony, I ducked as a police helicopter swooped well overhead. Dipping my head over the balcony, I saw a shiny Toyota Corolla rocketing down the road to the hotel, dragging about twenty cop cars in its wake like an electrified wedding veil. I was still pretty high, so the sound of those ghetto bird choppers and millions of police sirens coming at my head was indescribably intense. It was my worst nightmare.

The experience was too much. I turned away, back to my hotel room, and *saw it*. The TV screen—I was on it. Some TV cameraman covering the car chase had focused on me on the balcony to get a real time civilian reaction.

At the time, I didn't even understand what was going on. All I knew was that I was watching me on TV...watching me on TV...watching me on TV... watching me on TV...

This was my debut in L.A. They say the town is built for self-centered people, but this was ridiculous. For a lifelong narcissist like me, seeing a million Johnny Frattos watching a million more Johnny Frattos on a million TV screens...this was fucking Heaven! I had emerged from my own personal Hell in my own personal Paradise!

I made my national TV debut within an hour of landing in Hollywood.

I kept turning my head back and forth from the car chase to the TV screen, just to make sure I was still there. Within a few seconds, the car sped around the circular driveway at the Beverly Hilton like a NASCAR hanging a smooth curve and blasted out of sight. When I turned back to the TV, I was gone. I finally exhaled—it was a feeling of profound exhaustion and satisfaction like I had just finished fucking.

I crawled over to the hotel room bed. There was only one person to call: Dr. Greenfeld, my guru, my savior. I thought I was being nice, but the poor doctor had serious ethical misgivings when he realized the slurring, hallucinating, yelling maniac on the other end of the phone was the Iowan he had advised to engage his "creative side" in Hollywood. I was less than an hour into the treatment he advised, and I had already lost my mind.

After a long, doped-up night of sleep, I was taken up to Merv's floor at the hotel and escorted down a long hallway decorated with photos of Merv interviewing just about everyone who ever mattered on the Merv Griffin Show. I like to think I'm immune to being starstruck, but Merv whipped out some real trump cards for his "brag wall": there he was with Dr. Martin Luther King, John Lennon in 1965, and, last but not least, Moe *fucking* Howard of *The Three Stooges*.

Talk about your big guns!

Ushered inside an office the size of a Catholic basilica, I looked around in vain for Merv. Finally, I spotted the tiny speck hidden behind miles of carpet.

Merv was sitting behind a gigantic mahogany desk flanked by enormous elephant tusks, doing his best James Earl Jones in *Coming to America* impression. Merv never struck me as a Teddy Roosevelt safari sort of guy. On a nearby couch sat a beast from the deepest, darkest jungles: this enormous, savage dog that drooled like Slimer from *Ghostbusters* and sounded like Merv's buddy Orson Welles after a marathon.

As I took a seat across from Merv, all of the tricks of the conman trade I'd learned through the years were shouting over each other like a press conference in my head.

This is your one chance Johnny...You gotta charm this fucker...Act confident...Display your social value...Make him impress you...Don't oversell... Embody the power and prestige of your Dad...Make him pitch you...Own his respect, don't wait for it...Glamour him, glamour him hard...

And then—*Oh god, pretty please let this fucking guy like my story...Oh shit, what do I even say?...What the fuck can you even say to a guy who knows everyone and has seen everything?...This guy is the definition of an operator...I'm not in the same league!...What would Dad do?...Okay, okay, stick to the basics, say hello, Johnny...*

"Hello, Joh....Hi Merv," I said as I shook the hand of Dad's old friend. Merv was silver-haired, tan, round-faced, and still handsome. He was instantly charming in that iconic Hollywood gentleman way that no one since Carson and Merv's generation has been able to pull off.

"Hello, Johnny," Merv said smoothly. "Let's talk about making this movie!"
Wow, great job Johnny! That was quick!

Merv was sold on sight. He already knew Dad, knew our story, and knew what he wanted to do with it. Our meeting was just a formality: all I had to do was sign paperwork and empower Merv to change my life like the Great Oz.

"Listen, Johnny, let me tell you what I like about your story," Merv began. "It's the story that hasn't been told.

"Everyone thinks they know about the Mob; they've heard it all a million times. But this *isn't* the story you've heard. This isn't three guys from New Jersey or eight guys from Brooklyn. This is the Mob in *Des Moines, Iowa*... where the Mob couldn't possibly exist. Well, your story goes to show you that the Mob was everywhere, is everywhere, that it's a part of the American cultural fabric. It's a very powerful story, *Wonder Years* meets *The Sopranos*, a story of innocence and corruption in the American Heartland.

"It's perfect. All I need is a writer to get started on it...and for you to move out here to help me sell it. This thing makes sense to me, but you're going to need to be in the room to sell this thing. They're going to need to see...*you*," Merv said as he scanned from my *Bride of Frankenstein* hair down to my stylishly jerry-rigged jacket and the diamonds on my fingers, "to understand this project. I can sell it, but you can sell it in the *room*."

With Merv packaging the deal, I stood to be a producer with percentage points on a major Hollywood motion picture based on my own life. I was destined to make it like no wiseguy ever had in Los Angeles. With Merv on my side, how could I fail?

Every second I spent with Merv Griffin left me more and more impressed with him as a man and businessman. This guy was a real gentleman and inspiration. He was the Complete Businessman in the same way that Tony Accardo was the Complete Gangster. Merv had an air about him of comprehensive competence and know-how. You'd trust this man with your life after one handshake: his strength, dignity, and brilliance were immediately palpable. To know Merv was to respect Merv.

By the time I met him, Merv Griffin had been rich and famous for six decades, and he carried it effortlessly like the old pro that he was. For practically his entire life, Merv's job was to play the charming showbiz professional: first as a singer, then as a game show host, then as a talk show host for thirty years, and finally as the TV mega-producer who created *Jeopardy!*, *Wheel of Fortune*, and a real estate empire rivaling Donald Trump's. He closed deals with nothing more than a smile and "Hello, I'm Merv Griffin."

Despite Merv's incredible track record, after the initial high cooled off, my insecurities returned. You know that storyline on *The Sopranos* about every second-generation wiseguy having a shitty b-movie script to hawk and his name on the business card of a fictitious production company? That is the most accurate storyline of that entire series. I knew everyone back in Iowa and Illinois thought I would be a gigantic failure and would come back to Des Moines with my dick tucked between my legs like RuPaul.

For a creature of habit who had never lived outside of the Midwest and had just been certified as nuts by a psychiatric professional, moving to Beverly Hills to pursue a career as a movie producer was harrowing. Back when I swaggered and fooled myself into believing I was some bulletproof gangster, I could have bluffed my way through it, but I was no longer protected by my youth, by my secrecy, by my family, by my superstitions.

I had never done business in a place where the Farrell or Fratto name did not do half the work for me and my glamour/money did the rest. I had never lived anywhere without very powerful friends hanging around the neighborhood and a built-in network of connections to fall back on. I had always navigated waters that my dad, uncles, and brothers had extensively mapped out for me.

I knew exactly whom to see, how to talk, and what to avoid in Des Moines and Chicago. In Hollywood and Beverly Hills, however, I was a nobody who knew nothing. I was a fucking square in L.A. My name meant precisely dick. Nothing about me was special by L.A. standards.

Only one person believed I could make it: a longtime friend of mine named Walter Beich, a self-made pharmacy tycoon. Wally liked to daydream of one day retiring to Los Angeles to play film producer and financier, and he trusted that, if anyone could triumph where Cherry Nose and Johnny Roselli ultimately failed, it was me. To Wally, I was a regular Robert Evans. Once he heard that name Merv Griffin, Wally gave me a blank checkbook and said, "I believe in you, Johnny. Anything you need to close this deal, I'll make it happen."

That convinced me. If two business geniuses like Walter Beich and Merv Griffin agreed that I had what it takes to make it in Hollywood, then the rest of the world had to be wrong.

In traditional wiseguy style, I sealed my deal with Merv with a gift . . . a very strange gift.

Sun-kissed Merv liked to take meetings in the California sunlight around the pool or in the lounge of the Beverly Hilton. Every time we met with Merv outside, this one-legged pigeon would soar down from nowhere, land at his feet, and start murmuring for table scraps. Merv would always laugh about how this pigeon was stalking him, so one day I apologized that "the bird didn't get the fuckin' message the first time" and offered "to take care of the other leg" for him.

A few days later, I signed on the line with Merv Griffin Entertainment. As we popped the champagne, I produced a small jewelry box and gave it to Merv. Inside was a golden pigeon's foot on a keychain. "I told you I'd take care of the other foot!"

From that point on, Merv always carried his lucky golden pigeon's foot. When Merv introduced me to Nancy Reagan (the wife of another old friend of Dad's), who showed up but that little panhandling pigeon?

Merv winked at me.

"Nancy, see how that pigeon only has one leg?" asked Merv.

"Yes, how strange!"

"Well, it's not so strange. We know the story. That pigeon gave me a little trouble, so this guy over here taught him a lesson and brought me back *this* . . ." Merv pulled the golden pigeon's foot from his pocket, "as a souvenir."

26

THE BEVERLY HILTON HILLBILLIES

After that first meeting with Merv, I called Iowa and told Wally to send my busty blond girlfriend Jowanka along with the rest of my clothes and jewelry. I was home—the Beverly Hilton.

The cost of living the five-star life in this Beverly Hills institution was outrageous, but fuck it—Wally *did* say he was giving me a blank check. By the time I was done at the Beverly Hilton two years later, Wally would need one of those Publisher's Clearing House giant novelty checks to fit in all the zeroes.

Another reason why I chose to stay at the hotel is that I'm a guy who *needs* people. After spending my childhood living in Dad's bustling Mafia headquarters, privacy is a problem for me. I've always been defined as part of a group, seen my own reflection in the people around me.

That's why I've spent my life in clubs, bars, and lounges. I never want to be alone to examine too closely the sort of person I am and the life I live. Living in a high-traffic hotel with 24-hour staff would keep me from ever being alone with my thoughts. To make extra sure, I insisted that Jowanka and the now 20-year-old Lil' Johnny move into the two-bedroom suite to keep me company.

Unfortunately, blond Jowanka was Zsa Zsa on *Green Acres* in reverse. This girl didn't know nothin' besides Communist Poland and Iowa, and Beverly Hills was too much city livin' for her to take. She had never been away from her family for much more than an evening, and living in the most socially intimidating hotel in Beverly Hills with my pickup artist son and me was a pretty ambitious first flight away from the nest.

Besides, I had been with her since she was eighteen—it was like she was going away to college but sharing a dorm room with her grey-haired high school sweetheart. After a brief stay, Jowanka decided to go back home to find out whether she missed me or her family more. With Jowanka gone and my wife safely hiding in her Fortress of Passive-Aggressive Solitude back in Des Moines, I was a completely free man for the first time as a self-aware adult.

This was no mid-life crisis; this was a mid-life triumph! Johnny Fratto chilling all day at the pool, ordering lobster and steak from room service for every meal, smoking tons of high-powered California chronic while listening to Bone Thugs-N-Harmony in my suite, and going on a pussy-crazed rampage through the Beverly Hills socialite scene was anything *but* a crisis.

Of course, I didn't start off at full speed. I needed to warm up before I got around to breaking personal records. If I'm being totally honest, I guess I idled in "crisis" for a little bit. My first couple months in Beverly Hills were very fearful, very cautious. My only goal was to make it through the day without succumbing to my fears and insecurity and driving across the country back to Iowa. In fact, if Des Moines had been reachable by cruise ship, I wouldn't have lasted a week in Beverly Hills.

I was homesick, lonely, and full of doubt. The Hilton was so cultured and classy and *white* that I was more like a fish in outer space than a fish out of water. All I could manage to do was to maintain my routine and my tiny beachhead of normalcy at the Hilton for as long as it took for me to become acclimated.

I started my day right at 6 or 7 a.m. by crawling out of bed and dragging my swim trunks over my unwashed ass. I didn't waste time with hygiene, not even brushing my teeth; I just headed to the pool with my eyes still gummed shut from sleep. I'd slither up onto one of those floating chairs like the first fish ever to belly onto land and then pass out for two or three more hours under the baking sun.

The sunbathers around the pool got quite a performance every morning out of me. I suffer from some type of weird sleep disorder where I repeatedly slam my head face-first into the pillow for hours on end. People would stare at me braining myself on the chair, trying to work out if they needed to call an ambulance or not.

After a leisurely siesta, I'd wake up with a sunstroke headache and paddle over to the poolside bar to order some hot coffee and get some cigarettes delivered. For the next hour or two, I'd try to wake up by shitting up my morning breath with cigs and coffee so black it looked like a puddle of Wesley Snipes. My son would then usually join me in scoping out the girls around the pool. We'd grab some sandwiches from the bar and divvy up the available women in theory. Sometimes they'd go along, other times they wouldn't.

If there was nothing going on with the women, we would check out Merv's two hangouts at the Hilton, Griffs Restaurant and the Coconut Club, hoping for a chance run-in that would move our production schedule forward. If nothing was doin', I'd head back up to my room by dinnertime and order "the usual": cigarettes, ice tea, steak, and lobster. I'd settle in front of the TV, watch some Nick at Night, and gradually pop enough sleeping pills to pass out. In the morning, I'd crawl down to the pool first thing and start over.

I didn't have it in me to do much more than survive. I wasn't in fighting shape yet; my mind was still bent. I was very intimidated by the challenge of adapting to life as a single man in a hotel full of billionaires, royalty, and celebrities who looked down at me—a Fratto!—as a nobody. I had spent my entire life as the most cultured, sophisticated, and well-connected guy in my social circle; now people looked at me like I was a mugshot come to life or a Flyover Country redneck.

I felt unmoored from everything I thought I knew about the world. The mood was set by that car chase on the first day. I had been a married crook deeply entangled in the underworld my entire adult life, and now I was a single shipwreck in the most *overworld* place you can imagine. Everything was a trip at the Beverly.

A few weeks after our arrival, my son and I were in one of the elevators on the ground floor, waiting for the doors to close, when a bejeweled black hand reached inside and caused the doors to retract. Tits-first into the elevator marched the finest black chick I have ever seen in my life. I'll be goddamned if this woman wasn't wearing a skirt so short it required a haircut and a dress so low that her nipples were giving me a hard stare.

This girl was so distracting that it took me a moment to realize that the sweaty aborigine in a jumpsuit standing next to her was none other than James Brown. I was trying to decide whether to stare at one of the most influential musicians of my lifetime or one the greatest pieces of ass of my lifetime when the elevator screeched and came to a sudden stop roughly eight feet above the lobby floor. We were stuck.

Normally, a neurotic goofball like me would be sweating and compulsively scratching myself and screaming for help within seconds of being stranded in a jammed elevator, but this was different. I was stuck in an elevator with *James motherfucking Brown*, one of my personal heroes.

I turned to Lil' Johnny. "You don't know who this is . . ."

"Of course I do, Dad," he said in that smart aleck voice of his, "it's James

Brown." James politely nodded, not too eager to take his eyes off his lady friend for the benefit of two extremely tan honkies.

"No, Johnny, I'm tellin' you, you don't know who this is."

"Dad, it's fucking James Brown..."

"No, you *really* don't know who this is. Give this man the introduction he deserves."

I could see Lil' Johnny's autism begin to act up. It's very easy to drive him nuts. He's too rational and kind for his own good. He always thought I pick on him because I want to pick on him. He would be much happier if he realized that I never tease him to tease him; I only tease him to make myself look better to spectators. It's nothing personal.

I always know ahead of time when my antics will cause Lil' Johnny's voice to come out all high-pitched and exasperated, so I braced for it. "*Dad!*" There's the high-pitched whine I was waiting for! "What the *fuck* are you talkin' about?" my son squeaked like a chickadee.

"Johnny, see, I told ya you didn't know," I said with a superior smile and a grizzled chuckle. Now I had James' attention, and I knew just what this man wanted to hear. "Johnny, let me tell you who this is. This is Mr. "Try Me," Mr. "Please Please Please", Mr. "It's a Man's World"! This is the Hardest Working Man in Show Business, the Godfather of Soul... Johnny, without further ado, this is the one and fucking only, James *motherfucking* Brown!"

Right on cue, James yelled, "HAH!" and kicked out either foot, grabbed his belt with both hands, and did that little epileptic James Brown shuffle of his. You could tell the man appreciated the props in front of his girl, and the Godfather of Soul was yapping with me like old friends within seconds.

It didn't take long for me to realize what I had always heard said about James Brown from my friends in the music business was true: you couldn't understand a single fucking word he said. He was completely incomprehensible! James knew all of my heroes—the Beatles, Hendrix, Keith Richards, Marvin Gaye, Al Green—and I didn't have any way of obtaining his eyewitness insight into their characters.

I mean, I asked him, but all I got in return was, "Man, Hendrix man, I tella ya, he wadda shmedda moo, now now, c'mah fuh, downa cow, broke dat, balee dat! HAH! Hendrix man! HAH!"

There wasn't really anything I could say to that, but luckily James was pretty excitable in his cracked-out later years, and all I had to do was politely nod for him to go off on a long jibberish monologue peppered with "HAHS!" and catchphrases from his songs.

As I smiled vacantly at one of my heroes as he revealed himself to be the Godfather of Speech Impediments, I was struck by an epiphany: James Brown and my sweet old Aunt Edith had the exact same hair. I couldn't get over how two people otherwise so fundamentally different, genetically and personally, could end up with identical tar-black pompadours. I mean, they were matched down to the follicle.

As I was pondering this mystery, the elevator kicked to life and off we went to James' floor. James and his girl walked out as if they were not going to say anything, but James swung back around to us to deliver his parting good-byes. *God,* I thought to myself, *please let James Brown make sense for one fucking sentence so I have something to tell people back home . . .*

"GOODSON!" said James in this loud, throaty growl like he was hocking a loogie. There was absolutely no pause between "good" and son"; in fact, he said it so fast that it only covered about 1½ syllables. "GOODFADDER! GET OFF ON THE GOOD FOOT! WOW KADDA SHIZZA! HAH!"

The elevator door closed.

"Dad, do you have any idea what he said?"

"I was doing alright on that last bit until the end."

"What did the rest mean?"

"I think it meant we should treat each other well, y'know, as father and son."

There was a pause as we tried to let James' wisdom sink in. Unfortunately, my mind was already fully occupied.

"God, I want to fuck that black girl . . ." I muttered in awe. "And Johnny, did you notice that James Brown has the same hair as Aunt Edith?"

I drove Lil' Johnny nuts that night expounding at length about how meaningful it was that the Godfather of Soul and my Aunt Edith had the same hairdo. I don't why, but it made a big impression on me. I was like a stoned college student speculating that this showed that, no matter how different we all are, at heart people are all part of a brotherhood of mankind.

We are all one in James Brown's pompadour.

I was still feeling pretty goofy the next morning when I walked out to our penthouse balcony to take in the view and take in some cigarette smoke. Our balcony was right next to the roof on our wing of the building, so sometimes I liked to tool around on the roof and see if I could see people fucking in other buildings. When I stepped out into the sunlight that morning, what I saw on the roof was about a dozen men in plain clothes carrying AK-47s and sniper rifles converging on our balcony.

I dove back into our suite and started crawling on my elbows like Bruce Willis in *Die Hard*. I had no fucking idea what I had done to piss anyone off, but, take it from me, innocence is no comfort when you're shocked by a professional team of assassins first thing in the morning. The elite team of cold-blooded killers was casually peering down into our room as I pulled the phone beside me under the bed and called Merv's private number.

"Merv, there are fucking ninjas or assassins or some shit on my roof! They've got a fucking arsenal, and they look mean!"

"Ha ha ha," Merv chuckled like a yuppie on a yacht, not at all bothered. "Take it easy, Johnny, the King of Jordan is staying a couple doors down. That's his royal bodyguard. Just behave, and you'll be fine."

As I slowly got to my feet and peered with a friendly face at the scowling, heavily armed Jordanians in aviator sunglasses outside of my window, my thoughts turned back to James Brown. I hoped the poor old fuck kept his curtains drawn. If he woke up strung-out and hungover and saw all those assassins outside of his window, he was liable to lose that wonderful head of hair.

Then I had another revelation: *I bet if James lost his hair, at the very same moment so would Aunt Edith.*

Lil' Johnny did not appreciate this insight and refused to talk to me for the rest of the day.

27

THE CHRONIC WISEGUY

"*Baywatch* babe Nicole Eggert...is hot 'n' heavy with...Johnny Fratto, son of Midwest godfather and Al Capone's point man in Iowa, Louis 'Cock-Eyed' Fratto...So far, though, it's been a positive for Eggert in at least one way. The strained relationship with her ex-boyfriend...has improved drastically. Seems Fratto had a 'little talk' with [him]...Fratto, according to reports, was nabbed on drug charges in his native Des Moines in 1979. Cops at the time believed there was little doubt that Fratto, too, had become a made man."

STAR MAGAZINE

What do you call an organized criminal thousands of miles away from the organization? A lonely, paranoid motherfucker.

In the Beverly Hilton, I wasn't a gangster. I was too insecure. It felt like a persona, a part of my identity that only worked in the context of Des Moines and Chicago. Being a gangster even when you're all by yourself, far away from home, is the true definition of the species—Uncle Frank could have parachuted into Pakistan and ended up the crime boss of Karachi within weeks. As smart as Dad was, I have no doubt he could have ended up El Presidente in any random banana republic—hell, he pulled it off in *Iowa*!

And me? Without my muscle nearby, I was afraid to leave my hotel room in Beverly Hills.

I was cured of this crippling social illness by Dr. Anthony Henderson. Technically, Anthony Henderson is not an actual medical doctor, nor any sort of doctor besides whatever sort of doctor Dr. Dre is. Still, he's the only person who had the prescription for me.

I was brought to Anthony by our mutual friend, hip-hop manager Steve Lobel. I knew Steve going back a decade, back to when he was a tour manager for Run-DMC in the 1980s and visited clubs I was involved with in Chicago and Des Moines. We had always been tight as two abnormally cool white dudes who were down with the brothers and rap culture when that most definitely wasn't in style.

Once Steve discovered that the outgoing social predator he had known in the '80s was now a hermit who refused to leave the stuffy Beverly Hilton, he insisted I accompany him to a night at the studio with his top selling act, rap supergroup Bone Thugs-N-Harmony. Who knew Bone Thugs would end up being so therapeutic to know?

Anthony "Krayzie Bone" Henderson was the group's top star, and he was my savior. When Krayzie Bone handed me a blunt of the finest California chronic, he saved my life.

I was used to 1960s dirt weed, which was closer in potency to smoking bananas than the space age NASA weed hydroponically grown for Krayzie Bone. This wasn't the grass that made you giggle; this was the grass that gave you mental retardation. One or two hits of this shit felt like an elephant tranquilizer syringe to the brain.

And that's exactly what I needed. For the first time since I had moved to Beverly Hills, all of my crippling neuroses and fears melted away. I could actually think . . . albeit very, very, *very* slowly.

Krayzie Bone's chronic allowed me to relax enough to rationally concoct a strategy for success in Beverly Hills society. Until that point, I had been so paralyzed with fear that I couldn't even bring myself to *think* of confronting my new neighbors' stratospheric advantages in breeding, education, wealth, power, and connections.

Now that I had taken a few hits of *who gives a fuck?* from Krayzie Bone's weed, I was ready to hit the drawing boards. I got a couple pounds of top chronic and locked myself in my suite at the Beverly Hilton indefinitely. Just as the Buddha would not stop meditating under a tree until he attained Enlightenment, so would I remove myself from Beverly Hills society until I had devised my own path to nirvana.

To my son, my intense sessions of meditation and deep strategic concentration appeared to be nothing more than me zoned out in front of the TV, watching *Family Guy* on mute as Bone Thugs or Snoop Dogg or Tupac blasted from the stereo. On more than one occasion, Lil' Johnny walked into the room to discover me passed out next to my bong with a lobster claw hanging out of my mouth and liquid butter dried across my shirtless belly like candle wax. He did not understand that he was witnessing the aftermath of the moment when I had attained such transcendental insight that I had been transported to a place of perfect tantric peace.

I didn't hold Lil' Johnny's ignorance against him. As I always tell him, wisdom only comes with age. I'm the perfect example of that rule. I was well into my forties when I finally attained enlightenment as to how to carry myself in Beverly Hills. It was no surprise to me that Lil' Johnny could not detect any method to my madness. All he saw was madness. It seemed to get worse every day.

I went shopping and came back with grossly mismatched clothes. I would put together jarring outfits consisting of things like orange track pants, blue snakeskin sneakers, a red silk t-shirt, and an old tweed coat with leather elbows. To top off the look, I'd forego washing my hair and fuck it up with my hands so it looked like a snow white Lyle Lovett do.

I looked crazier than The Chin. And like Chin's act, it was all artifice. In other words, some of Dad's genius for intrigue, camouflage, and dissembling began to manifest itself in his black sheep son.

I began to mispronounce words Lil' Johnny knew I could pronounce, mangle names I had said correctly for decades, act lost in places I visited all the time. I would slouch upon sitting down to eat at a restaurant, pull up my shirt and scratch my belly while talking to strangers, and kick off my shoes at inappropriate moments.

In short, I intentionally did just about everything I could think of to mark myself out as a whacko and an outsider . . . but only *just about* everything.

I would never do *everything* wrong. I'd always leave one detail right: a beautiful custom wristwatch decorated with hundreds of diamonds, rubies, and black diamonds, or a tastefully chosen friend like Merv Griffin by my side. I always left a hint that the rest of my appearance was misleading.

This was my realization: the only way to compete with people who are better than you in every way is to signal that competing with them is beneath you. All I had to do was visually withdraw myself from the social rat race but leave one hint—usually a watch or piece of jewelry usually—that I probably had the resources to compete if it mattered enough to me.

I knew I couldn't match the Beverly Hills locals when it came to anything on a scale bigger than a wristwatch, so I *only* competed on that scale. I would throw on a $100,000 watch that I bankrupted myself to put a down payment on and let everything else fall into disrepair as if I didn't care what anyone thought of me. That bait and switch was irresistible to socialite types. Beverly Hills money people would see that $100,000 watch and extrapolate that I was so rich and powerful, I could get away with looking like a hobo.

This was my secret: mystique. Just like the mafioso derives power from silence, I realized I could transform my faults into strengths simply by shrouding them in mystery. All I had to do was reveal *just enough* to give strangers an inflated idea of what I was about, and then they would filter everything they *didn't* know about me through that prism. Instead of shoving a flashy persona in their face like a cheap conman, I would give them nothing more than a hint of the character I was portraying and let their imaginations fill in the rest of the blanks.

Inevitably, strangers liked the Johnny Fratto they made up themselves far more than they would have liked the real me.

Armed with my new powers of seduction, I fearlessly began to make a name for myself in Beverly Hills social circles. By explicitly telegraphing to everyone I met that I didn't give a fuck what they thought about me, I found myself honestly no longer giving a fuck.

The bluff worked on me, as well. I started collecting friends, allies, and admirers, building my own Beverly Hills network to replace the network Dad had constructed for me in the Midwest. Suddenly, the gangster part of swagger was back in my game. It worked according to the same principle: by not dressing or acting like a stereotypical Chicago gangster, when I dropped a hint here or there, I became intriguing. Hollywood is full of wannabes doing over-the-top New York wiseguy personas, so the fact that I was a godfather's son with a criminal record who looked like anything *but* made me intriguing. What was I hiding?

That was the question that returned poontang to my bedroom. The first catch came at a release party for Bone Thugs that Lil' Johnny and I attended. Father and son zeroed in on our targets: Lil' Johnny snatched this Amazonian black model, while I hypnotized this tiny honey with a narrow waist, big tits, and hair like a white girl.

The thing I dug most about these girls was that they weren't American black. They weren't café au lait black. These babes were 100% pure Zulu black; I'm talking so black they had that shiny purple sheen.

Johnny and I rushed our respective Nestle princesses back to our Beverly

Hilton suite. Don't get any sick ideas; we were in two separate bedrooms on opposite ends of a three room suite.

After such a long layoff, I have to admit I was a little nervous about getting back down to business, especially with a filthy hip-hop groupie who was built to fuck. So I made the mistake of taking a huge hit of chronic to calm my nerves. This shit didn't calm nerves, unfortunately; it *killed* them. I reached a point of such interstellar highness that I no longer *felt* any of my many body parts that were engaged in fucking a 20-year-old sex bomb. I might as well have been orbiting the moon. It was a weird feeling, like I was watching a porno starring myself from the point of view of myself but still couldn't feel anything.

Well, at least I'm not hallucinating . . .

Then I blinked. When my eyelids got around to slowly drawing up their curtains again, I was no longer fucking a coal-black Hutu hottie. No, I was fucking a gigantic Hershey chocolate bar. And instead of sweating, the Hershey bar was *melting*.

I was worried if I didn't come quickly, nothing would be left but a puddle of chocolate. By the time we were finished, my body and the entire bed was sopping, dripping wet with hot fudge syrup. I passed out thinking I had fucked the poor girl until she liquefied!

The next thing I knew, the room was filled with sunlight. I heard the sound of my bedroom door opening. I felt the sticky ass of my bedmate pressed up against my thigh. I was lying spread eagle, completely naked—I had no idea where the sheets on the bed went, but we were completely uncovered. There was no time to cry out. Whoever was opening my bedroom door was going to get a direct, unimpeded shot of my cock, balls, and taint.

The door opened. My oldest daughter Angela . . . whom I had given a key to our suite during an extended visit from out of town . . . was staring at *things that cannot be unseen.*

Angela ran from my bedroom across the suite with her fist in her mouth to keep from screaming. She was running for safety, but there was nothing *close* to safety in Lil' Johnny's room, where she encountered yet more *things that cannot be unseen.*

Back she went into the living room, trapped between two wide-open doorways. For a Midwest Italian princess, this was like Let's Make a Deal hosted by Satan—behind Door Number 1 was her naked little brother with a naked black girl and behind Door Number 2 was her naked Dad with a naked black girl. This was not the position most Italian daughters wish to find themselves in first thing in the morning. With nowhere else to run, Angela chose Door Number 3 (the balcony) and slid the screen door shut behind her.

If there ever was a job for Lil' Johnny and *not* me, this was it. He threw on some pants and talked Angela down from the ledge. I know it came at a steep cost, but she learned a valuable lesson about knocking before opening doors.

My next conquest was perhaps my all-time most notorious. If Krayzie Bone's groupie was the diametric opposite of "my type" of chick, then *Baywatch* bombshell Nicole Eggert was my ultimate dream girl: a young, blond, blue-eyed California beauty queen actress with Hollywood money and a filthy mind.

Nicole was *sick*, *luxurious*, just *creamy*, this perfectly edible little treat of a girl whom I just wanted to lock up in a dungeon and ruin. Nicole was one of the few girls whom I would see on TV and get *inspired* over. Whenever Nicole would flash on the screen, I'd turn to Lil' Johnny and inform him that, whatever it took, I was going to tap that ass.

"Whaddya mean, *you're* gonna tap that ass?" my son would ask, all brash and stupid.

"Listen up, Johnny, Nicole Eggert . . . now *that* is a job that daddy's gonna have to get done. I don't think you got it in you, boy."

The ultimate mark of the success of my new Beverly Hills persona was that I did not have to seek out Nicole Eggert. Nicole sought out *me*. That's when I knew I would be a success: when a famous sex symbol hunted me down without me doing *anything*. The money and acclaim wasn't there yet, but at that point I knew I had hit on my winning formula. Everything else would come in due time.

Nicole had heard so many bizarre rumors about the strange hip-hop pothead gangster who lived high up at the Beverly Hilton like the Phantom of the Opera that she just *had* to meet me. I had just finished smoking a serious bowl when Nicole Eggert was escorted into my hotel room by family friend Rick Bongiovanni as if she were royalty and Rick was her footman.

Naturally, I thought I was hallucinating and didn't take her arrival too seriously. Without even waiting to be introduced, I just started teasing her and playing with her and goofing around with her like I always did in my marijuana fantasies where we were dating.

And Nicole loved it.

That was my luck. If I had known she was coming, I probably would have flinched and pimped myself out with my flashiest suit, watch, and jewels.

I would have come at her correct; I would have flexed. And I would have struck out.

You see, Nicole had been famous ever since she debuted on the sitcom *Charles in Charge* at the age of 14. She had spent her entire sexual life being pursued by the rich, famous, and powerful. She had grown up way too fast, seen it all. It was impossible to run game on her or glamour her one bit. She was jaded, tired of being hunted by sport-fuckers and egotistical alpha-dogs.

So she was immediately attracted to the cerebral, spaced-out gangster sitting in a disheveled robe with a bong between his legs and *Married with Children* on the TV. Thanks to my incapacitating high, I could not have tried less to impress Nicole, and, when I did talk, what came out of my mouth was the sort speculative dorm room stoner talk that *no one* wasted on an intimidating blond bombshell like Nicole.

Within five minutes, Nicole had kicked off her shoes, thrown her jacket on my bed, and snuggled next to me and my bong. Sitting Indian style, she asked if she could have a hit of my chronic.

"What? You smoke?" I said, dazed and floating.

"Yeah, let me have a hit," she said with this chill, level *fuck me* gaze that I was digging.

"No, I mean do you *smoke*? This shit . . . this shit is no bullshit right here."

"Yeah, really. Let me have a hit."

So we smoked together.

And *days* went by. *Days* and *days* went by. At some point our clothes disappeared like pothead clothes do. Nicole and I got philosophical together, and by that I mean she did things to me that made me start believing in God and angels and miracles. And she also fucked up Lil' Johnny's world when he came home to find that Daddy had gotten the job done.

Nicole holed up in my suite for weeks at a time, really getting to know me inside and out. I understood exactly what she needed from a man. Due to her high desirability, Nicole's relationships with men seemed to me to consist of nothing but insecure men trying too much, pushing too much, taking too much, and worrying too much. It was like men were nothing but drama, stress, and work.

I knew that meant I had to be Nicole's playtime. From the very start of our affair, I kept my pimp hand strong. I told her to relax, sit back, and let Johnny take control. I wasn't going to fight for her attention or affection. She could hit the bricks . . . or she could trust me and let me take her for a ride.

There was no resistance on her part at all. Nicole, at least at that time in her life, was a shamelessly dirty sexual submissive. She wanted nothing more than to be freed from all the bullshit of dealing with prissy, insecure L.A. men and devote herself to serving a real man. She surrendered her heart, mind, and above all else her body—that *luxurious* body—to me. Absolutely nothing was off-limits. I said *nothing*. Anything you're thinking about, I did.

For the first time in her life, I gave Nicole the thrills that she missed out as a prematurely experienced teenager. She had her some fun in the Hollywood social scene, but I was going to push her until the sex became dangerous, exciting, liberating like it should be for an innocent-but-secretly-dirty hot little blonde like her. I was going to put the schoolgirl right back into her.

My favorite games with her involved power play. I would take her out on the roof of the Beverly Hilton in the dead of night and handcuff her to a post. Then I would leave. She would be standing out on this eerie roof all by herself, wondering where I was, getting scared, daydreaming that a stranger would find her helpless and take advantage of her.

After a while, I would show up by her side. She would think I was going to free her. Nope. I'd walk up to her, give her a kiss, and then roughly rip one piece of clothing off her body. Then I would leave again.

Ten minutes later, I would return and strip another piece of clothing from her as she begged me to let her go.

Eventually, she'd be completely naked and handcuffed to a pipe on the roof of Beverly Hills' most famous hotel, visible from any number of surrounding buildings and completely defenseless.

I'd take my time. I'd wait in the shadows.

I would smoke my cigarettes and watch her where she couldn't see me, getting off as her fear and excitement and adrenaline went out of control. I'd hold off until she was absolutely psycho . . . and then I'd pounce. I'd bend her over and take her in full view right on the roof.

And the next night, she'd be back again, teasing and dropping hints that she might want to head out to the roof for a smoke. Of course, sometimes I'd just chill out on the roof with her smoking a bowl, watching all the city lights and watching the ghetto bird helicopters. All the police helicopters circling above lit up the night sky like the reflections from a spinning disco ball.

My pervy power games weren't exclusive to the safe confines of the Beverly Hilton. I took my horror show on the road. Whenever Nicole and I would go somewhere, I'd make her my slave on the way. I'd let her in the passenger seat of the car, put the key in the ignition, and then tell her I wasn't going to leave until she gave me her clothes.

Once she had stripped and handed me everything but her high heels, I'd pretend like I was going to turn the ignition before yanking the key out and stepping out of the car. I'd leave her naked in the passenger's seat for a bit, wondering if I was going to come back, before returning and stuffing her clothes in the trunk.

Then I'd hit the road...with the retractable top of my convertible down. There was nowhere for Nicole to hide. She'd slide down as far as she could in her seat, but anyone in a tall SUV or truck could see her. I'd intentionally search out 18-wheelers on the freeway, speed up next to them, and start honking my horn. It was my way of saying thanks to the trucking industry, which had brought a whole lot of money to my family over the years.

As our affair progressed, Nicole and I started to get serious...serious about making love and getting high. Not all serious relationships have to be emotional. We were *seriously* into smoking a bowl and making love, and we did a *serious* job of it. Eventually, we wore each other out and settled down to being close friends.

And it's good our relationship calmed down when it did. She had been such a *delicious* distraction that I had barely noticed I had been in Beverly Hills for two years without accomplishing a fucking thing besides getting a press release with my name next to Merv Griffin.

You wouldn't believe how many motherfuckers I showed *that* thing to.

28

WHY DOES WILLIAM MORRIS HATE ME?

To paraphrase the great Moe Howard, you ain't gettin' no place fast. No matter what talent or advantages you have, it takes time to get anywhere in your career...

Unless you're in Hollywood. Then all you need is a name. You don't need talent; you don't need charm; you don't need that certain somethin' or even a fucking clue. All you need is a proven name to drop and you can become an instant sensation by proxy. Names are the currency of the movie business.

It's a lot like the Mob in that way; the individual ain't worth shit in either world. It's all in who you know and who you can get to stand next to you.

That's all show business is at its highest level: collecting names to collect paychecks. The people who actually make movies—the directors and the actors—just do the manual labor to fulfill contracts. The real money and power is with the producers, agents, and lawyers who attach enough names to a project to convince some German or Persian or Russian financier to put $100 million behind it. Once you get the names, you get the money, and sometimes all it takes is one good name.

And the ultimate, bona fide, untouchable billion-dollar name in Hollywood is William Morris. The agency of William Morris Endeavor Entertainment is the Outfit in Hollywood. You don't fuck with it, and it's not often you get to fuck without it. They say that, if you got William Morris behind you, you got a future in Hollywood ahead of you. Just like Lou Fratto could make you in the Midwest, William Morris can make you in Hollywood.

What I didn't understand when I first encountered William Morris is that this sort of power never goes in only one direction. Just like my dad, William

Morris can also break you down to absolutely nothing and make you sit there and fucking take it with a smile.

The only reason I found myself at the mercy of William Morris is the death of Merv Griffin. Merv had been my royal flush, the name I could throw down to make the money fall into my lap. Thanks to his half-century record of making *billions of dollars* in Hollywood and never screwing anyone over, everyone wanted to work with Merv, even if it meant they had to work with a goofball like me. All it took was for Merv to put his name next to mine on the pages of *Variety*, and within seconds producer David Permut (*Face/Off*), writer George Gallo (*Bad Boys*), and $75 million in financing fell from the sky. *Son of a Gun* was a go.

With Permut and Gallo in place to do the work, all that needed to happen was for Merv to stay at my side. He was the mother bird stretching out its wings to give the deal cover as it matured and got strong enough to venture out on its own. And it takes a *long* time for a movie to get strong, and Merv had cancer.

Cancer has killed every old man who had ever tried to protect me in this godforsaken world. Merv was the third to go. I recognized the signs immediately.

First Merv would schedule a meeting a week out, then two weeks out, then a month out—and then cancel at the last minute. David and George would be left hanging for weeks as they waited for Merv to take meetings with the financiers and sign off on decisions. Lil' Johnny and I saw less and less of Merv hanging around the Hilton, and every time we ran into him, he looked older, whiter, weaker. He never had time to spare; he was always rushing his body out of view.

Just like my father and uncle before, Merv was a powerful man retreating from the world in his time of vulnerability. The short window of time in which the extremely busy David Permut and George Gallo could make *Son of a Gun* was closing. They began to take on other projects, never abandoning *Son of Gun* but delaying any potential production schedule years and years down the road.

One day, I woke up and the financiers were gone. The rest of Hollywood had figured out Merv was finished. He just didn't have the physical power to get that last job done. Our only hope of fulfilling my dream was to move on and find new benefactors.

Getting serious about finding new partners meant I would have to clean up, leave the Beverly Hilton, and hit the streets. Lil' Johnny was sure that leaving the Beverly Hilton was the key to getting *Son of a Gun* made. He guessed, accurately, that I would have a hard time doing anything but smoking up and chilling in a hotel room where I could sniff the curtains and get a contact high.

As usual, I categorically refused to cooperate with Lil' Johnny's good advice. I am a creature of habit, and the accommodating staff of the Beverly Hilton had painstakingly enabled every ridiculous habit I could ever develop. I had grown pathologically accustomed to the luxury, security, and constant excitement of living full-time in a five-star hotel. I vowed to return to Iowa before I took a step down in my accommodations in Beverly Hills.

My son is stubborn just like me. He recruited allies. My ex-girlfriend Jowanka returned from Iowa, deciding that life as a pampered mistress in Beverly Hills was a *little* bit better than living with her Polish immigrant parents in Iowa. The spoiled Jowanka was won over to the anti-Beverly Hilton alliance by her entitled belief that she deserved better than bunking down in a cramped hotel suite with me, my son, and his girlfriends. Together, they nagged me, but as Sister Mary Esther and Frankie and Barbara had all found out, I am immune to nagging.

Getting desperate, Lil' Johnny tried to *shame* me out of living at the Beverly Hilton. This was an even dumber strategy than nagging me. I outgrew shame back in junior high school.

Lil' Johnny called down to the front desk and asked for a printout of the tab we owed after two years in a three-room suite with three room service orders a day. The bill that was dumped outside of our room door was the size of two phone books; it looked like the IRS records for the state of California. On the very last page was a total, and that total was roughly equal to the cost of purchasing six nice houses in Des Moines.

Lil' Johnny had assumed my refusal to leave hotel life had been based on an honest miscalculation of the amount of money I was spending. He figured there was no way I was so selfish, greedy, and wasteful that I would knowingly spend in the mid-six figures annually on a hotel room. He thought I would take one look at the price, gulp, and surrender to my decency.

"See, Dad?" Johnny said, "We could live just as well, or even better, at one third the price!"

"Actually, you're wrong . . ." I said, chuckling to myself. "I guarantee you the price is exactly the same . . . watch!"

I picked up my cellphone and dialed my business partner Walter Beich's number in Chicago. Five minutes later, the bill was paid in full. "See? The price *to me* is the same no matter what: zero!"

But I gave Lil' Johnny a lil' bit of my cleverness and just a touch of my evil. The next morning, I woke up early for my dawn nap in the pool. I went to the dresser to pick out my swim trunks, but the drawers were empty. The clothes I had draped over the furniture were gone. Everything in the closet was gone. My toothbrush and shampoo were gone. Even my girlfriend and son were gone. The hotel room was desolate. I opened the door and saw another, much smaller bill on the carpet covering the previous day.

I had been checked out. The only thing left behind was me.

While I was dreaming sweet dreams within a cloud of chronic smoke, Lil' Johnny and Jowanka snuck into my room with a couple bellboys and carried off all my stuff. They deposited my belongings in a fully furnished, beautiful penthouse condo in the heart of Beverly Hills, a couple blocks from Beverly Drive and Wilshire Boulevard. My closest ally, Wally, had fallen for their logic and financed the entire scheme to rip me from Merv's womb. Maybe he hadn't taken that Beverly Hilton bill as tolerantly as I thought.

When I entered the condo building for the first time, I secretly noted a good omen to myself: the penthouse was accessed only through a special elevator key that unlocked the ability to reach the top floor. I had seen this before—Dad had shown me the key Al Capone had entrusted to him that allowed the Lexington Hotel elevator to reach the Outfit's command center. When Dad got that key, he knew he was made and that Al Capone trusted him with his life.

Skulking around the small but beautifully furnished condo, I refused to let myself admit that Lil' Johnny and Jowanka had done well. I liked that I had the vast roof of the apartment complex to myself. From that roof I could see the Hollywood Sign, downtown LA, all of Beverly Hills, and the ghetto birds circling Compton like vultures. On that roof, I could see a future of conducting business on *my* terms: making everyone come to *me* just like Dad had, holding meetings on the top of the building like the last Beatles concert. Unlike any other office space, the roof allowed me to operate in my comfort zone of smoking, tanning, and sipping on ice tea.

No longer was I a visitor, a tourist in a hotel room. Now I could tell all of my cynical friends in the Midwest that I was a bona fide resident of Beverly Hills with my own penthouse condo.

I wasn't the only one who didn't waste time putting down roots. Jowanka had no intention of heading back to Des Moines. Within what seemed like minutes of returning to Beverly Hills, she had bought a little yappy demon dog and gotten herself pregnant with my unwitting assistance. I announced the news to Lil' Johnny as gently as I knew how: "Hey, Johnny, remember how you said you always wanted a brother?"

"Yeah, twenty years ago, when I was a kid."

"Well, better late than never, motherfucker!"

I thought I had won *that* round, but Lil' Johnny scored a knockout counter.

"Well, I guess it's time for you to kick the pot habit, huh?"

"Oh shit!" That hadn't occurred to me. I haven't smoked a joint since.

At first, the dog was more trouble than the new baby, Joey, who was 30 years younger than my first child Angela. To be honest, the dog wasn't really at fault; it was its nature to be a nasty little mongrel. The problem was with the elderly Russian landlord, who kept insisting that my lease agreement strictly forbade keeping dogs as pets on the premises. He'd bug me so often about the goddamn dog he eventually made a barbarian out of me.

One day, the little fucking Russian troll popped out of the elevator door and started right in lecturing about the little rat dog snapping at his ankles. That was it. I grabbed him by the throat and threw him against the elevator doors.

"Motherfucker? See that? What is that?" I screamed in his face.

"A...dog?" he said in a bewildered monotone that I can only compare to the voice of Howard Stern's dad, Ben.

"No, it's not. It's a fucking cat. It's a cat, motherfucker! Don't you see? IT'S A FUCKING CAT! Tell me, motherfucker, what do you see?"

"It's a cat! It's a cat! It's a cat!" the landlord yelped as the little dog ran around in a circle and barked repeatedly.

"That's right, and can I have a cat in this building?"

"Yes, you can have a cat!"

"Good, then leave my fucking cat alone!"

From then on, the landlord would always very politely ask me how my cat was doing before inquiring about my newborn baby or Jowanka.

I hadn't calculated on raising a newborn baby in Beverly Hills, where toddler shoes are imported from Italy and preschool costs $20,000 a year, so that meant I needed to get moving on *Son of a Gun.* I had left Merv's nest, and it was now time for me to fly or fall. Since Merv still held an option on the movie rights of *Son of a Gun*, we decided to give TV a twirl.

Our target was Jill Schwartz, the Vice President of Acquisitions at Fremantle Media, the gigantic European production company responsible for *American Idol* and *America's Got Talent.* Lil' Johnny and I had no experience whatsoever taking real meetings in Hollywood, so we came to Jill's office with nothing but a script Lil' Johnny had written and a pitch: *Sopranos* meets *The Wonder Years*!

Call it beginner's luck, or call it a brilliant pitch. Either way, Jill decided not to throw this silver-haired wiseguy and his pretty boy son out onto the street even though we had pitched an expensive dramatic series set in 1960s Iowa to a European company that produced reality TV shows.

"Listen, we don't do period pieces," Jill said with an indulgent smirk on her face, "but I like you guys. There's *something* I like about this. Why don't you get a camera and just film you guys hanging out, film your world so we can get a feel for you. Maybe we can do something."

Jill had not intended for us to shoot a professional TV pilot. She just wanted to see some home movies to see if her intuition that my family might have train wreck reality TV potential was accurate. But I didn't see the point of bringing a shaky, unedited, camcorder video to a formal meeting at one of the top TV production companies in the world. So I spent $80,000, hired a film crew and editor, and cut a 22-minute TV pilot.

Son of a Gun was pretty inventive for the time: half-reality TV series, half-scripted comedy. It was *Curb Your Enthusiasm* with a cast of nothing but real characters who were truly every bit the assholes in reality that Larry David was in his scripts.

After we showed the pilot to the initially skeptical Jill, she fell to her knees behind her desk and began to wring her hands as if she were pleading for her life. "Listen, guys, I can't *legally* ask you not to shop this around, but I *want* to work with you. It might turn out for the best if I have a little time to convince the guys above me. This sorta content is out of our area of expertise, but I think it can work!"

We trusted Jill, and in a couple months she delivered. *Son of a Gun* was optioned by Fremantle Media and referred to their packaging agent at the almighty William Morris Agency. Once I heard the words "William Morris," I knew I had arrived, and once I met our agent, Mark Itkin, I felt sorry for any misguided motherfucker that tried to get in our way.

Mark Itkin appeared to be everything I imagined a stone-cold William Morris capo was supposed to be: a broad-shouldered, hairy-knuckled, muscular icebox motherfucker with a gruff Clint Eastwood voice. One look at a bonebreaker like Mark, and I was popping champagne bottles and calling all my friends back home. With a reputed $10-million-a-year in commissions, Mark had the reputation as being *the* most powerful agent in reality TV.

Itkin didn't fuck around. He took us right to Mike Darnell, the president of reality TV at Fox and the man *The New York Times* called "The World's Scariest Programmer." As we walked into the meeting, Mark gave it to us straight. "Listen," he rasped, "Mike Darnell is going to kick us the fuck out in about five minutes. Don't take it personal."

In Darnell's huge office, Lil' Johnny and I did our spiel, and, to Itkin's shock, we managed to convince the skeptical Fox executive to watch our 20-minute pilot. Darnell looked fucking miserable, but he gave us a shot.

I watched Darnell stare with this blank, unblinking, unsmiling face as our pilot—which suddenly seemed every bit as cheap and amateurish as it was—played. After the pilot was over, I thought Darnell was going to call in security and have us tossed out onto the lawn like DJ Jazzy Jeff, but instead he simply cleared his throat and quietly asked to see the pilot *again*.

Even Itkin couldn't help but stammer a little bit at Darnell's unexpected request. Itkin got up, rewound the tape, and sat back down. He turned to me with this confused look, almost as if Darnell's request was a *bad* thing. Maybe Darnell was so appalled and flabbergasted at the shit we had just pitched to him that he just *had* to see it again to make sure he hadn't been hallucinating. Mark leaned over and whispered in my ear, "I've never seen Darnell ask to see something twice in my entire life. A guy this busy usually doesn't have the time to watch something *once*."

After another 22 minutes, Darnell swallowed and lightly nodded his head. Turning to Mark, he started to speak in a distracted, nonchalant voice, as if he were dictating his grocery list to his assistant. "I love it. I'm buying it. Let's do this." His facial expression never changed.

But mine sure as fuck did! We had just sold a show to the top reality TV programmer at the top TV network in the world! And we had done it in one meeting ... in the room ... *using a cheapass pilot that we produced ourselves with no experience.* I could see it now: *American Idol* followed by America's newest reality TV sensation, *Son of a Gun* starring Hollywood prodigy Johnny Fratto!

In the halls of Fox, Mark Itkin pulled me in close, all chummy like a bear on a honey high, and said, "I've *never* seen beginner's luck like that! You can stick around Hollywood for the rest of your life, and I don't think you'll *ever* see a meeting go that well, that easy, *that* high up ever again! You won't ever sell another thing in the room like that again!"

"No, no, Mark!" I said to him, gracious in my moment glory, "It was all you. William Morris is my lucky charm!"

If I only knew then what I know now.

The next morning (afternoon), I woke up to find a bottle of champagne on the kitchen table. On it was a note: "GET READY TO BE FAMOUS! From your friends at Fremantle Media." I popped that motherfucker open and got my drunk on first thing in the morning. I had never been so happy. My dreams of being a Hollywood player were finally being fulfilled. All I had to do was leave it to William Morris to handle.

Two months went by without an update, without even a scrap of news or a note from Mark Itkin. Finally, we received a short and cryptic message: Mike Darnell had been "overruled."

This was an insane message. Mike Darnell, second on the food chain at Fox TV, was *never* overruled. Did I accidentally screw Rupert Murdoch's mistress and not know? Fremantle was baffled; it was like someone saying that God had overruled Jesus. Darnell put anything he wanted on TV, even *Alien Autopsy* or *When Stunts Go Bad* . . . but not *Son of a Gun*, I guess.

Deep in the stash holes of my mind, I suspected William Morris had taken our deal into a crash landing. After all, we had done our job and sold it *in the room*. Why hadn't William Morris moved quickly to lock in Fox? Why did we end up waiting two months before getting an answer?

With Fox's surprise turnaround, Fremantle got a little insecure and decided that we needed to fortify the *Son of a Gun* package with a couple proven "showrunners"—the producers who actually manage day-to-day filming of a TV series. After Fremantle turned down eighteen established Hollywood showrunners, we finally found our guys: Jeff Stilson from the The *Osbournes* and Tim Gibbons from *Curb Your Enthusiasm*.

This duo was a motherfucking slam dunk. How could we go wrong with a showrunner from the most successful reality TV show ever made about a family and the showrunner from the best comedy in TV history? I thought there was no way anyone would turn down our pitch with Stilson and Gibbons, and I was right. We got an enthusiastic "YES!" from every TV network we pitched.

But the show was never made.

Why?

Well, I know *now*, or at least I think I do—Lil' Johnny swears to this day that I have sabotaged every autobiographical deal I've ever made (*after I get my up-front money*) to protect my mystique, my secrets. In his version of events, I made money for years accepting option after option, collecting advances and fees and favors on a multitude of projects based on our family, never fully intending to put the big spotlight on my life and the criminal career I had kinda, sorta let go.

One can judge the accuracy of this statement as you read this book.

Here's my theory why all of my deals died on the vine: Stilson and Gibbons were not represented by William Morris. Mark Itkin was a *packaging* agent who specialized in putting together shows staffed in all the key positions by other William Morris clients. That way, William Morris got all the commissions, all the credit, and all the negotiating power. This isn't greed, really; it's probably the only profitable and rational way to make TV shows where a single legal disagreement or contract dispute can tank everything.

Since Fremantle was so inexperienced at making scripted TV, they had no idea that adding Stilson and Gibbons had corrupted the deal for William Morris. They had spoiled the entire package. We were no longer worth the effort for William Morris, and Itkin wasn't about to educate us.

Or maybe he tried, and I didn't even notice—and he decided I was just an asshole who ignored his advice. Regardless, I would learn.

I was homeschooled. We sold *Son of a Gun* over and over and over again, yet I always ended up sitting at home. We had to keep reselling it to TV networks because William Morris kept appearing to tank each new deal.

We sold *Son of a Gun* to NBC Alternative Programming Head Craig Plestis in one meeting where he didn't smile at us, talk to us, or shake our hands. All he did was buy the series. Once again, Fremantle sent the champagne, and I drank it.

Once again, weeks passed... months passed... and whenever I called Mark Itkin's office, I was told he was on vacation at Fire Island. Finally, we heard from NBC that they were pulling out because William Morris would not send them the information they needed to agree on a budget.

Next came Ted Harbor and Lisa Burger at E!, who *also* bought *Son of a Gun* in the room at the first meeting. Itkin had been wrong; I apparently could sell *Son of a Gun* in one meeting *anywhere* in Hollywood. What I *couldn't* do was make William Morris close the deal. After two months of supposed Fire Island vacations and increasingly exasperated phone calls from the people at E!, the deal fell apart.

I was trapped in a bizarro world. Being represented by William Morris was supposed to automatically *make* deals; it wasn't supposed to automatically *kill* a client's project when everything else was going for it. Since I didn't understand the packaging concept, I was as baffled as a caveman who thinks the rain is God taking a piss. Everything in my experience led me to a single, indisputable explanation: *William Morris hates me!*

It was personal. It had to be. A lifetime among vendetta-carrying Italians had taught me *everything* was personal.

"Why does William Morris hate me? Why does William Morris hate me?"

I would repeat over and over to anyone who would listen, beseeching God and Lil' Johnny and baby Joey and Jowanka's little dog to explain to me why I had been cursed. "What have I ever done to William Morris?"

"Why do you hate *me*?" Lil' Johnny would ask. "Why do you blame everyone else when these deals go wrong? Why can't you just go to William Morris and fix this?"

I didn't. Instead, I puttered around my condo like Chin Gigante in my stained robe and ratty boxers and worn slippers, only I wasn't acting this time. I was going nuts from the stress, from the awful insecurity of not knowing *why* I was hated and being sabotaged by the most powerful people in Hollywood. There was no conspiracy theory too whacked out for me; I considered them *all*. There had to be an explanation.

My experiences in the Midwest had taught me two ways to deal with obstacles: violence and bribery. Violence wasn't going to fly in Beverly Hills, and the expensive gifts I sent to Mark and his spouse and donated to his favorite charities didn't help either. If anything, somehow these gifts made William Morris hate me *more*; now they refused to even *pitch* my show. I came to the conclusion that *Son of a Gun* was just going to sit until the option with Fremantle ended years in the future, in 2007.

I was on ice, and Mark Itkin was at Fire Island. I was on the shelf, and *Son of a Gun* was in the trashcan. My dreams in Hollywood were whacked. My reputation back home was poisoned; I had bragged to *everyone I knew* about my TV show being picked up not once... not twice... not three times... but four times.

And it was never made. I was a punchline, a deluded dreamer. I could hear Uncle Frank laughing from his grave. The fact that I was making money wheeling and dealing, hustling my way into owning pieces of various projects and pulling in cash for every imaginable option was beside the point: I didn't have *my* show.

I had come *so* close.

I couldn't have come closer.

I had made it to the Super Bowl, kept the game close to the very last minute, and pushed the football all the way down to the other team's one-yardline. I was one yard away from the game-winning score... and I kept getting stuffed at the line of scrimmage, inches away from achieving my dream.

What the fuck was I going to do with myself until the option on *Son of a Gun* expired?

LET ME TELL YOU A QUICK STORY...

ABOUT THE FROG AND THE ALLIGATORS

Not all Rolls Royces are created equal. I had this Rolls Royce once that looked beautiful but drove like dogshit. I couldn't get it to run properly, and I didn't have the knowledge, passion, or money to fix the fucker. So I put out the word that I wanted to sell it quick and clean to anyone in the market for a brand name hunk of shit.

One of my neighbors called me up and told he had a potentially interested buyer: this Indian guy named Bikram Choudhury. Unbeknownst to me, Bikram was not just any old rich Indian guy—he was an influential global spiritual leader. Bikram is the inventor of Bikram Yoga, or "hot yoga", the world's most popular style of yoga. "Hot yoga" is called "hot" because you perform the stretches in a steaming, sauna-hot room so that everyone smells of balls, ass, and armpit.

So I had no idea why the waiting room I was sitting in smelled so fucking horrendous. I was counting down the seconds on my watch when this pretty receptionist opened the door to the waiting room and beckoned to me with an angelic smile. "Sir, you look like a man who can settle disagreements. Come with me, please!" she said in a voice as sweet as rose water.

How did these fuckers know about my rep as a fixer?

I was escorted into this conference room where Bikram—a small, intensely muscular, pony-tailed Indian gentleman—and a number of his associates were having a friendly debate. "Mr. Fratto," Bikram said to me, speaking with a voice that sounded both serene and wise. "You appear to be a man of great wisdom and fairness. Please help us resolve our debate."

Why these accomplished businesspeople decided that a total stranger like me should be their final judge, I'll never know. It was probably some mystical telekinetic shit I can't wrap my head around. Anyway, I listened with the patience of King Solomon and handed down my verdict on their personal matter. I naturally agreed with Bikram, because he was the only person in the room who wanted to buy my shitty car.

Bikram nodded and smiled to me. "Thank you, Mr. Fratto," he said in his pleasantly accented voice, "I knew I made the right choice when I asked your opinion, you know? You have a very good aura, I see. You have the aura of an enlightened one."

Bikram gestured to his followers. "I have just met Mr. Fratto, but I can already tell a great deal about him, yes. He is like the little frog that lives in the pond with the alligators. Other frogs might be eaten, but Mr. Fratto is the one little frog that makes friends with all of the alligators. To the alligators, he is one of them, and to the frogs, he is just another frog.

"That is the secret of Mr. Fratto!"

Fuck, I thought to myself, *I must be really fucking stupid! Bikram just solved my identity crisis five minutes after meeting me!*

29

CASHTASTROPHE

June 11, 2003—that's the day I finally made my Dad proud.

There was no séance, no angelic visitation, no Ouija board compliment—but I could feel his pride.

I've always been Lou Fratto's son, and Lou didn't raise any fools. It just took a while for one of his children to realize that.

It just took me until three decades after his death to apply what he taught me. I was born too late in his life to master all the skills he wanted to teach me, but he planted the seeds in my memory and had faith that, as I matured, those seeds of wisdom would mature as well and bear fruit when I needed them most.

The precise moment I needed my dad's guidance most was the night of June 11, 2003 —the night I used Lou Fratto's wisdom to turn a Hollywood Hindenburg moment into a multimillion-dollar windfall. This was the moment where I was born again, the moment when I was finally made in Hollywood, regardless of what fuckin' William Morris had to say about it.

Incidentally, this was also the moment that made Paris Hilton. I defy you to find a TV piece on Paris Hilton before June 11, 2003. That was the night I took a local socialite best known for begging for attention by dancing on nightclub tables and elevated her up to the world stage. Paris already had a name, but I lit it up in big neon letters and put it on the marquee.

The story begins when Lil' Johnny and I got bored waiting for *Son of a Gun* to make us rich and decided to start exploring other business opportunities. We told our by-now many sordid associates in California to bring us ideas, and one of them delivered two rinky-dink, 29-inch-tall, 120-pound toy motorcyles with jerry-rigged lawnmower engines and elongated front ends. These contraptions were really just scooters dressed up like choppers for Halloween, but the concept instinctually appealed to me.

They were basically decorative motorcycles shrunk down to a size that they could be displayed in someone's house.

Though I was terrified of motorcycles and refused to ride one, I decided to give the motorcycle business a shot. Everyone told me you needed to be Harley Davidson himself (he was a guy, right?), or some German mechanic type, to even dream of making a profit with a new line of motorcycles, but I knew that all business boils down to marketing. Back when I was young, some guy came up with a way of marketing motherfucking *rocks* and made a fortune selling "Pet Rocks."

Midget choppers had to be easier to sell than that.

I decided to embrace the absurdity of the idea of marketing tiny, under-powered designer *choppers*, which were traditionally the sort of macho *Easy Rider* motorcycles that biker gangs rode. I came up with the perfect name for the company: Beverly Hills Choppers. Anyone expecting a seriously badass chopper would take one look at that oxymoron of a name and know I was in a different business. I was making "midi-choppers" for socialites who purchased tiny handbag Chihuahuas instead of real dogs.

I knew I was onto something when the first big fan of Beverly Hills Choppers was none other than Beverly Hills socialite Kim Stewart, daughter of singer Rod Stewart. The first time Kim Stewart visited our penthouse with Lil' Johnny, she saw two lipstick red midi-chopper prototypes shining in the sunlight on our roof and fell in love. She begged for permission to use them as red carpet props at the chopper-themed Maxim Hot 100 Party that weekend.

Her guest at that party? Paris Hilton.

I was dead set against staking a couple million dollars of legal liability on the chance that a couple hard-partying Beverly Hills socialites would correctly and responsibly operate these half-ass motorcycles at a crowded party. I saw the disaster coming from miles away, but I didn't see the opportunity within the disaster until it practically reached the white of my eyes.

All I could think about was the potential for a Lizzie Grubman scenario where these two sweethearts would kickstart *my* choppers and mow down scores of celebrities with great attorneys. I was sure it would be a catastrophe, but Lil' Johnny argued Kim's case with his usual persistence and annoyingness.

"I mean, c'mon Dad," he said in his kinetic Christian Slater voice, "what paparazzi photographer could resist two smoking hot billionaire heiresses throwing an impromptu photo shoot on the red carpet with sleek, stylish, lipstick-red choppers nestled between their thighs? It would be automatic tabloid candy, and great publicity for Beverly Hills Choppers."

"Fine, fine!" I said, waving my hands in the air to surrender. "They can do it . . . under one condition. Under no circumstances do you let those girls start them things! If I hear you started them fucking choppers, I'm going to lose my fucking mind! That would be my worst nightmare to see those rich white girls get hurt on my choppers! Don't fuck me on this, Johnny! We're going to owe the Hiltons a lot more than that hotel bill if Paris gets hurt!"

Kim agreed to the stipulation that they were allowed to do nothing with the motorcycles besides pose for pictures on the bikes and then slowly, gingerly walk them down the red carpet Fred Flintstone style. Grumbling to myself the entire time, I arranged for a limousine to escort Johnny, the girls, and their entourage to the party. They would be followed by a truck carrying the two bikes.

Under the perhaps too-watchful eyes of my son, the girls and their crew of Nicole Richie and rock singer Cisco Adler had the sort of fun in the back of my limousine that makes a chauffeur necessary. When they finally hit the red carpet, these veteran party girls were hopped up and ready to cause mayhem, and they did a professional job of it.

The photo op started beautifully: Kim in a slinky black cocktail dress and tall black fuck-me boots, Paris in a princess pink satin dress with black boots and a black cabbie hat, both looking absolutely beautiful as they straddled the midi-choppers. Dozens of paparazzi crowded the heiresses on the red carpet, each camera click worth thousands of dollars of free publicity to the girls and to my company. As long as the girls kept their word, everything would go fine.

Fortunately for me, the girls kept their word, but one of the people in *our* entourage didn't. Everything went insane in a moment. "Rev the bike!" a cameraman called out to Kim, looking for a nice growling sound effect for his footage. Kim obliged, but the bike was turned off—as promised—so no sound was made.

As fortune would have it, the goofball son of one of my business associates ran up behind Kim and pressed the automatic start button on the bike as Kim obliviously throttled the bike.

To her shock, the engine between Kim's legs roared to life like a Satanic vibrator and *zoom!* A crotch rocket was launched down the red carpet as Rod Stewart's screaming daughter hung on like Wile E. Coyote. After a 50-foot journey, Kim slid backwards off the bike into a face-first, spread-legged splat on the red carpet. She was splayed out like a crime scene victim, her ass in all of its thonged glory exposed to dozens of cameras with telephoto lenses.

The bike itself spun out of control and narrowly missed barreling into Pam Anderson and Carmen Electra, who had preceded the girls by a few seconds down the red carpet. The chopper finally sputtered onto its side harmlessly, thank God!

The paparazzi who didn't stampede over to capture exclusive shots of Kim Stewart's brown eye turned to Paris Hilton for a reaction shot. Sitting peacefully on her midi-chopper, Paris Hilton was ready for her close-up.

No matter what anyone tells you, that girl has *it*. You'll never convince me she wasn't born to be famous. She may not be calculating, but she has the instinct to make up for it. She defined her brand on the fly, doing what aspiring starlets spend decades failing to do.

Smiling and looking completely unconcerned about her friend, Paris with her best carefree Doublemint Gum commercial smile and spoiled Valley Girl voice delivered her star-making line: "Oh my god!"

Paris said those words with the innocent amusement of a little girl who had just taken a first sip from a delicious milk shake — not a full-grown woman whose best friend had just taken the sort of high-speed dive from a motorcycle that once scrambled Bob Dylan's brain so bad, his music never sounded the same.

Those three cheery syllables—"Oh my god!"—captured Paris' entire celebrity persona: the rich girl indifference to the suffering of others, the unflappable Marcia Brady smile, and the shameless pandering for paparazzi attention.

I first saw it as a breaking news bulletin on my TV screen: *Rod Stewart's daughter in a red carpet motorcycle crash!* They didn't say if she was alive or dead, crippled or scratched. My entire body went as cold as a first wife at bedtime; I had never considered the possibility that I might *kill* Rod Stewart's daughter.

My phone was blowing up within seconds. The general consensus was that Johnny Fratto was motherfucked. Royally motherfucked. Even the business partner whose son started the bike had the nerve to fax over his resignation from Beverly Choppers, effective immediately.

He had a point. The son of one of my business partners had turned on one of my motorcycles without Kim's permission or knowledge, sending her at top speed to the consoling embrace of Rod Stewart's high-powered attorneys. She could also make a good case that she had suffered serious emotional distress from the embarrassment of exposing her poonany and cigar cutter to every paparazzi camera in LA.

As soon I confirmed that Kim Stewart was still physically able to party, I shut off my phone like I was slamming the door to my underground bunker during an air raid. The bombs would keep falling, but I went into my bunker. I felt like an Outfit gangster who, after decades of luck, finally gets put in cuffs and told he's under arrest for murder.

Helpless and terrified, I instinctually turned to memories of Dad. I had never missed his wisdom and his calm more. Standing on my patio overlooking Beverly Hills, smoking a cigarette and massaging my forehead with one finger of the hand that was holding my silenced cellphone, hearing Jowanka bickering with our toddler son Joey through the glass sliding door—I tried to conjure Lou by recalling my memories of him.

I pictured him walking back and forth in his silk suit across our back porch, holding a rotary phone attached to a nine-mile-long cord in one hand and a cigar in the other, pretending to listen to my playground stories as he weighed decisions of life and death importance.

Either Dad was helping me out from the Great Beyond, or I just got lucky, but a new memory came to me. I remembered asking Dad as a little kid how he managed to succeed as a boxer despite his severe lack of height. I remembered Lou smiling and crouching down next to me with a smirk on his face.

"So, short stuff, this is how I did it," he whispered to me, hushed yet mischievous. "I'd never go off half-cocked. I'd calmly work my way inside, gettin' as close to the other guy as possible before takin' my shots. I might get hit five times gettin' in there, Johnny . . .

"*But*, when I got real up-close-and-personal, it only took *one* shot from me to end the fight. That's why I always tell you: take your time, don't move too fast! You rather be slow!

"It's like anything; in cards, you wait to show your hand until the other players have thrown down big bets. In war, you don't open fire until you see the white of your target's eyes and know you can blast 'em away. You got to learn to *thrive* in danger, thrive when you're in trouble, and never panic. It's only when you start taking a few on the chin that you really know you are close to your goal."

That was Dad's secret: he never panicked in danger and always waited for his moment. The man saw opportunity in danger and chaos for good reason. He had risen to wealth and power during Al Capone's bloody street battles during Prohibition. He had walked right into the punches of some of the best boxers in the world and faced down barrages of Tommy Gun fire to get at opportunity.

Dad never gave in. He would take a good, long, patient look at any crisis until he could see the way out before he did a thing. I'd watch him pace for hours, just focused on an obstacle, running his mind over it looking for a weakness. That's what made him Golden Tongue—the ability to think and then talk his way out of even the worst crisis that Frank Fratto could create and, somehow, profit from it. That cerebral side is what separated him from your everyday thug, what gave him his identity crisis.

Surely, if Lou had been in my shoes, he wouldn't panic and flee in the face of a crashed midi-chopper. This couldn't be as bad as it seemed. I needed to look for the way to massage this disaster into something good.

I walked back inside and faced the crisis head on. I watched the clip play on the local news a couple times—and heard myself laugh. *Laugh!*

I had my eureka moment: if I could laugh at my own misfortune, then people around the world were laughing at Kim Stewart's out-of-control kamikaze dive and Paris Hilton's carefree "oopsy-doopsy!" response. Even though I felt for Kim and feared for my livelihood, I had no choice but to laugh.

This thing would have legs; it would be played over and over again. All I needed to do was to leverage this publicity. This was no disaster; my life wasn't over. My life had just begun. All I needed was for this story to blow up—and for me to escape third degree burns despite standing right next to it.

Well, it did blow up. Kim Stewart's toppling chopper was tabloid crack. Kim's pratfall and Paris Hilton's hilariously indifferent reaction were played on every entertainment news show in the world. Not since Chevy Chase impersonated Gerald Ford has a pratfall gag been flogged so relentlessly. The crash was even named #1 on Vh1's *Best of the Worst Red Carpet Moments.*

As far as I know, Paris and Kim never spent another day without a paparazzi camera close by. For the rest of their youth, there was always some company willing to pay them *thousands of dollars* just to be seen wearing their clothes or partying at their club. It was the best thing that had ever happened to them.

Thanks to Dad, I was the only one who realized it was the best thing that ever happened to *me*, as well. To everyone else in the world, my life had just been ruined.

"Calm down," I assured my concerned friends and family, smiling too big and lapsing into a yawn. Just like Dad, I knew how to poker face people into a sense of security. I was as chill as Woody Harrelson. "I know exactly what to do. I've learned from the best."

Once it became clear this story was *my* moment, I immediately hunted down Kim Stewart on Beverly Drive with a big smile and embraced her like a long lost daughter. After all, I remembered how Dad had dealt with all of those ornery nuns and selfish politicians and greedy wiseguys.

"Listen, it was horrible what happened," I said with a porcelain-bright smile as I held Kim's pretty little hands in mine. "You deserve to be taken care of. You were such a trooper. I'm going to take care of you. You've gone through enough. Let me take care of you," I cooed, running my fingertips along the inside of her wrist.

"Let me tell you what I'm going to do. To make good what you went through, I'm going to build you and Paris your own custom-made, deluxe, hot-pink choppers done any way you like—with encrusted jewels, fine leather, anything you want! It's all yours, for free, as a sign of my gratitude for being such good sports."

Kim smiled her Barbie smile and nodded her head. I defused a multimillion-dollar lawsuit with a gift of two $6000 midi-choppers with lawnmower engines. Paris' was encrusted with hot pink Swarovski crystals, while Kim requested a pink paint job with tiger stripe flames.

Of course, I stole another million dollars' worth of free publicity by throwing huge events commemorating the bribe I paid to Kim and Paris. My two favorite celebrities accepted their custom Beverly Hills Choppers in front of a cavalcade of cameramen and journalists. Paris, savvy as ever, lied through her teeth and inflated the cost of her chopper to $250,000, which was picked up and replayed endlessly on the E! Entertainment Television special *The Fabulous Life of Young Hot Hollywood*.

Overnight, everyone in Beverly Hills wanted a Beverly Hills Choppers *specifically because of the inflated price*. Our brand was also helped by the fact that the bikes were so exclusive—we didn't have any! There was no company, no factory, no store, nothing! Just a name and a publicity stunt. Because our bikes were expensive and hard-to-find, *everyone* wanted one.

I was made.

A brand was born.

I had been just as oblivious as Kim Stewart when Beverly Hills Choppers surprisingly kickstarted to life between my legs. Unlike Kim, I did not land face first. I corrected mid-fall and rode that fucker right to the bank. It was a veritable cashtastrophe. Only a Fratto would decide to launch a motorcycle company on the back of a motorcycle crash.

Celebrities such as P. Diddy, Martha Stewart, Lil' Jon, Kelly Ripa, Snoop Dogg, Fat Joe, Damon Dash, Jermaine Dupri, and Fergie were snatching photo opportunities with Johnny Fratto and one of his Beverly Hills Choppers. Eventually, we built a few choppers and granted their wishes. We did specially commissioned bikes for Russell Simmons' company Phat Farm, Kimora Lee

Simmons' Baby Phat, and MGA Entertainment's Super Bowl release party for their movie *Bratz!*

A few months later, this publicity would bring Beverly Hills Choppers, a nearly nonexistent company based out of my penthouse apartment in Beverly Hills, a seven-figure licensing contract in Japan. A consortium of Japanese billionaires flew us over and deputized the Japanese police *and* the Japanese Mafia, the Yakuza, to escort us to the grand opening of the first Beverly Hills Choppers store in Tokyo.

With cops on one side and the gangsters on the other, I was the middle to Good and Evil, just like Dad.

When our limos pulled up, it was like Beatlemania: people were screaming, paparazzi were fighting for position, hot Japanese girls were pulling at my son's long black hair. We could've sold out the Budokan for an appearance. We were stars.

That was just the beginning. Though I couldn't keep selling *Son of a Gun*, my newfound celebrity and cachet combined with my Mob Network connections allowed me to talk, glamour, and hustle my way into a preposterous assortment of TV, film, music, and magazine deals. The Beverly Hills branch of Fratto Inc. was suddenly doing the sort of business the Chicago and Des Moines branches had been doing for decades.

Even Tweety Bird wanted a piece of me.

When younger sister Nikki Hilton got jealous of Paris' crystal-studded bike, Warner Brothers jumped at the opportunity to grab a Hilton family and Beverly Hills Chopper publicity stunt. To get us to appear together at the grand opening of the new Tweety Bird store in Manhattan and remind everyone of Kim Stewart's red carpet fall, Warner Brothers commissioned a crystal-encrusted Tweety Bird-branded Beverly Hills Chopper to present to Nikki at the event.

And that appearance happened to put us in New York, the home of a certain radio show. It took one fortuitous accident to get me to Manhattan and the green room of *The Howard Stern Show*, the biggest radio show in modern history.

LET ME TELL YOU A QUICK STORY...

ABOUT THE MINIATURE MAFIA

Let's enjoy a short flashback to the late 1960s . . .

"Lemme tell you somethin', size ain't everything!" Uncle Frank said, interrupting my brother Frankie after he joked about how opposing athletes never expected a short kid like him to be such a force of nature.

"Yeah, I tell you, don't let anyone say you're too small to do anything. Frankie, I'm going to tell you a story that shows how even a three-foot-tall midget can have gigantic fuckin' balls."

That was the first time I had ever heard the word "midget." And after Uncle Frank's story, little people (*really* little people) became an obsession of mine, just like vampires.

"You see, there once were these two little Italian midgets in Chicago in your Dad's crew named Jesse and Lil' Al," Uncle Frank said. "These two guys were real-deal fuckin' *gangsters*, and they weighed like sixty pounds apiece. You should have seen how everyone laughed at them and busted on them when they climbed up to a card table, but those two fucking hustlers would clean out the entire table in thirty minutes. They were fucking genius gamblers.

"Well, one night, Lil' Al pissed off the wrong guy and got shot up outside your grandma's house in Chicago. I ran out to see about the commotion and got out there too late to see who done it, so I picked up Lil' Al, carried him up the stairs, and laid him out on your grandma's table. As he bled out, I couldn't think of nothin' but how much room there was left on the table . . . I mean, the guy was just *this* big, poor little fucker!

"So, in through the door come these two Italian cops to watch Lil' Al as he dies. They keep begging him in Italian to snitch who shot him so they can go out and get'em. With his dyin' breath, the little guy looks up, shakes his head, and says, 'I ain't beefin'!' And then he died!"

Uncle Frank turned serious, nodding his head with respect. He was showing the respect that he only gave to the dead. "Man, I always said that was a classy move, one of the classiest moves I ever saw. *I ain't beefin'!* He wasn't tellin' those cops nuttin. I can't help but brag on the class of that little midget."

ABOUT WHY YOU SHOULDN'T HUFF EMBALMING FLUID

The noble fall of that great gangster began my fascination with midgets—and I say that word without malice or apology. I'd be a phony if I pretended that I don't say the word "midget" because a couple busybodies printed up some stationery and started writing letters to politicians and TV stations. I'm not being hateful; it's just the word that makes sense to me and feels honest.

"Little person" isn't specific enough of a term. Lil' Wayne is a little person, but he ain't no midget. Hell, *I* have always been a little person, but I've never been a midget.

I haven't *earned* that word—I love and admire midgets for overcoming their shortfalls.

I especially admire evil midgets.

My first experience with an evil midget came as a young man. I was in the passenger's seat of my lifelong best friend Mike's car, enjoying an afternoon drive. Mike had spent years dropping LSD and huffing embalming fluid at his Dad's mortuary, which combined to transform him into a totally paranoid, cracked-up burnout.

During our leisurely drive together, Mike suddenly screamed "IT'S THE MIDGET!" and swerved our car into oncoming traffic. At the last possible moment, he shanked the car onto the sidewalk, only to narrowly avoid running over a grandma by gunning the car down a one-way street the wrong way. After the scariest thirty seconds of my life, Mike swung into a dark alley and slammed on the brakes. His hands were like talons on the steering wheel, and he was sweating buckshots and crying.

I was too shocked to even scream. I slowly turned my head, blinked a couple times, and calmly asked my old buddy what the problem was. "There is an evil midget..." Mike panted, staring at me with a melancholy, hopeless look that reminded me of Anthony Perkins in *Psycho*. "...An evil midget named Nathan. Nathan is hunting me down. He's following me. Everywhere I go, he's shadowing me. He has *evil* plans for me..."

"Because he's an evil midget?"

"Yes...because he's an evil midget. He's chasing me."

"Now listen up, buddy," I told Mike as I bravely ventured to put a reassuring hand on his tightly clenched shoulder. "It's my pleasure to inform you there is no such thing as an evil midget, and there are *definitely* no evil midgets that go around chasing people."

Mike, I'd like to apologize. I'm sorry, buddy; I had no way of knowing.

If I knew then what I know now, I would have definitely believed that Nathan existed. After all, I was chased by an evil midget more or less constantly for many years. I'm just lucky that *my* evil midget did it on the radio so everyone could see I hadn't gone insane.

30

SAY HELLO TO MY LITTLE FRIEND

The story of the third generation of the alliance between the Fratto family and midgets begins on June 21, 2006 in New York City. Lil' Johnny and I were in Manhattan to present Nikki Hilton with her custom Tweety Bird Beverly Hills Chopper for Warner Brothers. Since we were in the city at the same time, my son's roommate invited us to accompany him to the studios of *The Howard Stern Show* for an interview he had scheduled there.

My son's roommate was no stranger to the most successful morning radio show in American history: my son was living with none other than K.C. Armstrong, Howard's recently fired but still beloved associate producer. K.C. was a Stern icon, a muscular jock with serious anger problems and a thin skin when it came to homoerotic song parodies and impressions.

After getting abruptly and secretly fired for being a volatile loon, K.C. headed west to become a movie star or the kept man of some rich aging Hollywood socialite, whichever came first. In one of the greatest strokes of luck in my family's history, K.C. happened to quickly meet, befriend, and move in with Lil' Johnny. They made perfect roommates: two handsome twentysomething pussyhounds whose looks camouflaged their paranoid neuroses.

Feeling sorry for K.C., Lil' Johnny gave him a job as a scout for The Beverly Hills Angels, the team of red-hot bikini spokesmodels we used to advertise Beverly Hills Choppers bikes and clothing. You'd think "finding hot chicks at clubs" would be the one job besides lifting weights that K.C. could do, but K.C. scared away all the talent by fucking the girls and then weirding them out by talking about Illuminati and aliens and Freemasons.

We tried to get K.C. off our payroll by nudging him back into the one thing he had ever been good at besides high school amateur wrestling: radio.

Instead of capitalizing on his huge name recognition and getting a new job in radio, K.C. spent his days pulling out Lil' Johnny's phone lines in search of wiretap equipment, disassembling and reassembling their computers to make sure they contained no CIA-implanted chips, and sleeping in a closet with a baseball bat.

When Lil' Johnny asked K.C. why he had dissembled all of his electronic equipment, K.C. grumbled in his grizzly bear voice, "I just want it to work bettah!"

This got me rolling. I'd yell at K.C. for hours. "Work better? *What?!* You think a meathead like you knows better than fuckin' Sony?"

One night, Lil' Johnny came home and K.C. had thrown out the garbage can. He would never tell us why. We suspected K.C. had heard the garbage can talking to him like John Wayne Gacy's dog, the lid flapping up and down like a mouth.

K.C. was losing his mind, and a jacked-up jock squandering his good looks and his incredible career to battle imaginary enemies is *great* radio. It's no surprise that Howard decided to let K.C. come back on the show to explain his disappearance and his bizarre psychological state. Naturally, we were invited.

On the big day, we were already in Manhattan when K.C. called from what he said was Los Angeles Airport and told us to head up to the green room and wait for him there. As we were sitting on the ratty couches outside of the studio at 5 a.m. in the morning, I leaned over to Lil' Johnny and bet him that K.C. would never show.

"What? Are you crazy? Why would he fly all the way out here and not show? He's been dying to come on the show and get his side of the story out!"

"You *goofball*," I said, shaking my head at my son. "K.C. ain't takin' no flight. You had to dope me up halfway to death to get me on the airplane out here, and I'm ten times less paranoid than K.C. He ain't gettin' on no fuckin' airplane this morning. He thinks Al Qaeda is out to get him."

I'm wrong all the time, but Lil' Johnny is my lucky charm: it's rare that I'm wrong on anything he disagrees with me about. It's like God must have a similarly annoying time with Jesus and never wants me to be wrong with *my* know-it-all son. Roughly one second after I finished my prediction, my son's cellphone rang. It was K.C. He said he got lost on the way to the airport, even though we had given him a GPS receiver that gave him street-by-street directions.

Thirty minutes later, he had somehow gotten laid over in San Diego and was waiting for another flight.

Then *that* flight was delayed.

Then somehow he was back in Los Angeles.

Then he assured Lil' Johnny that he'd still make it cross country in a couple hours one way or another. "What? This motherfucker gonna to charter a Concord?" I asked.

At around 9 a.m., Lil' Johnny and I were still sitting in the green room, killing time. Since the show also had time to kill and K.C. wanted to divert the attention from his no-show, he called up Stern's producer, Gary "Baba Booey" Dell'Abate, and told him to put me on the air since I had great Mob stories.

A couple minutes later, I was escorted into the studio all radio fans knew so well: Robin Quivers was in her little Plexiglas booth that made her look like a high-security prisoner waiting for a visitor; sound effect virtuoso Fred Norris was hunched over in a cluttered corner, grunting into the microphone as he did his gay caveman K.C. impersonation; bloated comedian Artie Lange was gnawing through a big sandwich fresh from the deli; and Howard Stern himself was presiding over his radio control board, as commanding a presence as Captain Kirk.

It's impossible to exaggerate the intensity and intimacy of Howard Stern's bond with his radio audience. For decades, he has been the friend, therapist, entertainer, and tastemaker for millions of fans, who have formed a daily partnership with him during their lonely and miserable morning weekday work hours. He takes the worst part of their lives and transforms into a time of hilarity and fun, with a cast of characters that are as familiar and as flawed and as comfortable as family. His fanbase isn't just huge and loyal—it is bonded to him on a profound level.

Think of the scale of their interaction—Howard spoke directly and honestly to his audience for hours, uninterrupted, every single workday, for decades. Even today, while working a more relaxed schedule, he personally produces and performs hundreds of hours of entertainment for his fans annually. Most hardcore Howard Stern fans have listened to his voice more than any other person in their entire lives. They know him better than they know their own spouses—hell, they know his newsreader, producer, sound effect guy, and limo driver better than they know their own families.

If you make it with Howard, you have made it with over ten million radio listeners.

If you fail with Howard, a huge segment of the world hates you, forever.

There's no bullshitting around the truth: I have never been more nervous, more terrified. Without warning or a chance to prepare, I was called in to do an impromptu appearance on the most notoriously intimidating talk show on the planet. This was my ultimate challenge as a conman and bullshit artist. I was now face-to-face with the most gifted, clever, and challenging broadcaster in multimedia history. I would be going one-on-one with Howard Stern, a man who had successfully improvised and self-promoted his way into a multi-billion dollar fortune in a dying industry.

If I killed, I would have so much notoriety that I could do anything I wanted with Beverly Hills Choppers and *Son of a Gun.* This was another pivotal moment in my life. In that moment, I knew my future might depend on how I approached this challenge.

Instinctually, I did the same thing that saved my ass during the Kim Stewart crisis: I thought about Dad. I felt myself calm down, cool down, and exhale. And then the stories started pouring out of me: Dad stealing the space capsule, Dad shaking poor Michael Landon like a bobble head, Dad making the Harlem Globetrotters play in my backyard, Dad taking away Blinky's ability to blink, Dad hitching rides on the back of a garbage truck in his silk suit—all of my favorite childhood memories.

As always, Lou showed me the way. I had the hardest room in America exploding with laughter, one story after another. I went into that room an anonymous goofball—the first thing Robin said to me was she thought I was some strange Arab guy due to my tan—and killed for an unprecedented *70 minute* interview. I got seventy straight minutes of promotion on the top radio show in America! For free! Spur of the moment!

I have never been prouder than when Howard finally brought the interview to a close with the following goodbye: "Johnny Fratto, you're great! Johnny Fratto and son, Johnny Fratto Jr., *welcome to the show!* Great to have you here! The *next* time you come back, you're gonna tell me about when *Nicole Eggert* was your girlfriend. I like that!"

I bet Howard did; when he ran for Governor of New York, Stern had promised to make Nicole the Official State Girlfriend.

Unless you've experienced it yourself, you cannot imagine the incredible cultural reach of *The Howard Stern Show.* After my appearance played on air and was put up on Howard's On Demand TV channel, I started getting recognized not only every day but every *hour.* It was a humbling experience. Here I thought that the Mafia had built an impressive empire over the past century, and come to find out that a disc jockey from Long Island had constructed a multimedia empire and social network that put Tony Accardo to shame.

The best way I can explain Howard's incredible reach is by comparing how I was treated in Hollywood before and after I went on Howard's show.

After I got rolling with Howard and the option with Fremantle lapsed, I was instantly given an option for *Son of a Gun* on the History Channel. They gave us everything we wanted, including money to film a new professional pilot with professionally shot flashback scenes.

And in the end, it was *me* who walked away from the chance to put *Son of a Gun* on TV. (Yes, Lil' Johnny, I just confessed.)

Why? Because the offer I had on the table wasn't good enough. I was getting so much interest and play in Hollywood after Howard "made" me that I could carefully *pick and choose* how I wanted to make my TV and film debut. No more begging for me—now I could make millions just sitting on my ass, collecting money on TV and film "options" I never ever intended to honor. Why come clean when I could make millions coming dirty?

Once I understood the incredible promotional potential of Howard's show, I took him at his word when he said "Welcome to the show!" Though I had no intention of getting on a fucking airplane and flying back to New York, I was happy to call in from Beverly Hills just about every night that my insomnia medication, Ambien, didn't work.

The mind-bending side effects of Ambien added a certain maniacal charm to my calls to Howard. I'd be sitting at kitchen table, mumbling into my cellphone about how the bar code on my ice tea bottle looked like Eric Roberts, and this lunatic gibberish would be broadcast to millions of cars, homes, and offices across America.

Ambien made me funny: I would call in so numb and oblivious that I didn't realize that, while I was talking, I was also *very* loudly chomping on some macaroon cookies directly into the ears of 20 million listeners. On one famous occasion, I called in so drugged up that I simply passed out mid-sentence and snored through the rest of my call. Any other broadcaster would have just hung up, but not Howard. Howard left my rhythmic snoring playing in the background as the show continued, providing a steady groove like The Rolling Stones' rhythm section.

But there's a secret to my "sleeping" calls into the *Stern Show*, which happened more than once. The fact that I was always sleeping on the toilet is actually the least embarrassing part of the confession I'm about to make.

If you happen to walk by the bathroom in my Beverly Hills Penthouse when I am using it, the gap at the bottom of the door glows like I'm being visited by the Virgin Mary.

That's because of my deepest, darkest secret: I tan on the shitter, and I've been broadcast to tens of millions of radio listeners while tanning asleep on my toilet on more than one occasion.

Though I'd tell Howard Stern that the tan Robin Quivers described as "Arab" comes from an Italian driving a convertible around California, the reality is I jerry-rigged a tanning apparatus next to my throne. All Italian family men of a certain age cherish their time in the bathroom, but, unlike those who like to read, I enjoy laying back, sunning myself, and keeping my tan crisp.

There's just one problem with this otherwise brilliant set-up: tanning makes me sleepy.

That's right, if you ever listened to me on Howard Stern's radio show, there's a high likelihood you listened to a distinguished Italian gentleman as he tanned on his toilet. If you ever heard me asleep on the phone on Stern's show, I can basically guarantee you that I was tanning on the crapper at the time.

What else was I supposed to do while on hold for hours at 3 a.m. California time besides bathroom sunbathe?

Even with Howard's help, I might have worn out my welcome with the audience a long time ago if it wasn't for a chance phone call from an evil midget far more terrifying than the fictitious Nathan.

I was standing on my patio, having a smoke and listening to my Sirius Satellite Radio receiver, when this unknown Sacramento number started blowing up my cellphone. I finally got so annoyed by the persistent, incessant calls that I picked up. "Hello?"

"He...lo, is this...Johnny...Fratto?" The voice on the other line was slow, raspy, and somehow mechanical. It sounded like a robot that needed to reboot its batteries every few seconds.

"Yeah, who are you?"

"I...am...Eric Lynch."

"And who the fuck is that?"

"You...may know...me...from the Stern show. They...call me...Eric the Midget."

"Yeah right," I said, laughing to myself, "I wasn't born yesterday, Richard and Sal. Go fuck yourself." I hung up the phone. I wasn't going to fall for a phony phone call from Howard's pet touchtone terrorists. There was no way that was the *real* Eric the Midget, the King of the Wack Pack.

A moment later, the Sacramento phone number called again. A growling, venomous, demonic voice seethed through my phone. "Listen...motherfucker...this is not those cunts Richard...and Sal...this is the real...

Eric . . . the Midget . . . but don't . . . call me . . . that . . . but this is me, shit . . . fucking . . . head!"

Now *that* sulfurous rage could only be the real-deal Eric the Midget. No one else could replicate that Satanic Hervé Villechaize anger. Now I felt bad for hanging up on the poor little guy.

"Alright, Eric. I'm sorry," I said, sincerely apologetic. "What can I do for you?"

"Well . . . I have a crush on Kelly . . . Clarkson . . . from *American Idol* . . . and I heard . . . that you . . . are connected in . . . Hollywood . . . and can maybe hook . . . me up . . ."

And from that moment, Mike's nightmare became my reality: an evil midget was chasing me.

For those who don't know of the only evil midget to become a clue in the *New York Times* crossword puzzle (which actually happened), Eric Lynch was God's special little voodoo doll. He was a 3'5", 85-pound, misshapen little creature with countless disabilities. He suffered from a preposterously horrible condition called Ehler-Danlos Syndrome that came with every shitty symptom you can find in a circus freakshow tent. He had a Gorbachev ink blot on his forehead, a club foot, weak lungs, bug eyes, stumpy legs, and gnarly claw-hands that Jimmy Kimmel once shook and compared to rotten plums.

Basically, Eric looked like the misbegotten love child of Yoda and Rick Moranis. He was truly pitiable in every way. The only thing about him that wasn't cursed was his spirit; he had a gigantic, over-the-top, take-no-shit personality trapped forever in a tiny, tortured body.

When Eric first called into Howard's show, he was a virgin who had never held a job, walked, driven a car, or experienced the dignity of taking a shit without another person's assistance. His only joy in life was watching *American Idol* and pro wrestling—and masturbating by dog-humping a special fuck pillow in his bed.

Looking at this laundry list of bad luck, it was impossible to feel anything but pity for Eric. And therein lies the problem. Poor Eric spent his entire life prior to calling into the Howard Stern show being coddled, accommodated, and lied to. No one ever checked the kid when he got out of line; they just kowtowed to him. When combined with the justifiable resentment he feels for his lot in life, this ass-kissing behavior turned Eric into a pathologically arrogant, aggressive, entitled, insulting, and rage-filled little person.

Basically, Eric was the world's biggest or littlest asshole, depending on how you look at it.

And the incredible thing is that, until calling into Howard Stern, Eric had no idea his personality was unlikable. He foisted himself upon the most merciless and critical audience imaginable, oblivious even to the possibility that he might receive some sort of negative response.

At first, Howard indulged Eric, giving him cash prizes every time he waited on hold for two hours to bitch about them calling Kelly Clarkson fat or pro wrestling gay. This initial kindness was taken by Eric as encouragement to bully the Stern show. Any time Howard said a single syllable Eric disagreed with over the breadth of a five-hour broadcast, Eric would call right in to insult, berate, lecture, and condemn the entire Stern staff with psychotic vitriol.

Howard, with his unerring comedic instinct, zeroed in the most hilarious part of Eric's bizarre psyche: the entitlement. Eric sincerely believed he was above dating anyone besides white-hot celebrities, and it was *outrageous* that America's most popular radio show didn't immediately put him on the air every single time he called and let him ramble, *forever*, about any inane topic he chose. Whenever Howard gently disagreed with Eric, the midget would respond by e-mailing Howard's producer Gary messages like these actual all-caps excerpts:

"FUCKER BOOK ME ON THE FUCKING SHOW NOW!!!! ASS-HOLE, AND GET YOUR LIE DETECTOR PERSON IN THERE. I WILL COMPLETELY SUBMIT MYSELF TO A FUCKING LIE DETECTOR TEST TO FUCKING PROVE YOUR ASS WRONG, AND SHUT YOU THE UP ONCE AND FOR ALL.... I SO WANT TO MAKE YOU EAT YOUR FUCKING WORDS AND SEE THEM PASS YOUR HUGE LIPS, AND TEETH.... I DID WHAT I DID DO TRY TO GET BACK AT YOU BIG TIME, AND TO GET YOU TO FUCKING APOLGIZE TO ME FOR THE SHIT THAT YOUR FUCKING RETARD ASS OPINIONS OF ME HAVE BEEN CAUS-ING ME ON LINE.... KEEP YOUR FUCKING OPINIONS TO YOURSELF."

This sort of letter would come in just about every day, and so would the phone rants. Eric's lovely personality gradually won him the title of the most viscerally hated person in all of radio. Even Daniel Carver, the KKK leader, was regularly voted more popular than Eric on Howard Stern fan sites. Eric made public appearances at comedy shows or strip clubs, and, despite looking like one of Jerry's Kids, he would get booed and catcalled like Hitler at your local Jewish Community Center for *minutes on end*. It was incredible to see.

Instinctually, I think Eric knew the only way he could escape being an object of sympathy was to be an object of hatred. In fact, I think, deep down, Eric appreciated when the Stern Show staff teased and argued with him because they were giving him the respect of treating him like the total asshole he is, not a "poor cripple" to be pitied.

After that first phone call, Eric the total asshole was now my problem. He unilaterally adopted me as his sugar daddy, making excessive demands on my time and finances despite the fact that we had never met. It was pure extortion: one day the little fucker just decided I had to give him whatever he wanted or else. Though I realized this situation was absurd, I felt sorry for the kid and let myself be exploited. Still, Eric was never satisfied.

One day, Eric made the mistake of bitching to Howard about my insufficient generosity. Howard knew immediately that this was a storyline too good to be true: a reformed wiseguy being ruthlessly bullied by a parasitic evil midget. Individually, Johnny Fratto and Eric the Midget were once-a-month callers.

Johnny and Eric as a comedy team became a daily part of *The Howard Stern Show*. A collection of all our appearances on Stern runs to over 50 unedited hours of primetime national exposure, replayed for thousands upon thousands of hours in re-runs. In a life of unlikely circumstances, accidentally becoming a part of a massively popular unpaid radio comedy duo with a tiny disabled gentleman has to be the most surreal experience.

Don't get me wrong, my abusive relationship with Eric was real. Like with the motorcycle crash and K.C. flaking out on us, I just did my best to exploit a bad situation. Over time, I lost my pity for Eric and began to conspire with the Stern show staff on ways to torture the little fucker for his disrespectful attitude. There have been way too many great pranks, phony phone calls, and dirty jokes to rehash, but here are some of my favorites.

One of our longest and most popular ways of tormenting Eric was to try to convince him to let us tie him to a bundle of children's balloons that would lift him up and let him "fly" around Howard's studio. This made Eric apoplectic with rage for reasons no normal human mind can wrap itself around. The entire humor of the gag was Eric's insanely vicious response to the mere mention of the word "balloons" like Pavlov's angry Chihuahua.

Another favorite was Howard's threats to build a life-size latex sex doll replica of Eric that he would give to all of the Midget's least favorite Stern show regulars to repeatedly violate and use as a "cock puppet." I scored one of my biggest hits when I leaked Eric some "legal research" that stated the "landmark case of Bergen versus McCarthy" made the sex doll stunt illegal. When Eric repeated the name of the case on air, it took a couple minutes for someone to pick up on the joke: Bergen & McCarthy were a famous ventriloquist act.

Probably the most popular Eric routine among Stern fans is the infamous "You know what to do" message. This kid from Eric's high school had been calling into the show to discuss how Eric had nearly bankrupted the school district by insisting all sorts of ramps, pulleys, and special accommodations be installed specifically for him. This justifiably enraged Eric (I mean, the guy doesn't deserve to go to school?) so much he left an ominous message on my answering machine saying that he wanted the motherfucker who had disrespected him "taken care of."

"Johnny," Eric said with all the gravity of Don Corleone. "You know what to do!"

The midget had not *asked* me to murder a complete stranger... he had *ordered* me to murder a complete stranger! This little fucker was the new Uncle Frank!

And let's not forget the cherished memory of when Eric threatened to forcibly fuck country musician Natalie Maines of the Dixie Chicks in the ass for criticizing him on a *Celebrity Superfans Roundtable* show!

As much as I love those Eric moments, I have to admit that my all-time favorite Eric memories took place on his cursed JFSC.tv *American Idol* webcam show. And for the first time ever, I'm going to reveal the dirty little secret of those shows.

Since Eric constantly complained that Howard cut him off from delivering his hour-long dissertations on every *American Idol* episode, I decided to give Eric the soapbox he wanted by building a website for him, JFSC.tv (The Johnny Fratto Social Club). On the JFSC, I underwrote the cost of producing Eric's own webcam commentary show to run simultaneously with *American Idol*. That way, Eric could give his *American Idol* opinions at length to all of his adoring fans... and I could fuck with him mercilessly.

You see, Eric never dreamed that, when I paid for a camera and microphone setup to be installed in his bedroom, I also had my guy secretly install controls that would allow me to remotely interfere with the audio and video streams of the show. Eric thought he had finally found a platform to speak about *American Idol* without interruption or interference, but he was wrong. He was no longer at Howard Sterns' mercy; he was now at Johnny Fratto's.

Every single episode of Eric's *American Idol* recap show was plagued by what Howard called "audio difficulties." That's a euphemistic way of saying

I was fucking with the audio stream on my computer like a DJ manipulating a turntable.

I would drastically raise and lower the volume, over-modulate Eric's voice, cause loud microphone feedback, make the audio skip like an old vinyl record, insert the sound of jackhammer blasting away concrete, and even pipe in a police scanner directly into the feed. The only thing I enjoyed more than sabotaging Eric's self-indulgent and otherwise unlistenable *American Idol* show was listening to Howard, Robin, Artie, and Fred dying with laughter as the clips were replayed the next day.

Of course, I did plenty for Eric to make up for all the teasing and ball busting. I hooked him up with a brothel and got him laid for the first time in his life. I directed tens of thousands of dollars in strip club appearance fees, endorsement payments, and outright charity his way. I tried to put together a contest to staff a modeling agency for Eric to fuck around with, but the demented little control freak fucked that up by insisting on seven-year contracts that stipulated the girls must live in his basement.

I even fulfilled Eric's lifelong dream to drive. I flew that ungrateful prick down to Beverly Hills, bought him a child's electric Cadillac Escalade toy, and took him on a pimping joy ride around Wilshire Boulevard that TV gossip show *TMZ* broadcasted around the world.

If I were the crying type, a tear or two probably would have fallen down my cheek watching Eric cruising in his miniature Cadillac Escalade down the sidewalk with all the pride and swagger of a teenage boy driving his convertible for the first time. I really did love that little fucker like a son I thank God every day I didn't have.

31

A SUSPICIOUS NEIGHBORHOOD CHARACTER

It was 9 a.m. The fucking sun was sickeningly bright. I didn't want to be up this early. Unfortunately, I owed Steve Lobel too much to turn him down. He wanted to meet at a local jewelry store so I could negotiate with the hard-job behind the counter for a good price on a watch he wanted.

I was too groggy and distracted by my own grumbling to notice anything unusual when I pulled open the door of the jewelry store. It wasn't until I heard the sound of glass crunching under my sneakers that I snapped awake. Pulling down my sunglasses, I saw a completely ransacked and devastated showroom. This place had been *very* recently robbed and pillaged. I stood frozen.

"MAKE ONE MOVE AND I'LL SHOOT!" screamed an unidentified voice behind me. Here's a little tip for you law enforcement officers out there: don't *startle* someone with a threat to kill them if they move.

"HANDS UP SHITHEAD!"

"This is bullshit!" I squealed as my hands were wrenched into cuffs, "I just walked in like a minute ago. I got an appointment with a friend to talk to the jeweler. I mean, do I *look* like I'm dressed to rob . . ."

I hesitated. I probably shouldn't have let on that I had intimate experience with the customary wardrobe choices of a jewelry store burglar. I also realized that my indignance at being suspected of a jewelry store burglary was probably a bit rich considering my past as, you know, a jewelry store burglar.

"Well, officers, you'll see this is all a mix-up," I said in a much more sedate tone. "This will be cleared up in a second when my good friend Steve Lobel gets here . . ."

Right on cue, Steve walked up to the door to see me in cuffs. "Johnny?!" I swung my head to my old buddy, knowing he would clear matters up . . . "Johnny, what the fuck *did you do*?"

"NOTHING, motherfucker! Why the fuck did you go and say that? I was just waiting for your late ass when I noticed this place was all busted up and . . ."

"Sir, we've found the owner," called out a cop from across the room to the meathead frisking my pockets. "He's tied up in the back."

"Thank God," I said. "Now, he can clear this up, and you guys can let me go!"

So out came the jittery, crazy-pale jewelry shop owner with rope burn on both wrists. I gave him a big, friendly, Lou Fratto teddy bear smile. He was not too happy to see some guy in handcuffs smiling at him. "Hey buddy, can you clear this up for the cops and let them know I wasn't the one who robbed you? Can you please tell them Steve Lobel and I have an appointment with you?"

"Yes, yes you do," said the jeweler with a nasty little squint that I thought was a classic example of psychological displacement.

"So, who is this guy?" the cop asked the jeweler, referring to me.

The jeweler looked right in my eyes with a look of disgust and said for everyone to hear, "Oh, *him*? He's just some suspicious neighborhood character!"

"*You motherfucker!*" my brain begged my tongue to say. I knew the store had a surveillance system that would exonerate me, so I just stood silent and stewed.

But . . . a suspicious neighborhood character? Are you fucking kidding me? That's the story of my time in Beverly Hills and Dad's life in Des Moines. Here I am, trying my very best to be good just like him, raising my kids in a nice area and spoiling them rotten, and still people assume the worst of me. No matter how nice I smile, or how much sugar I pour, or how many PTA meetings I attend, or how good a job I do as the block Neighborhood Watch captain, I'll still just be a suspicious neighborhood character to all these white folks out here.

I try to tell them that I am just as horny and pent up as the rest of them, but they don't believe me. They don't understand that every time I get my hands on Jowanka, the parental sex alarm will go off in one of my little fuckers' heads— and either 8-year-old Joey will come knocking at the door asking for some rare *Transformers* action figure, or the *new* new kid, William Pius Fratto, a little toddler with two fangs just like a vampire, will start crying for titty milk.

I want to tell that little fucker that it's time for *daddy* to get some titty milk, but he don't listen. That isn't surprising, since Willie's named after the Pope who stuck by the Nazis through thick and thin—not to mention my stubborn little brother.

Not that I can blame him. The Fratto name just doesn't wash completely clean. I'm reminded of this unchangeable fact all the time.

One day, we were filming some footage for one of the *Son of a Gun* pilots at my condo when the sound guy stopped the shoot because he was getting some type of interference with the audio. "It's like we're getting microphone feedback or something," he explained, very confused about why a microphone would be hidden in my living room.

I knew why. I searched the house up and down and found it: an electronic bug in my light fixture. Figures; the feds will be recording me to the day I die. I knew better than to fuck with it myself or tell my family. I discreetly called an expert to come over and extract it the next day.

As I was sitting on my couch in the living room waiting for my electronics guy to come over, Jowanka walked in carrying the laundry basket with an apologetic look on her face. She lifted up a pair of wrinkled jeans with a wad of soaking wet cash sticking out of the back, looked up at me with her big beautiful eyes, and said the dumbest fucking thing she could have ever dreamed of saying.

"Johnny, I can't believe I just laundered all of your money!" *Oh shit.* I imagined an FBI asshole in a van pumping his fist and saying, "Finally! We got him for money laundering!"

"JOWANKA," I screamed very, *very* loudly, loud enough for the tiniest microphone to hear. "I KNOW THAT YOU MEAN THAT YOU PUT MY CASH IN THE WASHING MACHINE!"

"Why are you yelling, Johnny?"

"Why AREN'T you yelling, Jowanka?" I screamed back, all flustered and wide-eyed. "Tell them you meant that you got my fucking cash wet, woman!"

"Tell who, Johnny?"

"For fuck's sake, woman, say it was just the washing machine!"

"Shit, Johnny, you need a smoke. Maybe you need to start smoking weed again . . ."

"FUCK! DON'T SAY THAT!"

It was hopeless. I was sure I'd hear that conversation in a courtroom one day, and no one would believe that Jowanka was honestly holding up a pair of wet blue jeans with cash sticking out the back pocket like a crumpled green corsage. It's just my luck.

Once I went to a Halloween costume party thrown by Hollywood script-writer Shane Black and refused to dress up. I just came as myself in a nice silk suit. I've never received more compliments: "Awesome costume!"

"But I'm not wearing a costume!"

"Yes, you are! That's the best John Gotti costume I've ever seen!"

This put me in a grumpy mood. I took it out on one of actor Vince Vaughan's friends who needlessly picked a fight at the party. I grabbed my huge cellphone, thrust it forward in my coat pocket like a pistol, and thrust it in the guy's back. "Listen up, motherfucker, start walkin' or I'll blow a fucking hole in you!"

This was one time when the stereotype paid off—the guy took me at my word. I escorted him all the way out of the party at "gunpoint", the entire time praying for my phone not to ring. If it had, I definitely would have gotten my ass beaten—making my unintentional John Gotti costume even better since he had just been in the news for getting *his* ass beaten in prison.

Here's another good one. Being a sleazy guy by nature and by profession, my porn photographer buddy Victor likes to trade in on my name. In this instance, Victor met a retailer who happened to be a Mob junkie and promised to introduce him to me in exchange for some deals on some merchandise.

So Victor brings this kid who's obsessed with the Outfit up to my penthouse. The kid was stupefied when he saw me, as if I were an unchained lion. He was gawking at me like he was in the presence of Death itself. One wrong move would kill him.

I tried to make small talk, but it was hopeless. Normally, I do anything I can to avoid answering my cell phone, but this time I picked up on the first ring. "Hello, Meestah Faratto, youse shipment is in!" said the friendly immigrant fellow from my favorite gas station. My regular delivery of ice tea was waiting for me.

They say people are 80% water, but Johnny Fratto is 80% Lipton's Pure Leaf Ice Tea (Sweetened, No Lemon). This blue-labeled bottle of ice tea is the only thing I drink; I'll drop twenty bottles in a day, filling each one with cigarette butts when I'm finished. For some reason, it's normally impossible to get this tea outside of the deep, dark, depths of the inner city ghettos—you'd think it was made with Menthol. I have a better chance of finding a bottle of Soul-Glo Jheri Curl Activator in Beverly Hills.

Back in my pot smoking days, I'd take Lil' Johnny and Nicole Eggert on crazy suicide expeditions to Korean grocery stores in Compton or Inglewood just to get my tea. Since I have young kids now, I pay my gas station good money to wholesale order cases of it that I can pick up.

Figuring this Mob junkie would finally be good for something, I told this kid to come along with me on an errand. I sensed he thought he was about to be riding shotgun on St. Valentine Day's Massacre-style rampage, so I told him we were just going to the gas station.

I backed my Mercedes up to the gas station's loading area and told the kid to get out. It was broad daylight in Beverly Hills, but he was swerving his head right and left as if I had Uncle Frank and Milwaukee Phil lying in wait for him.

"Meestah Faratto, your shipment is in!" called one of the gas station workers.

"I know, I know, that's why I'm here."

"We get it right now!" The Mexican guys at the station were scrambling to be the first to roll the cases out to my trunk; they knew how well I tipped.

Once the cases of tea bottles were sitting by my trunk, I motioned for the kid to help us load them into my Mercedes. When he didn't move, I looked up to his eyes and saw he was on the verge of tears. This was a bit much.

"Um, *buddy*, what's wrong?"

"I...I...I..." The kid was stuttering and shaking.

"Why don't you just help us load the tea into the trunk?"

"I can't. I've ... *got a family* ..."

"Um, so do I, and if they were here, they'd help."

"Really, Johnny, d-d-d-d-don't make me do it," the kid pled. "I'm-ma-ma-ma, I'm'-ma-ma-ma, I'm a good person! I don't want to be involved in anything criminal.

"*Criminal?!* What the fuck are you on?" I wanted to scream "What's your major malfunction, numbnuts?" at the kid like Gunnery Sergeant Hartman in *Full Metal Jacket*. "What *exactly* do you think is in these bottles? Here," I said as I plucked one out, opened it up, and offered it to the kid, "Take a sip."

"*Please! I have a family!*" the kid just about screamed. He must have thought it was poison.

"For *fuck's sake*, look!" I happily drank a delicious, if warm, swig of Lipton Iced Tea. "See? It's nothing to be afraid of. Take a sip."

With a trembling hand, he took the bottle. Looking down at it like a cocked pistol, he raised his teary eyes up and asked, "D-d-d-do I have to?" I nodded. He pooled his courage and took a sip. His eyes sprung open in surprise; he gingerly swallowed. "What? It's-sa-sa-sa, it's just tea?"

"Yes, it's just tea."

Suddenly, the kid's impression turned sour. He looked downright pissed. I had ruined his fantasy; I was a fraud. "How on Earth do you break the law with a bottle of tea?" he asked with a bitchy tone.

Apparently, gangsters have to be outlaws even when enjoying a refreshing bottle of ice tea. Before I could smack the kid upside the head, one of the workers at the gas station piped up from behind me.

"Well, we always thought it had something to do with the bottles!" the attendant offered helpfully. "Maybe, y'know, Meestah Faratto took some bottles and melted 'em down and there was cocaine hidden inside."

When I looked at the gas station attendant like he was mental, he too got a sour look on his face. I had disappointed him, too. Apparently Johnny Fratto wasn't all he was cracked up to be.

Unbeknownst to me, my local gas station attendants were under the impression they were participating in an international drug smuggling ring under my direction. My gigantic drug profits were the reason for my exorbitant tips, not my native generosity. They could not have been more depressed to discover I was just a normal, good person—not a gangster.

And in that lies part of the solution to my identity crisis.

Dad fought a losing battle to change everything about him that hinted at his gangster side: his wardrobe, his language, his reputation, his cars, even his name and his hometown. He went to war with his past and his very nature. He thought he could hide in plain sight.

I think the only reason why he died with a murder indictment hanging over his head is because he tried to act like a civilian in the first place. If Lou Fratto hadn't worked so hard to appear soft, then Alan Rosenberg would have never dared to threaten his children. Alan would be alive. By suppressing a large part of whom he was, Lou invited trouble and stifled his healthy predatory energy.

And it was all for nothing. Once A Gangster, Always A Gangster—Period! You can't scrub that shit off, no matter who you are or what you do. It's the scarlet profession, the mark of the beast. You gotta own it or be owned by it.

That's why I no longer run away from the word "gangster" like Dad did. It just doesn't work. It makes people more suspicious, and it fosters a self-loathing within yourself for a part of you that cannot be eliminated.

That's one reason why Hollywood is where I belong. It's the only place where the gangster stigma is as comfortable as a track suit. In Hollywood, everyone and everything is so phony that the locals assume even the real deal is just as fake and harmless as them. In L.A., a gangster reputation is like being a rock star whose instrument is a gun.

Besides, everyone in Hollywood is so immersed in famous Mob movies that they take on all the characteristics of a gangster like fashion accessories. I don't stick out at all in a town where every Persian with slicked-back black hair renames himself Gambino and every coked-up actor threatens to cut off the heads of his adversaries and brags he can get away with murder.

To these people, I'm just the gangster next door. The fact that I have an *actual* record, *actual* connections, an *actual* real-world reputation . . . well, that just makes me a little bit cooler and sexier than them. I just have more street cred, like the rapper with a couple extra bullet wounds. It just means I can stamp their G-card.

Like any successful person in Hollywood, I have to give the people what they want.

And what they want out of Johnny Fratto is "Johnny Diamonds" and "Handsome Johnny."

Some smartass said "All the world's a stage." Someone even smarter said "Perception is reality."

Well, if you cast me in the role, a gangster I will play.

32

HOW TO GET AWAY WITH MURDER

In May of 2010, I was a guest on the Spike cable channel's top-rated original program, *Deadliest Warrior*, as an expert on Al Capone. On that show, I got paid top dollar to do what Dad and Uncle Frank risked the electric chair and Hell to do. I did the most depraved gangster shit imaginable to the amusement of an international audience of millions of upstanding citizens.

The angle? They were going to have me try out all of the weapons of the Capone-era Chicago Outfit under scientific observation to gauge how effective these tools of death would have been in a hypothetical time-traveling street war with the posse of Wild West outlaw Jesse James.

I know—it's a convoluted concept, but all I cared about was the fun I was about to have play-acting as my Dad!

I put on my nicest suit and jewelry, got comfortable in the passenger seat of a 1926 Hudson Super 6 Coach luxury automobile, propped my Thompson Sub-Machine Gun with the classic "cheese wheel" drum magazine on the window sill, and told the driver to slam on the gas. At speeds of over 40 miles-an-hour, I unleashed a thunderous spray of steel on five life-size targets . . . cursing and laughing the entire time.

The exhilaration and evil joy I experienced in those five seconds cannot be compared to any other lawful activity in America. I imagined how that much power and freedom from morality would have felt to my powerless teenage Dad in Prohibition Chicago... and I understood the incredible force that pulled him, against his nature, towards Evil.

Then came my turn as Uncle Frank. The producers of *Deadliest Warrior* handed me a switchblade and led me to a high-tech, blood-filled, gel dummy fashioned by scientists to be as identical to the human body as possible. They told me to do my worst. Looking at a friendly, silver-haired Beverly Hills father like me, they never suspected a thing. They had no idea what a nephew of Frank Fratto had learned about using a stiletto.

I flicked open the blade and smiled. Once they gave me the go-ahead, my pleasant face was distorted into a twisted, demonic, obscenity-spewing Halloween mask.

"YOU MOTHERFUCKER YOU!" I screamed as I swooped in and went to work. In a blink, I gave the dummy a Joker Smile from his teeth to scalp, severed his throat from his skull, messily disemboweled and gutted his midsection, and finally jammed the blade between the ribs and into his heart. This frenzy of street surgery happened so quickly, so instinctually that *Deadliest Warrior* had to replay the slaughter in slow motion to make my handiwork visible to the naked eye. There was nothing human in what I had done.

The blood was dripping from my diamond-studded "JF" ring, and my bottom lip was dented with the imprint of my fangs as I returned to humanity. I was suddenly very self-conscious. I had revealed the most dangerous, demented, sick fuck side of my soul. Before an audience of millions, I had unmasked the predator, momentarily let slip my Beverly Hills smile to reveal the beast whom Uncle Frank had called the most dangerous force in the underworld. I thought the jig was up.

I turned to *The Deadliest Warrior*'s hosts Geoff Desmoulin, Dr. Armand Dorian, and Max Geiger. Their faces were pale, their eyes wide. I thought they were going to ask me very politely to leave the set. Instead, they smiled, began to laugh, and poured on the compliments. They had never seen such a small weapon inflict such catastrophic damage.

Though Uncle Frank would never have said it out loud, his black heart would have been proud. Watching the slow-mo of the knifing captured something telling about myself, something I never would have noticed otherwise. As the blood gushed from the dummy's gut, a teeth-sucking look of predatory ecstasy appeared on my face.

On closer inspection, however, something even more revealing could be seen. I watched my hand as it expertly jiggled and zigzagged the blade to maximize the gore produced. It was like watching a painter deftly flicking his brush over a canvas. I looked up to my eyes, half-obscured behind my sunglasses, to see the look of intense concentration and falcon-like focus on my handiwork.

In that blood-splattered, gruesome moment, the very essence of my personality was exposed. In that moment, I was revealed in full: the gangster and the artist were one.

33

THE EVELYN SITUATION

"You got to appreciate what an explosive element this Bonnie situation is. If she comes home from a hard day's work and finds a bunch of gangsters doin' a bunch of gangsta shit in her kitchen, ain't no tellin' what she's apt to do."

JULES, *PULP FICTION*

"Birth of daughter [name redacted], to subject, EVELYN GLASSER, on [date redacted] at Chicago, Illinois, verified but no information developed as to marriage or present whereabouts of EVELYN GLASSER or daughter... On August 26, 1958, Doctor ROOS... advised that he recalls having delivered a female child to LOUIS FRATTO and his wife, EVELYN, about 30 years ago, but has not had any contact with them since a short time after delivering the child..."

FEDERAL BUREAU OF INVESTIGATION
September 11, 1958
FILE 92-243
Delivered directly to FBI Director J. Edgar Hoover

I was born into a family where secrets—serious, heavy-duty secrets—were part of the deal like siblings and church on Sundays. Most people who know me assume I inherited all the answers, like I've got a mental map of where all the bodies are buried in the Midwest from the 1920s until next week. I don't. Even the secrets I *do* know just lead me to other more interesting secrets I'll never unlock.

There are some secrets, however, that have always plagued me. These secrets, unsurprisingly, concern Dad and his identity. I am still in such awe of the idea that a man like Lou Fratto was my dad, I can never feel completely satisfied with what memories of him I have. I have always felt like I'm one tiny detail away from finally understanding him and thus, somehow, understanding myself.

It turns out I was right!

Of all the secrets about Lou Fratto, you already know the one in particular that has always bothered me: why did he *really* leave Chicago and become the Mafia boss of Des Moines? I figured Dad's case of split personalities—half excessively affectionate family man and half hardened gangster—must be explained on some level by whatever caused a proud Chicago Italian like him to abandon his name, his hometown, his history, and his reputation to become a completely different person: Lew Farrell of Des Moines, Iowa.

Though Uncle Frank often told me about how Dad moved to Des Moines because he was attracted to Iowa's wide-open rackets and low profile, I sensed there was something more. Dad loved Chicago and loved his family; he wouldn't leave them for purely business reasons. I judged by how quickly the normally rambling Uncle Frank changed the subject when it came to Dad leaving Chicago that he was hiding something—something that even *he* felt uncomfortable talking about.

It wasn't easy to get Frank Fratto to snitch, but I got a little something out of him. After Dad and Frankie's death, Uncle Frank was constantly drunk and talking. He was vulnerable, and I'm good at exploiting vulnerability. I approached Uncle Frank indirectly.

"Hey Unc, do you think Dad had any regrets about leaving Chicago for Illinois?"

"Besides the puckin' pact that I wouldn't be around to beat you into shape?" he snarled, jiggling his screwdriver glass.

"No, seriously, did Dad have any regrets, you think?"

"Yeah, of course, about that little girl of Evelyn's." I recognized Evelyn as the name of Dad's Jewish high school sweetheart in Chicago, whom he briefly married long before coming to Iowa.

"Who's Evelyn's little girl?"

"Uh, puck off, Charlie Manson. I'm done with you." Uncle Frank swatted at me, but I was too quick. I knew not to push him any further.

At least I had a lead now: Evelyn's girl. The odd thing was that Uncle Frank, the notorious gangster, was probably the most loose-lipped source of information about Dad and this little girl. Just about everyone else clammed up like I was a cop the second I dropped her name. Finally, I made enough people uncomfortable that an aunt sat me down for a short talk.

"Listen, Johnny, you know your dad was married once before in Chicago, right?"

"Yes, for a short time. Then the woman divorced him and eventually he met mom."

"Well, Johnny, that woman had a daughter, and even though your Dad never saw her, some people say she was his. But it was probably just a rumor."

This should have a bigger impact on me than it did, but I decided not to go digging around in Dad's past in search of malicious rumors. I didn't want to sully Lou's memory with this sort of sordid business, nor did I really believe a loving father like him could have endured being estranged from one of his children for decades.

Over the years, I would hear little whispers here and there at family functions from elderly relatives about Dad's pushy first wife, about the little girl, and even about rumors that Dad had arranged clandestine meetings with the girl on empty beaches in Illinois. I didn't take it too seriously; at the same family functions, my relatives ascribed all sorts of lovechildren to me that had no basis in reality.

Then, in 2007, it happened. I found out about Delores.

I'm always searching for new information, testimonies, court records, and archival FBI records about Dad to put up on my website dedicated to him, MidwestMafia.com. My search for new dirt on Lou Fratto eventually led me to discover that one of the many patronage jobs Al Capone had gotten for him as a young man was a gig as neighborhood interviewer for the 1930 federal census. This meant I could look up the paper records of the 1930 census and see what Lou Fratto wrote about his own family in his own handwriting.

I felt a moment of pride when I first saw Dad's signature—Louis T. Fratto—written on that census form as flamboyantly as if it were on the Declaration of Independence. As I compared "Louis T. Fratto" to the rest of the names on the page, it was clear he had whipped out a much thicker and darker pen to write his own name, and he had pressed it deep into the page. He was literally making his mark on history.

Much less grandly written were the names of the rest of his household. In his own hand, Lou named the following members of his family as living with him at 5406 West Wellington Avenue in the Belmont Cragin neighborhood of Chicago: Louis J. Fratto (21 years old), his wife Evelyn (17 years old), followed by Evelyn's mother, two siblings, and nephew.

Youngest of all was Delores Dawn Fratto, eight months old—my long-lost sister.

This census sheet listing my sister's name in Dad's handwriting was the only connection I had with Delores. I didn't want to get too sentimental about a piece of paper, but deep down I had to admit to myself that I suddenly felt like I *missed* someone. I *missed* someone I had never met and had only recently learned existed! Really, half the time I could do without the siblings I have, but this Delores was also part Lou Fratto. She was a part of my dad, a part of his life and even a part of his genetic code, that I had never seen.

I wanted to know her. I tried the Internet and found nothing. There was no record of Delores or Evelyn under the Fratto name or the maiden name. My initial excitement waning, I got scared of what I might find and I gave up.

This brings us to this book's writer, Matthew Randazzo V (Matty the Fifth, aka. MRV, aka. Merv, as I call him in honor of my last great collaborator). Matty took the liberty of boring me with some details about the research his lovely wife, Melissa, was doing about his own family. As you can probably deduce from his decision to go walking around with an ancient Roman number tacked onto his nametag, Matty is pretty obsessed about his family's history down in his hometown of New Orleans.

Matty was explaining to me how his wife Melissa had traced his family history back to the time of the Vikings, shaking his family tree so all sorts of kings, emperors, pirates, and revolutionaries fell out ... and with them, a fair number of big-nosed Mafiosi (yeah, my writer on this book comes from families in Palermo and Corleone, Sicily—big surprise).

"Melissa can find anyone; she's the best researcher I've ever met," Matty bragged, which is his usual form of communication.

Only half-listening to the stories of Matty's cavemen ancestors' inventing linguini thousands of years ago, my ear luckily caught his claim that his wife could find *anyone*. "Oh yeah?" I asked. "Well, if she can find anyone, then she can find my long-lost sister, Delores." With his usual impulsiveness, Matty guaranteed his wife would find Delores' whereabouts within two weeks.

I figured Randazzo's wife had little chance of finding my long-lost sister starting from scratch seven decades after her disappearance. At best, she would find an obituary letting me know I had missed the opportunity to befriend my father's first child. After all, eighty years had passed since that census sheet had been handwritten by Louis T. Fratto; Delores had most likely either died or covered up any connection to her family's embarrassing past.

My doubts only increased when Randazzo uncovered that FBI Director J. Edgar Hoover himself had been personally briefed in 1958 on his agents' unsuccessful attempts to find Lew Farrell's long-lost wife and daughter. You may ask why J. Edgar Hoover would be wasting tax dollars hunting for dirt on my family, but that's how the old blackmail queen worked, especially if you were friends with his mortal enemy Jimmy Hoffa. Surely, Melissa Randazzo wouldn't succeed where that sassy bitch J. Edgar Hoover, with all of her resources, had failed.

Melissa Randazzo proved me wrong: just as her husband promised, she did the impossible in less than two weeks. One night in September of 2009, Matty called me up and told me to check my e-mail. Inside a blank e-mail was an attachment—a photo of a small, handsome, dark-skinned teenage boy. My reaction was instantaneous . . . and a little hysterical.

"*Them is one of us!*" I screamed into the phone, momentarily losing control of my grammar. "I can spot a Fratto anywhere. That boy is a Fratto!"

"Well, Johnny, it's a girl," Matty said.

"No, that's a boy! I'm looking right at the photo, that's definitely a boy," I insisted, squinting hard at my computer screen, "and I bet you money it's a Fratto."

"Yes, yes, but that's not what I mean. There's been a new addition to the family."

"What, Melissa's pregnant?" I asked, now completely confused. For a writer, Matty can be a pretty poor communicator.

"No . . ." Matty said. "Melissa found Delores. She's alive, well, and lives less than an hour away from Beverly Hills in Escondido, California. That boy is a nephew, the great-grandson of your dad. He is a Fratto. Check your e-mail *now.*"

Right there, in my e-mail inbox, my long lost sister's e-mail address and Facebook page appeared. Not only was my 80-year-old sister alive, she was an Internet dynamo!

After fifty-five years, I finally talked to Delores Fratto. Within twenty-four hours, my other three surviving siblings and I had all spoken for the first time to our father's other child, a sweet and beautiful woman who grew up constantly thinking about us.

Our family was no mystery to Delores: she knew all about our dad and his new life in Des Moines. When our Frankie's death made national headlines in

1969, Delores cried uncontrollably, grieving over the little brother she would never get to know.

I asked Delores why she had been too afraid to get in contact with us since she always knew where we were. I figured that such a lovely, sentimental woman must have had a good reason to isolate herself from her family.

I was right. After a little coaxing, Delores voluntarily told me the story she was given for why she could never contact my father and his children. Nearly eighty years after it happened, I finally learned about the Evelyn Situation, the accident that made my life possible and caused Dad to leave Chicago for its underworld satellites.

If not for the Evelyn Situation, it is very likely that Delores would have grown up the daughter of the boss of the Chicago Outfit—instead of me growing up as the son of the boss of the Des Moines Mafia Family.

The Evelyn Situation occurred in 1934 in a bungalow home in Skokie, a suburb of Chicago. Louis, Evelyn, and young Delores Fratto had just moved from Skokie into a suite at the Seneca Hotel in downtown Chicago. Yes, over six decades before I stepped foot in the Beverly Hilton, Lou moved into the most expensive hotel in the big city to make it big.

His new neighbors in the hotel were the families of Dad's then partner-in-crime, Sam "Teets" Battaglia, a young enforcer so nicknamed because of his buckteeth, and a grim young man named Anthony Joseph Accardo—Tony Accardo, then widely known as "Joe Batters" for his calling card of beating people with a baseball bat.

A sophisticated, prissy, spitfire Jewish woman with strong morals, Evelyn hated Accardo and Teets for being "savages", and she complained to Dad that she could never be comfortable living so close to such scary people. Dad could hardly explain to his oblivious Jewish wife that their new home in the most lucrative underworld district of Chicago was a sign that the Outfit expected Lou Fratto to join Teets and Joe Batters in one day managing the greatest criminal empire on Earth.

Evelyn deeply resented having to move from suburban Skokie to the hustle and bustle of the Seneca Hotel. She made a point of showing her displeasure by transporting their family's possessions as slowly and in as many trips as possible. If she never finished the move to Chicago, Evelyn could hold out the hope that it could be more easily reversed.

After a few months, Evelyn gave up and drove back to their old home in Skokie to collect the rest of her belongings. Pouting over the entire thing, she made no attempt to inform Dad.

As she walked into the kitchen of her vacated home, Evelyn stepped onto a tarp. Looking up, she saw Teets, Dad's cousin "Milwaukee Phil" Alderisio, and an unidentified man whom I can almost guarantee was my very young Uncle Frank. These three close associates of my father were standing around Evelyn's kitchen with meat cleavers and bone saws in their hands; they were caked in dried blood and viscera. On the kitchen table where Evelyn had spoonfed her newborn daughter was a dismembered human corpse.

Without a word, the three men watched Evelyn slowly back out of the house the way she came. Dad may have been Golden Tongue, but nothing he could say could convince Evelyn she "was in no danger since the Boys trust Louis' wife." With regret, my father handed her a large sum of cash and a divorce so she could flee for safety with his little Delores.

To escape from the hit team she wrongly thought was pursuing her, Evelyn changed the spelling of her last name and disappeared into a new life. She also decided her little girl could never risk her life by seeking out a relationship with her father. That's why Evelyn told Delores about what happened in that kitchen in Skokie: to scare her away from Dad.

Delores never considered the idea of speaking with her dad's side of the family for the rest of her mother's life—which turned out to be a practical eternity. The woman once known as Evelyn Fratto died at the age of 89 in 2002. She was perhaps the last person living who intimately knew Tony Accardo, Sam Battaglia, and Lou Fratto as very young men in the Chicago underworld. Who knows the stories she could have told?

By the time Evelyn was dead, Delores was already well into her seventies...too old, she thought, to start a relationship with a new family. Like me, she wondered about us mostly to see what information we could give her about Lou, whom she barely remembered. On that day in September of 2009, Delores not only gained three new brothers and the sister she always wanted, but she gained the knowledge that losing her was our father's one great regret.

My sister also learned that, throughout our childhood, Dad took my little brother Willie and I to a synagogue in Des Moines every Saturday, where he impressed the local Jews with his mastery of Yiddish and all the Hebrew holy prayers. At the time, I figured my father was just punishing us by making my brother and I go to twice the church as the average Catholic. Talking to Delores for the first time, I realized that going to temple was probably Dad's way of keeping in touch with the little Jewish girl he left behind in Chicago and praying for her wellbeing.

Ironically, when I told Delores this touching story, she acted dumbfounded. After Evelyn left Dad, she erased her family history in order to cover her tracks. Delores was not raised as a Chicago Jew, but as a French Presbyterian! No matter how often Delores' aunts and uncles revealed a certain suspicious familiarity with Yiddish, Chanukah, and good delicatessen, her mom continued to act like a Conehead by stubbornly insisting over and over that "WE ARE FROM FRANCE."

It turns out the full-blooded Italian Frattos spent their childhood in temple, while the little half-Jewish girl never learned the meaning of kosher.

It also turns out that the little boy who was obsessed for years with the riddle of whether his father was a gangster or not...well, he only existed because some poor motherfucker got chopped up on a kitchen table in Skokie, Illinois.

How about that gangster shit? Dad's identity crisis was simply a crisis of conscience. He was once every bit the gangster the FBI said he was, but, in the last thirty years of his life, he made a sincere attempt to change within the confines of what he could get away with without drawing suspicion, betraying his oaths, or getting killed.

Like me, he saw the ultimate tragedy of the gangster lifestyle, only he learned it in the hardest way imaginable: he lost his wife and little girl. He lost his family. He swore he'd never make that mistake again. His spoiling, hands-on, always-available fathering of his new family makes perfect sense in retrospect—he was wounded, guilty, and haunted by what happened in Skokie, and what he lost because of *gangster shit.*

In the end, almost every gangster pays in the damage he does to his family. Every year that goes by, the more true that becomes. The old days, and the old timers, are gone.

Their End was my Beginning. But that doesn't mean my Beginning was the End.

I knew it way back in Des Moines. Like the bison that once roamed the plains of the Midwest, I could see the pack was being thinned to extinction. We were down to the Last of the Mohicans. There was no air left to breathe.

I knew this life was no longer for me. I just had to get away.

I didn't want to go to jail for an institution that was, in itself, a prison to me. I didn't want my legacy on Earth to be that I had sacrificed my family for a crime family that had served to encourage the worst and stifle the best in me. I wanted to follow in Dad's footsteps, but *keep walking*, walk all the way past the things that held him back like I know Frankie would have.

Their end was my beginning.

I *exploit* the Sin. It serves my purposes and my purposes only. No one puts it on me like a Scarlet Letter. It's a beautiful silk suit that I put on and take off as I wish. I'm an actor who may or may not be acting in a gangster movie that may or may not be real. Around my neck is a necklace showcasing a medal of St. Dismas, patron saint of thieves, given to Dad by Al Capone, and on my middle finger is a diamond-studded skull ring. I've learned how to transform GANGSTER into an accessory. It is the shiniest of the many diamonds I own.

Let the neighbors gossip. Let the FBI listen in. Let the local muck-ety-mucks call me a suspicious neighborhood character.

They're right. I *am* suspicious. I'm suspicious of all you motherfuckers who act like you've got nothing to hide!

Go right on and think the worst of me. Whatever you think I am, I'll be the first to tell you I'm probably worse. I mean, have you *read* this fucking book?

The only thing that matters to me is my family and my honor. Whatever else you say about me, I have managed to keep hold of both, despite all of my sins and all of my faults. I look forward to succeeding my Dad in the most important way of all: dying a free man, beloved by his family.

I just thank God that, unlike my poor father, I never had to lose a child in order to see through the glamorous illusion of the Mafia.

ACKNOWLEDGMENTS

Johnny Lew Fratto succeeded where it counted most. Johnny died a free man surrounded by his family on December 5, 2015. He was a 61-year-old victim of cancer. Funerals were held for him in both Beverly Hills and Des Moines, with over a thousand people in attendance.

A little over a year prior to Johnny's death, his longtime friend and comedy partner Eric Lynch also died from complications associated with his disabilities. Better known as "Eric the Midget" and "Eric the Actor", Eric aggressively volunteered to be interviewed for this book. Eric asked me to ensure that the world knew that he completely disagreed with Johnny's version of how they met (Eric swore Johnny sought *him* out), as well as to repeat for the record that he thought Johnny's hair and dress style both looked stupid. Finally, Eric asked me to make sure the world knew he truly loved Johnny and considered himself (not Johnny) a great friend.

And yes, I can confirm from extensive firsthand experience that Johnny truly adored Eric, and vice versa, each in his own very bizarre way.

Johnny himself gave hundreds of hours of his time to this project over many years. Every story contained within this book was directly told to me by Johnny in detail on multiple occasions and blessed by him to be published. Identifying details about multiple crimes were removed from the manuscript, but only after Johnny had provided me with enough information to broadly corroborate the stories themselves.

The rest of the Fratto Family, beginning with Johnny Fratto Jr., were fantastic to work with in preparing this book for publication. Johnny deserves full credit for making this project a reality in the aftermath of his father's death— I know Johnny Sr. would be proud. I'd also like to thank Rudy Fratto, Peter Piccione Sr., Michael Piccione, Nicole Eggert, and Johnny Costello for their help confirming and filling out stories.

Johnny Fratto Jr. also asked me to express our gratitude to everyone at *The Howard Stern Show* for all of their support and friendship through the years—Howard, Robin, Fred, Benjy, Gary, Will, Brent, J.D., Shuli, Ronnie, and everyone else ... including Scott Salem, whom we didn't forget!

Neil Strauss and Anthony Bozza deserve credit for being the original publishers who greenlit this book. Bill Tonelli was the excellent original editor. Though Johnny ultimately pulled out of the deal before the book was published, the foundations for this book were laid under Neil, Anthony, and Bill's expert supervision. It was also Neil who introduced us to the great Tyler Shields, who contributed the photograph for the cover of this book.

Personally, I'd like to thank Kenny "Kenji" Gallo, the co-author of my book *Breakshot: A Life in the 21st Century American Mafia*, for introducing me to Johnny in the first place. You can learn more about Kenji, his life in the underworld, and his current work as a writer and philanthropist at kenjigallo.com.

Finally, I need to thank the team that salvaged this book and ushered it to publication. This book was ultimately published thanks to Sean Meenan, the CEO of the Isaac Olivia Company, who always believed in this project. I owe a major debt of gratitude to Danielle Deschenes, the brilliant designer who created the cover and interior design, as well as formatted the book for print. I'm also deeply appreciative of my research assistant Joseph Landoni IV, my lead editor Heather Matthews, and the friends and family who assisted on the final edit, including Jeannie Morris, Diana Lofflin, and Dr. Ranjan Chhibber.

Lastly, I want to thank my wonderful family, my wife Melissa and daughter Olivia, for everything I cannot put into words. In addition to her exploits as a researcher and genealogical investigator, Melissa is the best friend, wife, mother, and partner I could have ever met.

MATTHEW RANDAZZO V
September, 2017

Made in the USA
Monee, IL
16 January 2024

51876642R00167